**Library of
Davidson College**

Colección Támesis
SERIE A: MONOGRAFÍAS, 181

TIRANT LO BLANC: NEW APPROACHES

TIRANT LO BLANC

NEW APPROACHES

Edited by

Arthur Terry

TAMESIS

© Editor and Contributors 1999

All Rights Reserved. Except as permitted under current legislation
no part of this work may be photocopied, stored in a retrieval system,
published, performed in public, adapted, broadcast,
transmitted, recorded or reproduced in any form or by any means,
without the prior permission of the copyright owner

First published 1999 by Tamesis, London

ISBN 1 85566 068 7

Tamesis is an imprint of Boydell & Brewer Ltd
PO Box 9, Woodbridge, Suffolk IP12 3DF, UK
and of Boydell & Brewer Inc.
PO Box 41026, Rochester, NY 14604–4126, USA
website: http://www.boydell.co.uk

A catalogue record for this book is available
from the British Library

Library of Congress Cataloging-in-Publication Data
Tirant lo Blanc : new approaches / edited by Arthur Terry.
    p. cm. – (Colección Támesis. Serie A, Monogrfías: 181)
Includes bibliographical references.
  1. Martorell, Joanot, d. 1468. Tirant lo Blanch. I. Terry,
Arthur.
PC3937. M4T538 2000
849'. 933 – dc21   99–40573

This publication is printed on acid-free paper

Printed in Great Britain by
St Edmundsbury Press Ltd, Bury St Edmunds, Suffolk

CONTENTS

Preface by Arthur Terry	vii
The Chivalresque Worlds in *Tirant lo Blanc* JESÚS D. RODRÍGUEZ VELASCO	1
Comedy and Performance in *Tirant lo Blanc* RAFAEL BELTRÁN	15
'Poets and Historians' in *Tirant lo Blanc*: Joanot Martorell's Models and the Cultural Space of Chivalresque Fiction JOSEP PUJOL	29
Tirant lo Blanc: Rehistoricizing the 'Other' *Reconquista* MONTSERRAT PIERA	45
Tirant lo Blanc and the Muslim World in the Fifteenth Century MARÍA JESÚS RUBIERA Y MATA	59
The Eschatological Framework of Tirant's African Adventure ALBERT HAUF	69
Language and Intimacy in *Tirant lo Blanc* THOMAS R. HART	83
Death in *Tirant lo Blanc* JEREMY LAWRANCE	91
Nine Problem Areas Concerning *Tirant lo Blanc* JOSEP GUIA AND CURT WITTLIN	109
Bibliography	127
Index	141

PREFACE

More than 500 years after its publication, *Tirant lo Blanc* remains deeply enigmatical: a major work of art, certainly, but one which defies classification and whose ambiguities – deliberate or unintentional – are far from being resolved. Riquer's distinction between 'books of chivalry' (the earlier romances) and 'chivalresque novel' (the *Tirant*) is useful in that it places the emphasis on imaginative creation; yet any attempt to assimilate it to the modern novel should be resisted: whatever else it is, the *Tirant* is a late-medieval work, to which notions of unity and authorial intention seem hardly relevant.

Plot it certainly has: roughly speaking, it is the story of an imaginary knight – a 'Breton of Arthurian descent', to use Hauf's phrase – whose greatest achievement is to deliver Constantinople from the threat of the Turks. After the early scenes, which take place at the English Court, the action centres on the Mediterranean. Tirant, by now a famous general, takes part in the French expedition to Rhodes and becomes commander-in-chief of the Byzantine armies; later, after a series of adventures in North Africa, he returns to Constantinople, marries the Emperor's daughter, Carmesina, and dies of an illness shortly afterwards. To summarize the book in this way, however, leaves out a great deal of what is really interesting: Tirant's protracted wooing of Carmesina and the setbacks this entails, the surprising juxtaposition of the erotic and the spiritual, and the way burlesque is continually used to defeat the reader's expectations. Moreover, it is clear that the manners and customs of the Byzantine Court are an accurate reflection of those of Valencia, though Martorell's realism is so convincing that it is often difficult to say where his social observation gives way to invention. One of the most striking features of this society is its love of ritual, which affects everything from personal relationships to the elaborate protocol that surrounds the most brutal behaviour. The common factor in all this is language: the characters of the *Tirant* take as much pleasure in drawing up an elegantly worded challenge as in postponing their sexual pleasures with fine talk. And in both areas of experience, ritual is linked with strategy: not only detailed schemes for defeating one's enemy in war, but also the deliberate manipulation of potential sexual partners.

So much would be obvious, one imagines, to a sensitive modern reader. However, there is one further dimension of the book which would appeal to a fifteenth-century audience, but which we may possibly underestimate. This is its encyclopedic nature, the way it can be made to serve as a compendium of knowledge on all manner of things, from social behaviour and the kind of speech this entails, to the qualities of a good knight and the detailed conduct of war. And this affects the actual structure of the book, the way much of this comprises a mosaic of previous writers from Homer to Boccaccio, including a number of Catalan sources. This is where modern ideas of 'originality' and 'plagiarism' are merely distracting. For Martorell, who comes near the beginning of a vernacular tradition of fiction, this recourse to previous authors is not so much a matter of plagiarism as of establishing authority, of bringing to bear the wisdom of the past on a strictly contemporary enterprise. And this is where the idea of a compendium is most effective: in providing his readers with a mass of authorities, many of whom have a bearing on actual conduct, he is deliberately stretching his fiction to achieve the encyclopedic dimension for which it must originally have been valued.

I referred earlier to the ambiguity of the *Tirant*. This operates at both an external and an internal level. Externally, there is the question of its relation to known fact: Martorell began his book around 1460, seven years after the actual fall of Constantinople to the Turks; since he makes no mention of this, is he attempting to rewrite history by putting real events into reverse? And what is his stance towards chivalry itself? Does he regards it as still valid, or, despite his admiration for its values, does he recognize that it is becoming a thing of the past? More specifically, is he re-creating this world in fictional terms in order to demonstrate the imaginative truth of chivalry to a society whose values are becoming progressively less aristocratic? (This would perhaps explain why he admits certain non-ideal elements, not with the intention of undermining the ideal, but as a way of making it more meaningful.)

Much of the internal ambiguity of the *Tirant* has to do with the objectivity of the narrative. It is hard to think of another work before the sixteenth century in which the author's guiding hand is so conspicuously absent, or which is so free from moral comment. For all the gaiety with which he treats sexual relationships, Martorell never allows his humour to soften the impact of what he is describing. His only concern seems to be to persuade the reader that this is how things must have happened, and it is for the reader himself to allocate praise and blame – hence, for example, one's difficulty in knowing how seriously to take the ending. Is the apparent solemnity of Tirant's death undermined by our awareness of his earlier sham deaths, as Jeremy Lawrance claims? And how does the final burlesque of Hipòlit's marriage to the Empress reflect on the earlier episode?

Finally, there is the question of the joint authorship of the book. Was Galba simply a copy editor, as has sometimes been claimed, or did he have a more active part, either in the later chapters or throughout the book? Or – and this is one of the most striking developments of recent scholarship – was there a third author involved, and, if so, to what extent?

*

The essays which follow address these, and many other, questions, opening up new lines of approach without providing any easy answers. Jesús Rodríguez Velasco carefully examines the different conceptions of chivalry prevalent at the time of writing and explains how Martorell rejects the idea of 'Roman chivalry' then in vogue and associates Tirant with the monarchic order, which stresses the importance of prudence rather than mere strength. Rafael Beltrán, in a wide-ranging essay, discusses the part played by performance or 'representations' in the *Tirant*, placing the three major examples – the 'rock', the Arthur-Morgana episode and the Viuda Reposada's plot – on a scale which goes from the more or less direct imitation of real-life events to the relative freedom of literary elaboration. Josep Pujol scrupulously records Martorell's debt to previous poets and historians, particularly Guido delle Colonne, and shows how these various borrowings act as superimposed strata in the composition of a work that accommodates fiction to history, thus 'bringing it into an area of writing which is not affected by clerical prejudice'.

Several of these essays are concerned with the relation of the *Tirant* to real life events and practices. Montserrat Piera, after rightly claiming that Cervantes dehistoricizes the novel, goes on to show how the fate of Byzantium reflects the decline of Aragon itself after the Compromiso de Caspe (1412), and how the ending of the book reveals a 'tragic sense of hopelessness' and a reversal of Martorell's previous strategy. ('Earlier Martorell undid history, now he undoes fiction.') María Jesús Rubiera, a noted Arabic scholar, examines the way the Muslim world is depicted in the *Tirant* and provides the most conclusive evidence so far of its dual authorship by showing how in chapters 301–49 – presumably the work of Galba – Martorell's relative familiarity with the Muslim world, based on his knowledge of the *mudéjares* of Valencia, suddenly lapses, only to be resumed at a later stage. Albert Hauf's essay connects interestingly at several points with both Piera and Rubiera. Starting from Tirant's prophecy in chapter 300 – the beginning of the North African adventure – he explains how this corresponds to the contemporary sense of approaching apocalypse brought on by the severe social and economic crisis Valencia was experiencing. On this reading – a thoroughly convincing one – Martorell's fiction (as in the case of the Fall of Constantinople) would be a compensation for what in real life did not happen: 'His hero, now become a prophet, avoids . . . the great disaster which history could not prevent, and offers his readers the substitute of a longed for, but imaginary, reality.'

The next two essays are more strictly literary. Thomas Hart skilfully analyses the means by which effects of intimacy are achieved in the novel, despite the lack of characterization in the modern sense. Though Martorell does not show us the characters' thoughts as they actually develop, he creates a sense of ambiguity which exists for the characters, but not for the reader.

Or, as he puts it: 'Part of the fascination of the *Tirant* lies in the opportunities [he] gives to look directly into the consciousness of characters who seem to be almost always on show and to see things they do not.' Jeremy Lawrance comments subtly on the profound ambivalence of Tirant's and Carmesina's deaths – 'mingled tragedy and disenchantment' – and reviews a number of previous interpretations. These he finds plausible up to a point, but, as he says, '[They] all founder . . . on the rock of the narrative's seemingly inexhaustible range of conflicting tones and attitudes.' This, as he interestingly claims, may have to do with a distinctive late-fifteenth-century view of tragicomedy, visible also in the *Celestina* and perhaps in the *Tragèdia de Caldesa*. Thus the ending may fulfil an artistic, rather than a moral purpose: 'The tonal complexity of such a story . . . seems too extraordinary to bear any single moral. We are drawn to consider a final explanation . . . , which is that the narrator intended the protagonists' deaths to mix tragic and comic effects, not for any didactic purpose, but for reasons of art.'

Finally, Josep Guia and Curt Wittlin, two of the critics who have thought most pertinently about the authorship question, identify nine 'problem areas', each of which they examine with a compelling mixture of common sense and exact scholarship. Though at present much of what they say can only be tentative, they pose very real doubts about previous theories of authorship. In particular they raise the question of the participation of a third author – Joan Roís de Corella – which on the face of it seems extremely likely, though for the moment the extent of this remains a matter for speculation. Perhaps we shall never know exactly what happened to Martorell's original manuscript between his entrusting it to Galba and its eventual publication in 1490; however, the problems Guia and Wittlin rehearse are ones which future *Tirant* scholars will need to continue to investigate, and they at least indicate the directions their work is likely to take in the coming years.

It would be a mistake, however, to assume that such exact scholarship puts the *Tirant* beyond the range of ordinary readers. Though any attempt at an overall interpretation, as these essays show, must remain open-ended, the narrative itself, as many generations of readers can testify, serves as an endless source of fascination, not the least because it comes from a mentality very different from our own. Because it makes so few concessions to conventional morality, the *Tirant* is a disconcerting book, and this in itself is a sign of its vitality. In the end, however, it is the scope and depth of the vision which make it a masterpiece, a vivid and densely populated fictional world which still retains its power to convince and to draw its readers into an endlessly ramifying process of discrimination.

Wherever possible, we have quoted from the English translation of the *Tirant* by David H. Rosenthal (London: Macmillan and New York: Schocken Books, 1984), with permission of the present holders of the copyright, Pantheon Books, a division of Random House, Inc., New York.

Arthur Terry

The Chivalresque Worlds in *Tirant lo Blanc*

JESÚS D. RODRÍGUEZ VELASCO

To Carlos, Alejandrina and Edgar

In 1460, when Joanot Martorell claims to have finished *Tirant lo Blanc*, European chivalry was once again absorbed in a search. The institution was at its peak, but its frame of reference was not. The courtly world had aged, and the various chivalresque patrons, kings for the most part, had tried to give statutes to increasingly restricted sections of chivalry with the object of redefining the chivalresque function and its ethical world. The result is the lay chivalresque orders which flood monarchical Europe from the middle of the fourteenth century (Boulton 1987). But this is insufficient explanation; the proof is that, apart from these 'chivalries', there remains chivalry itself, the shapeless mass that descends from courtly culture. For that reason, in the course of the first half of the fifteenth century, the theorists and doctrinaires of politics and the civil world create what we might call the ideology of Roman chivalry, an ideology according to which medieval chivalry is the direct descendant of the Roman *equites*, an *ordo* which combines military, political and administrative functions and which, furthermore, is juridically linked to the nobility in accordance with the institution of Justinian (*Codex*, tit. XXXII, 'De equestri dignitate').

In the course of his novel, Joanot Martorell shows himself to be perfectly familiar with this ideology and, like any knight who had lived in the first half of the fifteenth century, he must have known of the enormous success it had among kings and nobles, and surely recognized that many knights of more obscure lineage felt seduced by it. In fact, Martorell makes use of its literary procedures, of the precise form in which fifteenth-century chivalry interpreted the knowledge that came from Humanism and which, based on ethical descriptions of character, in Ciceronian-type speeches and in historiography, affects siege techniques, tactics and strategy in accordance with the models found, above all, in Vegetius and Frontinus (Badia 1983–4; Contamine 1992; Rodríguez Velasco 1996). Far from representing a practical option, a permit for realism, all these literary procedures are, so to speak, self-referential: they are born, develop and die in the literary work, except for the ethical and political paradigm which stems from them, and which will conform to the frame of reference associated with the 'Roman' knight (Rodríguez Velasco 1996a:367–73). But Martorell never reaches this point. And he fails to reach it, not through lack of knowledge, but because his idea of chivalry has nothing to do with this world which is extending itself throughout Europe.

Martorell was not unaware of the fact that the majority of the doctrinaires and polemicists of the new chivalry were speaking from the point of view of a conflicting reality. From the middle of the fourteenth century, their voices were heard throughout Europe: those of jurists like Bartolo de Sassoferrato, educated clergy like Honoré Bouvet, professional politicians like Leonardo Bruni or Buonaccorso da Montemagno, historians like Georges le Chastelain or Olivier de la Marche, third-rank knights like Diego de Valera (Rodríguez Velasco 1996a). Faced with these numerous interventions, the chivalresque, monarchical and aristocratic orders continue to grow and to restrict chivalry itself; there emerges on all sides a plutocratic chivalry proceeding from the merchant class, and courts like that of Burgundy take delight in ancient courtly pleasures sufficiently evoked (and wrongly seen as a universal norm) by Huizinga at the beginning of this century.

And just as he was not unaware, he had no interest in remaining neutral. From the very beginning of the novel, Martorell declares openly that he is about to compose a 'treatise' (*tractat*), which, at least in principle, suggests an essay form or a doctrinal exposition. Like so many of his contemporaries, he is convinced that stylistic crudity is less important than that others 'may enjoy the fruit which belongs to it' (ibid.). I am absolutely certain that Martorell thought this fruit would be 'the reinforcement of the noblest chivalric values', but I doubt very much whether he believed this could be done through 'the replacement of old, hollow values that had become outmoded and virtually useless for the fifteenth-century military situation', as Aylward states (1985:45), at least if one takes it that this old chivalry is courtly chivalry (as Aylward seems to imply; on the other hand, courtly chivalry was the only kind which could be considered outmoded). On the contrary, Martorell, who, when all is said and done, is a professional knight, does not opt for any of the fashionable theories concerning chivalry: he does not advocate the most modern of all, 'Roman chivalry'; there are no signs of courtly chivalry, which, as we shall see, is the object of strong criticism in the course of the debate between the Empress and Carmesina, and he even allows himself to transform it in the part dedicated to Guy of Warwick; he rejects as too partial the chivalry of the knightly order, and only praises it in the context of other complementary dimensions of chivalry which we shall go on to examine.

Apart from this, one accepts the doubt which Albert Hauf (1995) has expressed very clearly concerning the possible anti-chivalresque nature of the *Tirant*, through the introduction of moral interpolations and social points on the basis of various texts of Joan Roís de Corella. Whether such introductions are or are not the work of Martorell, whether they correspond to a literary dismantling and subsequent reconstruction on the part of the tiresome Martí Joan de Galba, is something we must of necessity leave aside for the present. But what is certain is that throughout the *Tirant* one experiences an ideological tension with regard to the concept of chivalry which verges on contradiction. And this tension, whose main characteristics I have mentioned in the previous paragraph, is very similar to another work which came originally from the courtly milieu, which grew in the monarchical world and which was reformulated, or rather reconstructed, amidst the culture of Roman chivalry, with the intention of showing the validity of a chivalresque world now concentrated on the new Christian knight. I refer to *Amadís de Gaula*.[1] Perhaps this contradiction, or the desperate attempt to resolve it, is the mark of a period that has seen the decadence of chivalry, but since this supposed decadence is belied by contemporary and slightly later events, it seems necessary to defend other hypotheses (see, for example, Kamen 1986 and, more recently, Scaglione 1991). For the moment, we need to see what the chivalresque worlds of the *Tirant* are like.

The Courtly World

Let us say immediately that Martorell transforms the world of courtly chivalry. He rejects it to the point where, at those moments when he is compelled to introduce it, he poses serious objections to it. The most obvious instance comes in the part dedicated to Guy of Warwick, which proceeds quite certainly (as Riquer clearly demonstrates [1990a:257–71]) from the fourteenth-century prose narrative known as the *Romant de Guy de Warwick et de Herolt d'Ardenne* (Conlon 1971).[2] Both the *Guillem de Vàroic* of ms. 7811 and the *Romant* are deeply attached to the courtly world. The novelesque French version, because it summarizes the affairs concerning the dynasty of the counts of Warwick contained in the primitive Anglo-Norman poem, and continues to breathe the same ideology of chivalresque feudalism. Ms.7811, because it adds the Lullian reflections on *militia christiana* and the

---

[1] On the composition of the *Amadís* across the centuries, see Avalle-Arce (1991), who dates the first version from the time of Sancho IV. In my edition of the *Amadís*, I give reasons for thinking that the date of the first version should be taken back to the personal reign of Alfonso XI.

[2] The problem posed by Riquer himself concerning the influence of both the *Guillem de Vàroic* of ms. 7811 and the *Romant* on the *Tirant* is still unresolved. In my opinion, ms. 7811 is merely a manuscript composed of notes which Martorell could have found interesting for his project, a form of working suggested by Hauf (1995:113), and with which I am in complete agreement. As I see it, the *Guillem de Vàroic* of 7811 is a reworking on Martorell's part on the basis of his readings of the *Llibre de l'orde de cavalleria* and the *Romant* already referred to; nothing prevents him later, on including the *Guillem de Vàroic* in the *Tirant*, from going back to these primitive notes, now enriched by other passages or linguistic echoes of the *Romant* and, probably, with techniques proceeding from some treatise on strategy and siege warfare. (I do not venture to give a single title, since there are procedures which could have been found, *in nuce*, in Frontinus, Vegetius, Egidius Romanus or Valerius Maximus, to give some examples.)

thirteenth-century courtly code which it shares, for example, with the prose *Lancelot* (Ramos 1995). By contrast, *Guillem de Vàroic* gives a completely different twist to its sources, in the first instance because it converts Guillem the knight errant, the subsequent hermit who remains attached to certain customs much praised in the courtly world, into someone completely foreign to this world: a captain whose essential virtue is that of strategic skill. Martorell dwells much less on Guillem's socio-political history than on the way he handles grenades, barbs, and the like. In the second place, because the hermit who first takes on a Lullian aspect, and then, to our confusion, appears as an archtypal doctrinaire, an ex-knight who is now a hermit (like so many knights of the Arthurian cycle, including Lancelot himself), is suddenly humanized, brought up to date, presented as absolutely contemporary, and prepared to take a passionate interest in the chivalresque feasts which are described to him, first by Tirant and then by Diafebus (chapters 41–98).

The second time Martorell confronts the courtly world is precisely in his account of the English feasts. I do not think there can be a better literary moment for exploiting courtly ideology than the trappings involved in any kind of feast. In a great many novels from Chrétien de Troyes onwards (in *Erec*, for example), this moment has been the occasion for courtly crisis, for adventure or, on more than one occasion, for love and all that this entails. Nor do I think there can be a better occasion for exhibiting the voluntary and subjective gifts of the courtly knight, in which he can demonstrate, as well as his strength and courage, his good nature and his talent for knowing when to forgive and when to act piously. But in *Tirant lo Blanc* all this courtly nucleus is also changed. Perhaps the least important thing is the fact that the account of the English feasts is cast in the Burgundian style, with a setting which yields nothing to the feasts which gave place to the series of vows known as the *Voeux du Faisan* (De Courcelles 1996), described by Matthieu d'Escouchy and Olivier de la Marche. It is more important that each of the warlike actions, whether single or collective combat, whether those which are *à outrance* and those which are *à plaisance*, should be overshadowed, over and above the courage of the individual knight, by the law which determines his behaviour and to which he must imperatively submit.

Despite what one might think at first sight, these laws are not those of the courtly world. In their place, there will be found the complex formulations which the Europe of the knights has received from the hands of jurists like Giovanni Legnano (*De bello, de represalis et de duello*), Bartolo de Sassoferrato (*De insigniis, De dignitatibus*) and, above all, the vast chivalresque encyclopedia of Honoré Bouvet, the *Arbre des Batailles*. All of these, and those which appeared in their wake in compilations and adaptations like the *Tratado de armas* of Diego de Valera, have as their regular object that which canon law had condemned: the shedding of blood beween Christian knights for relatively 'sporting' motives such as personal duels or tournaments for airing long-standing enmities. And in the *Tirant*, they are all brought to the fore, from the forms of personal duels, with due regard for the choice of arms, to the possibility that the capture of a banner may signify that a master of arms goes to the Great Sultan with the sole intention of warning him that he is infringing the laws concerning the display of banners (chapter 152).

The third time the courtly world is questioned is, if I am not mistaken, the harshest and most explicit. I am referring to the debate involving the Empress and her daughter Carmesina as to what is the most important virtue in a knight. The Empress adopts the courtly model, arguing that the knight's essential virtue is *fortitudo*, while Carmesina opts for a very different vision, which I shall later discuss in detail, in which she advocates the knightly excellence of him who can use wisdom.

The significance of the Empress's defence of *fortitudo* must be linked to her genealogy. She comes from the only truly courtly world which persists in Europe, since she is the daughter of the Germanic Holy Roman Emperor, an illustrious example, in the *Tirant* (and in other works, like the *Amadís*) of an institution anchored in the past, and clearly overtaken by that earlier and historically more genuine empire, that is to say, the Greek: the only one which can be said to be a direct descendant of the Roman Empire.

The Empress would never have been able to value wisdom as a knightly virtue, but the only cultural reason in support of her attitude is the fact that the courtly world always separated the material and warlike functions from the cultural function. The courtly dichotomy *chevalerie / clergie* is, up to a point, irreconcilable, since both qualities cannot exist in the same person, but will always be separated in the two levels of society it represents. If on occasion we find warrior bishops or hermit knights, it is only for literary reasons: not even Chrétien, who formulates the dichotomy, dares to join it in a single sector of society; not even Ramon Llull, who exploits this literary argument in the *Llibre de l'orde de cavalleria*, allows himself to create a definite fusion of the two worlds, and, in the final instance, will show that, in any case, the functions of one and the other, though complementary, are different (*Llibre de l'orde de cavalleria* VII,9; also *Doctrina pueril* LXXXI,2).

Martorell finally disqualifies the Empress's courtly vision, and the agent of this criticism is the Emperor no less, who finds in favour of Carmesina and her defence of wisdom (chapter 186). But this does not mean that the courtly vision of the political and chivalresque world fails in the *Tirant*. In fact, one could spend a long time discussing what might be Tirant's intention in constructing a novel in which the worlds which finally triumph are precisely those of the characters who best represent the old courtly chivalry tied to irascible appetites and physical strength. I shall not go into intolerable moral judgements over the love scene between Hippolytus and the Empress before their family tombs, though I have not the least doubt that Martorell, in describing this scene, wishes to provoke moral judgement, the rejection of two characters who throughout the novel have been anchored to this courtly world – the Empress, even, by means of a long argument, as I have already indicated; Hippolytus through an attitude which comes directly from the images of the principal Arthurian lover, Gawain, created by the courtly novel up to the fourteenth century, a true playboy, as Riquer calls him (1992).

Monarchic Chivalry

One must not overlook the fact that Martorell shows his preference for a monarchic chivalry; and not for any one, but for the monarchic chivalry that arises in the last quarter of the thirteenth century with the work of Egidius Romanus and is formalized in the second half of the fourteenth with the princely European proto-states, in particular the French (Guenée 1991; Krynen 1993), for which Martorell expresses his admiration, as Riquer has also shown (1992:116–19).

One of the chief discoveries of monarchy is the acceptance of courtly chivalresque ideology and its transformation by way of adapting it to the political needs of a growing sacralized absolutism (Kantorowicz 1957; though for its actual practice, see Boureau [1988]). The first strategy of adaptation consists of creating lay chivalresque orders, with rules imitated from the military orders, and endowed with juridical mechanisms of fraternity and blood relationship, and a procedure of union with the master of the order. The virtues of this idea are essentially the work of Alfonso XI of Castile, whose Orden de la Banda is the first to have this structure and legal statutes enacted by the Crown (which is the sole source of legality – another discovery of monarchic ideology). In imitation of this order, others spring up throughout Europe.

Tirant lo Blanc is a paladin of the most important one of all: the Order of the Garter, created by Edward III of England in 1348. The fact that the function of the Order in the course of the novel is on the whole slight may seem of less importance. As on so many other occasions in the *Tirant*, the original plot imposes itself on the extratextual references in such a way that these serve as narrative reinforcements, as procedures for the characterization of an attitude rather than as narrative vehicles for the attitude itself. In this sense, Tirant's belonging to the Order of the Garter reinforces the hero's essentially monarchic character. And it is still further reinforced when we realize that Tirant, the character, knows exactly which honours he wishes to receive and which not: *aut Caesar aut nihil*, Tirant rejects the title of Duke of Macedonia (the greatest non-regal dignity which can be considered) in full awareness of what he is doing. Likewise, if Tirant had not believed in everything the Order of the Garter signifies, we might think that logically he would not have agreed to be invested with it.

But the chivalresque orders, their constitution and meaning, proceed from the courtly world, so much is obvious. They are formalized and regulated imitations of the Arthurian company. To a great extent, they are the realization of the Arthurian world in territorial society. Even the image of King Arthur is ratified by the monarchs of the second half of the fourteenth century and the fifteenth throughout the whole of Europe. The great difference is that Arthur's is an exclusively literary world, while later monarchism is essentially tangible, as the lay orders clearly prove. By way of insisting on the divergence of these two chivalresque and political worlds, which nevertheless refer back to the same literary tradition, the *Tirant* gives place to one of the most enigmatic interventions concerning politics and chivalry, the interlude of the enchanted King Arthur. The content of his discourse is fundamental to the creation of a frame of reference of monarchic ideology in the *Tirant*, not so much for the topical elements he expounds in answer to the Emperor's questions as for the conceptual framework in which Arthur himself is going to move (chapter 182), one in which the foundation of nobility is indicated by the virtue and ability of the prince to grant nobility to the virtuous person – an idea which only makes sense in the anti-feudal monarchic world, as opposed to the sole reason of lineage proposed by the high nobility of the thirteenth century in the face of chivalresque aspirations (Köhler 1991).

This same idea is what steers the narrative towards its actual ending: both Tirant, Caesar of the Empire, and Hippolytus, Emperor, to all purposes, on the death of the elderly Greek Emperor, are tied to a lineage and show a dignity which on no account would have allowed them to reach the point they have arrived at at the end of their lives. The person who best explains these circumstances is Plaerdemavida when, in a speech she makes to Carmesina, she opposes the view of lineage defended by the Viuda Reposada to the reality of the virtue which Tirant can, and does, demonstrate:

> All your noble deeds have been Tirant's doing, as he routed the Sultan and foiled his plans. Those infidels thought they could defeat our aged Emperor, but instead the Turkish kings had to retreat to Bellpuig – not calmly, but as fast as their terrified legs could carry them. Tirant deserves a reward for his courage, and if I held the royal sceptre I know what I would do, but we damsels foolishly strive for honours, rank and dignity, whereby many of us come to bad ends. What good would it do me to be King David's daughter, if I lost it all for want of a good knight? Arm your soul, my lord, since you have not risked your body in battle, and do not think of giving her to another ... Shall I say it? I must: bestow her upon Tirant.
>
> (chapter 229)

Virtue, then, makes a man worthy, over and above his lineage. The courtly world does not exclude this possibility, to be sure, but it is no less certain that, behind the progess of Lancelot or Percival to the highest levels of dignity, there lies the lineage of which they were unrightfully dispossessed, as perfectly conscious prose narratives like the Arthurian *Vulgata* or *Li hauz livre dou Graal* take it upon themselves to explain.

Apart from this, the courtly world bases this possibility on isolated individual prowess, that is to say, on the heroic career of the knight errant who constructs his life solely in terms of the strength of his arm and the speed of his horse. It is here that the *Tirant* gives a complete twist to this conception, and turns to the idea of a chivalry conceived in the light of monarchic ideology. For Martorell, chivalresque virtue, though constructed on the axis of an individual, in this case Tirant lo Blanc, does not show itself in him in isolation, but this individual prowess is now projected into his ability to lead the chivalresque forces at his disposal. This attitude is already to be found in the transformation to which Martorell submits the narration of Guy of Warwick, through the introduction of a narrative layer whose interest consists in the description of the strategic systems the hero employs. Certainly, he does not fail to maintain the isolated individual strength of his hero, who is a figure of Tirant, above all in his intervention in the face of the King of the Canaries (chapter 19), just as he takes pleasure in what is the prehistory of Tirant gaining individual honour at the English feasts – always, to be sure, in close connection with the hermit.

This attitude refers us, as we have said, to the monarchic, not to the courtly, world. The chivalresque formation conveyed by the courtly novel often places us in battles of armies against armies, but what dominates them is the account of the deeds performed in the midst of battle by the various knights errant assembled there and, on more than one occasion (I am thinking of the battle between Galahad and Arthur, and the role Lancelot plays in it), the simple fact that a particular knight takes sides with one of the armies is sufficient to tip the balance of the battle, not through his strategic skill, but by the force of his arm. On the other hand, the vision of chivalry we call monarchic always conceives the presence of a more important ordering intelligence, one which, in reality, is not so obviously present *in* the battle as *before* it. For that reason, the theorists of the monarchic vision of society preferred the essential virtue of the knight to be centred in his prudence, rather than in his strength. I need only refer to Egidius Romanus, who maintained, following Vegetius, that, more important than the numbers and strength of the combatants, was the prudence of the knight who led them,[3] going on to describe in terms of preparation and strategy the components of the said knightly prudence. On this point, Egidius was contradicting his master, Thomas Aquinas, who could not believe there could exist a knightly prudence or virtue applicable to each one of the knights who take part in a battle, though he himself

---

[3] 'Nam ut plurimum bellorum industria plus confert ad obtinendam victoriam quam faciat multitudo vel fortitudo bellantium' (*De regimine principum* III, iii,1), and then he adds, on the same point, that 'opus autem bellicum continentur sub militari', and, in the project for this part of the book he announces that 'sciendum igitur militiam esse quandam prudentiam, sive quandam speciem prudentiae'. He goes on to enumerate the five kinds he considers in the political milieu and places the military one both in the head, which is the king, and in each of those whom the king delegates.

admitted that the virtue of knightly prudence could always be granted to the leader of the forces:

> Ad primum ergo dicendum quod militaris potest esse ars secundum quod habet quasdam regulas recte utendi quibusdam exterioribus rebus, puta armis et equs: sed secundum quod ordinatur ad bonum commune, habet magis rationem prudentiae.
> Ad secundum dicendum quod alia negotia quae sunt in civitate ordinantur ad aliquas particulares utilitates: sed militare negotium ordinatur ad tuitionem totius boni communis.
> Ad tertium dicendum quod EXECUTIO MILITIAE PERTINET AD FORTITUDINEM: SED DIRECTIO AD PRUDENTIAM, ET PRAECIPUE SECUNDUM QUOD EST IN DUCE EXERCITUS (*Summa Theologiae* 2–2, q.50, a.4).

Notice the distinction Thomas makes between knightly action and direction, one which is fundamental to our understanding of the space in which we are moving. I would emphasize that the world of courtly chivalry takes pleasure in chivalresque action, whereas Tirant, whose prehistory, vicariously related in the presence of the hermit, is based on direct chivalresque action, reveals himself, in direct narration, to be a strategist of the same kind as his master, Guy of Warwick. In one way or another, he undergoes a natural evolution from the courtly world until the moment when he is integrated in the monarchic order, first when he becomes a Knight of the Garter, and then in his functions as a strategist.

In fact, Tirant is the true executant of the ideas maintained by Carmesina before her mother, at the heart of a debate part upon which I have already commented. And it is precisely this vision which Carmesina is defending when she claims that wisdom is a much more essential virtue in a knight than strength. Carmesina puts all her force into considering *saviesa*, which, in my opinion, was often thought to be part of prudence or a *sine qua non*. Although I have dealt with this subject elsewhere (1996a:343–7), I shall add two short notes which may justify this opinion. In the first place, one of the two Castilian translations of the *De regimine principum* of Egidius Romanus, that of Juan García de Castrojeriz of around 1345, instead of translating *prudentia* as 'prudence' (as does the other version, which I believe to date from 1434), systematically gives it as *sabiduria* ('wisdom'). In addition, we might note what Llull has to say on the cognitive position of prudence:

> Prudence is between wisdom and knowledge, for through wisdom it loves the good and hates evil, and through knowledge it knows what is good and what is evil. And that is why prudence brings together wisdom and knowledge: wisdom and knowledge make up prudence, and prudence is not without wisdom and knowledge (*Doctrina pueril* LVI,4).

In effect, Carmesina brings up one of the arguments which the European chivalry debate foregrounded at the moment of attacking the courtly models of chivalry and defending a new monarchic chivalry which, as seems evident, led to the cultural model of 'Roman chivalry'. In particular, it was the fifteenth century which found in Cato, via Sallust, the idea that Rome had increased its power not through force of arms:

> Nolite existimare maiores nostros armis rem publicam ex parva magnam fecisse. Si ita res esset, multo pulcherrimam eam nos haberemus, quippe sociorum atque civium, praeterea armorum atque equorum maior copis nobis quam illis est (*De coniuratione Catilinae* LII,xix–xxiii).

All the reasons which then are given are centred by fifteenth-century intellectuals on prudence or wisdom (Weiss 1992), and Carmesina is thinking along the same lines when, to end her first set of arguments, she states:

> 'Then Your Majesty can look at the Romans, who, though small in number, conquered the world through wisdom, nor could any fool, however brave, be a Roman consul or senator. Their empire lasted as long as they maintained this custom, but once they ceased to choose wise emperors, they were quickly vanquished . . .' (chapter 181).

Roman Chivalry

In fact, as I pointed out earlier, the whole cultural apparatus of Roman chivalry runs through the *Tirant*, though Martorell's preferences, I believe, tend to the side I have just described. It would be impossible for the frame of cultural references to be absent from the *Tirant*, for solely chronological reasons. The range of literary examples which is put forward by the various characters in order to justify or explain their attitudes belongs to the ancient world, and they serve both Carmesina, when she claims that the best knight is the wisest, and her mother, when she maintains a completely opposite view. This way of arguing is the sign of a particular period, but this sign does not entail the acceptance of everything it implies. The background, as Sales has remarked (1991), is a mixture – quite natural in the fifteenth century – of the Breton and the Roman worlds, that is to say, a correct compendium of what the chivalresque literary traditions signify. In the case of the use of ancient tradition, of its texts, its discursive forms, its strategic systems and so on (though not its political paradigms), although Badia (1988) rightly prefers not to speak of humanism, it seems, nevertheless, that the influence of the humanists in the exploitation of this tradition is decisive. However, this falls short of a depiction of all the concepts of Roman politics. No speech conforms to a world whose frame of reference is based on republican politics and

Stoic ethics. To be sure, the terminology of Roman chivalry, of Roman politics in general, is brought into play, but Martorell does not feel easy in this world, and avoids it at all costs.

The most obvious instance is the long political, chivalresque and moral speech made by Abdala Salomon in chapter 143. In it, effectively, the entire republican terminology is stated: the state is a republic directed by a prudent prince who has a fraternal, not a paternal, relation to the people; the said leader is, furthermore, the natural outcome of the warrior who in his early years stood out because of his strength and now, following the precepts of academic politics, has gained prudence with experience, and so on. Besides the terminology, the speech of this Moor of semi-Christian origin contains the whole system of argument based on Roman historiography, which is not only a source of examples, but also of doctrine. We could go much further: Abdala Salomon's speech is a Ciceronian speech in two senses. In the first place since it is an *oratio* perfectly structured in terms of classical rhetorical models, though it falls into the occasional Asianism. But this hardly matters: the most important thing is that it is Ciceronian because it is profoundly republican, profoundly anti-imperial, in its arguments; in each of the Roman arguments it puts forward, the model of action and thought is not a Roman emperor, but Scipio Africanus; and this republican way of arguing reaches the point where only rarely does the figure of Julius Caesar appear in Abdala Salomon's speech, except for his qualities as general and not as prince, whereas Scipio is described as 'magnanimous prince', with true admiration. The Ciceronianism of Abdala Salomon's speech could also be pinned down to various Stoic parameters, deriving from the Ciceronian party and from Senecan philosophy, above all when the speaker insists on friendship as the foundation of correct political action:

> Let the prince be ever mindful of Sallust's teaching: that neither soldiers nor money can defend a king, but only friends won by good deeds, merit and honesty. Therefore, a prince should live in concord with his subjects, as concord makes small things flourish whereas discord fells great ones. Marcus Agrippa was one example: a man who strove mightily to achieve concord. A good prince will be every man's brother, comrade, friend, or worthy master. After God and charity, let him hold friendship dearest, never banishing those who merit love from his councils, but rather following Seneca's advice and taking counsel with trusted friends (chapter 143).

But soon this same speech turns aside to consider the thirteenth-century political topic of how to distinguish friends from flatterers, of the problem which arises between friendship and power, and other questions that appear in the literature of practical advice so common in the Peninsula and the rest of Europe towards the end of the thirteenth century (Jonsson 1995; Haro 1995; Haro 1996; Rodríguez Velasco 1996b). In general, this literature derives from two traditions: on the one hand, the mirrors of princes of a monarchical type, duly freed from their treatise aspect and made into rapid guides to eminently practical phrases; on the other, they come from a princely tradition dear to Islamic political theory, represented in treatises by Al-Farabi or Avicenna, when they comment respectively on Aristotle and Plato, but, above all, conveyed in a literature that delights in presenting the prince in the bosom of his council, and the strategic and dialectical systems which allow the prince to resolve political problems after listening to and evaluating the opinion of his counsellors. It is here, above all, that Abdala Salomon's speech takes its place, though it seems to allude to the Roman world: in his long monologue, he reviews each and every one of the extremes of practical knowledge to which I have just referred.

Views of Chivalry

All this is far from excluding the fact that the characters of the *Tirant* take a particular view of chivalry. In a certain way, this view allows the confrontation of the different conceptions, over and above the ideological positions we might notice in the preceding pages. The view of mythical chivalry has been sufficiently emphasized by Emilio Sales (1991), and there is no need to insist on it. But alongside this we must remember that practically each one of the sensibilities that are opposed in the novel offers some manifestation of a chivalresque type. I do not need to recall that the Duke of Macedonia tries to counter Tirant's great prestige in the Greek Empire by opposing his own idea of what chivalry is, and by reproaching Tirant for the importance he gives to the strategic systems which, as we have seen, are an essential part of his notions of chivalry. The Duke, on the other hand, prides himself on a courtly idea, based less on opportunity than on the individual strength of which I have already spoken.

Beside this concept, the fearful lords of the infidels (chapter 164) or the preacher who offers his sermon on the occasion of Diafebus's marriage and his subsequent elevation to the Dukedom of Macedonia show their own respective conceptions; in the latter case, the preacher contents himself with providing an *abrégé* of chivalresque formation in virtue and knowledge. Notice that, before the possibility of expounding a Lullian concept of chivalry, as the situation might suggest, he prefers to summarize the content of something very similar to what Egidius Romanus sets out in his *De regimine principium* (Book III, Part iii).

For this reason, the account of the formation of the warriors of Enedast (chapter 239) is very significant:

> Enedast ... is a fertile and abundant province. As soon as a male child is born the King takes charge of his training. Once the boy is ten years old, they teach him to ride and use a sword, and after he has mastered these

skills they place him in a forge, that his arms may grow strong and good for smiting Christians. Having taught him to wrestle, throw a lance, and wield all other weapons, they place him in a slaughter-house where he becomes accustomed to hacking flesh. This King's cruel and hardened knights quarter Christians without pity. They are the bravest warriors in pagandom, and ten of them are worth forty of the others.

It is not surprising that the natives of this people are especially cruel. But the content of this description is not an exaggeration constructed by Martorell for the occasion, but a careful textual reference, easily recognizable and strategically transformed. The monarchic tradition of chivalresque doctrines had freely made use of the contents of the *Epitoma rei militaris* of Flavius Vegetius, transforming them in turn in order to adapt them to a completely different society. Although Vegetius already notes that warriors should be distinguished by a certain spiritual quality as well as by their strength, it was the political treatise of Egidius Romanus and the *Siete Partidas* of Alfonso X that emphasized the need for the strength or brutality of warriors to be balanced by a modicum of nobility and gentlemanliness which would provide them with the necessary shame for behaving in battle. This meant that, in the event, one and another of the Christian monarchs signalled their preference for nobles, though they might be weaker, over cruel warriors accustomed to harsh trades like smithying or butchering. Since the *Segunda Partida* was translated into Catalan by (or, rather, for) Pere III in the part dealing with chivalry, it seems logical to suppose that Martorell could have extracted from it this opposition of worlds:

And in their choice they looked out for three things: the first, that they should be hard-working, that they might know and could undergo the great labours which may occur in wars and battles; the second, that they should be used to suffering, that they might kill and overcome their enemies better and more quickly, and not easily be put to flight while fighting; the third, that they should be cruel, so as not to care about robbing and taking what is their enemies', nor about wounding and killing.

And that is why in ancient times, in order to make knights, they took huntsmen from the mountains, men used to suffering much labour; and carpenters, blacksmiths and stonebreakers, since they are used to striking and have strong hands; and likewise butchers, since they are used to killing living things and shedding their blood. And they looked out for one other thing in making knights: that they should be well formed in their limbs, and strong and light.

And the ancients used this way of choosing for a long time; but often seeing that such men, being without shame, forgot all these things, and instead of defeating the enemy, defeated themselves, those who are wise in these matters held it good to choose for such business men who naturally felt shame. And a wise man named Vegetius, who spoke of the order of chivalry, said to this effect, that shame prevents the knight from fleeing from battle, and that that shame makes him a conqueror (Pere III, *Tractats de cavalleria*; Bohigas 1947:113–14).

From this description, anyone who knows about medieval chivalry will gather a great deal of information; above all, this people of infidels is characterized not only as infidel but as ignoble. What is more, since the interpretation of these extremes is essentially monarchic, it also brings into relief the world which is preferred by Tirant's companions

By Way of Conclusion

In short, it was not a question of making great demonstrations, but rather of showing the narrative function of ideas about chivalry in Martorell's novel. It seems that we cannot regard the opposition of the different worlds of chivalry as a crucial element in the plot, though, in the same way, I have not the slightest doubt that, for those who were aware of the different ideologies of the time, the fact that the novel brought into play these systems of opposition must have seemed highly significant, and would have helped them to make the appropriate identifications.

In all probability, it would be no less important for them that, from all this stagnation, there should emerge an idea – the monarchic one – which was not exactly in fashion, but which, to middle ranking knights had offered throughout history, and through the whole of Europe, a strong reason for supporting it, as against the feudal privileges of the highest nobility, clearly prejudiced, above all, by the monarchic ideologies of France and Castile.

A novel, naturally, of history and fiction, as Riquer has called it, it makes use of the systems of its time to create a powerful world in the enormous laboratory of reality which is the literary work.

Translated by Arthur Terry

Comedy and Performance in *Tirant lo Blanc*

RAFAEL BELTRÁN

In chapter 275 of *Tirant lo Blanc*, the Emperor decides to organize a great feast in honour of Tirant. The most ostentatious and symbolic part of the proceedings is to be the preparation, entrusted to master craftsmen, of an unspecified number of banners, as many as the battles he has won, and also 372 standards bearing the arms of Tirant, corresponding to the number of castles and cities he has conquered for the Empire in the course of the four-and-a-half years he has spent in Constantinople. The banners will be placed in the church of St Sophia and the standards around the principal altar of the same church. What happens a little later, in chapter 282, must be understood within the framework of this homage. The Emperor sends urgently ('a gran pressa') for Tirant. He orders him to sit at the table alone. While the Emperor himself, his wife the Empress and his daughter, Princess Carmesina, serve him with dishes, the others listen spellbound to a recitation:

> The other guests listened to an old knight experienced in arms, an eloquent jurist who began to recount Tirant's deeds. And thus both lords and ladies forgot about their food, hearing what great honours Tirant had obtained to that very day. When Tirant was finished eating, the elderly knight ceased his recital, which had lasted for three hours (chapter 282).

After this curious recital, which lasts throughout Tirant's copious meal, all the courtiers rush to the marketplace, where wild bulls are fighting, and entertain themselves with more feasting and revelry. Once night has fallen, after supper:

> the dances, with farces and interludes, lasted as long as was needed to show how Tirant entered into battles. This feasting went on almost the whole night (chapter 282).

It is certain that literary emulation in the Middle Ages often led to the practice of genuine acts of imitative staging (Keen 1986:265–70). Thus these two quotations make clear how, in a single day, there take place two levels of literary transmission of Tirant's actions: reading or recital ('recount[ed] Tirant's deeds') and performance ('show[ed] how Tirant entered into battles'). The reading, on the part of an elderly knight who is both a soldier and an educated man – he is neither a minstrel nor a priest – occupies the minds of his listeners for three hours, and such is their rapture that they forget to eat. The performance, the pantomime of the 'interludes' – the anonymous translator of the Castilian version of 1511 renders the term as 'mummeries' (*momos*) – probably staged a selection of the passages the guests had listened to some hours earlier.

An oral recital and a festive performance. Action and commemoration. A war-like and ceremonial rehearsal of victory. A profane, chivalresque ceremony, but also a religious one, like the banners and hundreds of standards with Tirant's arms in the church of St Sophia. To what extent are these two levels of narration, the reading and the performance, present and differentiated in the *Tirant*? The biography of the character Tirant in the novel is constructed as a sequence of pictures of public and private activity.[1] The former, from the scenes of fighting in battles or tournaments, to the wedding, and eventually to his death, since they are open, sometimes require the narrator to divide himself into some of the various perspectives from which they might be seen in the real life they reflect. Thus the linear account of Tirant's deeds is compatible with another level, where some of the character's vicissitudes are seen from a different angle: readings on a different stratum, which bring with them different dimensions of Tirant and of other characters in the novel.

Point of view, in the modern sense, presents the partial realities experienced by each character and encourages the reader to reconstruct a totality on this basis. The discovery of intratextual recipients requires the multiplicity of readings, documents, letters, books, edicts, sermons, eye-witness accounts, monologues, messengers, symbolic languages (the language of banners, for example) and so on. And a polyphony of registers, within these indirect communications between narrator and reader, which goes from oratorical emphasis (the epic reading at the meal and the feast) to visualization in the form of a spectacle. As Segre says, referring to *Tirant lo Blanc*:

> The succession of deeds is subjected to a fluctuating illumination, so that reality is revealed to the different characters under very different aspects. The characters are often victims of this illusionism; but the reader also, if attentive, meets with genuine surprises (Segre 1993:582).

When the impersonal narrator temporarily delegates his voice in the story or in the composition of a ceremonial script to another character, the latter may initiate a new circuit of reception within a particular situation in the novel. There is a perfect example of this in the change of internal narrator for

---

[1] The novel follows the linear account of a historical chivalresque biography and the narrative is structurally very coherent, as Perujo has shown (1995). Martorell scarcely leaves his main character in any of the intercalated episodes, and he has little recourse to *entrelacement*. Nevertheless, he seeks 'illusionary effects frequently, and in a most modern way' (Segre 1993:582).

the account of Tirant's deeds in England. When Diafebus gives a detailed inventory of Tirant's victories (chapters 56–84), the latter listens to him with humility and resignation; he is listening, for the first time in the novel, to the literary expression of part of his life, which he hears with discomfort and embarrassment at seeing himself magnified in the mirror of the recitation. Similarly, when the Emperor is planning the homage in chapter 275 he summons a Royal Council for its approval, but when 'he learned why the Imperial Council had been convened, Tirant hastily returned to his lodgings. He refused to attend lest he hear himself praised . . .' Nevertheless, in the majority of cases, this secondary mode of discourse (the recital or performance) is not based on a distant past, but has to do with a present which implicates the protagonist in the deeds which are shown. On these occasions, Tirant is not only a referent but a reader / spectator, like we ourselves, of his past and present, and his own reading of history can be a determinant in the developing actions of the plot.

We have spoken of pictures of public activity. The same illusionary and polyphonic effects are to be seen in those of private or intimate activity, those of the bedroom, which are usually represented through the lens of occultation, hidden or converted into dreams (like that of Plaerdemavida on the night of the 'secret weddings') or deviant fantasies (like the loves of Hipòlit and the Empress).

Are there scripts for the representation of one and the other? The public sphere, as we shall see, has script models in a whole series of representations, tied on the one hand to the palace settings of royalty or nobility and to urban spaces, which produce feasts and courtly spectacles, and on the other to performances in churches, which produce liturgical spectacles. By contrast, the private sphere – always understood as the most intimate – can only be represented by recourse to models and codes related to exclusively textual literary sources.

Comedy

We start, then, from the idea of comedy as a text that is read (which naturally, since we are dealing with a medieval work, does not exclude the dramatized reading nor the group hearing, that is to say, oral transmission), and from the idea of representation as an act performed as a spectacle (which does not exclude the use of a text, but is always dependent on the presence of other signs of non-verbal communication). The idea of the comedy as text comes from our knowledge of what the term 'comedy' originally meant in the Middle Ages: a story with a happy ending.

We therefore do not take into account, for medieval literature, the identification of comedy and representation. Thus, the elegiac and humanistic comedies form a unit which, strictly speaking, does not belong to the dramatic genre, that is to say, to the medieval theatre (so difficult, incidentally, to delimit), though it is certain that its basic simplicity, the obscenity of its themes and the rhetorical use of a low, and by extension, comic style, contributed decisively to the development of the theatre. This is the case with the *Pamphilus*, probably the most widespread elegiac comedy, attributed in the Middle Ages to Ovid. Juan Ruiz, the Archpriest of Hita, paraphrases a good part of this text in the *Libro de buen amor* (coplas 583–891). For some time now the *Pamphilus* has been recognized as one of the main sources of the *Celestina*. What is curious is that Joanot Martorell shows that he knew it, since Carmesina's dramatic monologue (chapters 436–7), when Tirant succeeds in conquering her and entering the castle of her body – to use the author's clumsy military image – is a fairly faithful version of Galatea's speech when she reaches a similar situation with Pamphilus (*Pamphilus*, vv. 680–8). Pamphilus therefore, however rudimentary his origins, provides the same remote literary origin for such apparently different characters as the I / Juan Ruiz of the *Libro de buen amor*, Tirant the lover and Calisto (Beltrán 1990).

Owing to this common source in *Tirant lo Blanc* and the *Celestina*, we see that the famous night of the 'secret weddings' (chapters 162–3), with Estefania's amorous soliloquy and Carmesina's final surrender already mentioned (chapters 436–7), have a perfect replica in Acts VII, XIV and XXI of the *Celestina*, as in other Hispanic texts, such as the dramatic monologue of the Archpriest of Talavera on 'How women speak to those they love, of whatever age'.[2] Both the dramatic monologue of the deflowered maiden and the prayer which follows it (Sosia, in the *Celestina*, calls it an 'oration') were very familiar to university students, and also to moralists like the Archpriest of Talavera, who states, after giving his variant of the prayer as an example of female deceit:

> They say this and other things to make themselves honest, but God knows the strength they put into it, or the vehemence with which they flee or resist . . .; they appear to put all their strength into it, seeming to express grief and annoyance.

'They appear to put all their strength into it', that is to say, they are feigning or representing. Does this mean a theatrical performance, a staging within the novel (like those we shall see in a moment)? Of course not. We are

---

[2] They are not simply lexical coincidences, but moments of intertextuality, which have their ancient origin in the final episode of the *Pamphilus*. Thus, the use of force, with ill treatment of the maiden: 'Quod me sic tractas!' (*Pamphilus* 688), which in the *Tirant* becomes: 'By your gentleness, do not treat me thus'; useless cries of resistance, such as 'Desine! Clamabo! . . . Quod agis? . . . Perfida, me miseram' (*Pamphilus* 689–90), which becomes: 'Watch out, wretch! . . . I shall shout! Watch out, I am going to shout'; the final lament, the amorous surrender, etc. For further details, see Beltrán 1990.

simply faced with the effect or the illusion of being able to capture a concrete, vulgar, daily reality, an effect proper to low speech and, in particular, to comedy.

When Erich Auerbach (1953:20–43) comments on the use of this expressive comedy language in the *Satiricon* of Petronius, he emphasizes its limitations: in Antiquity (and we could extend it to the Middle Ages) the criticism of vices is posed as an individual problem which never touches social life or the historical background. But this same limitation, which comes from a lack of sufficient historical awareness, leads to the presentation of other kinds of life in an ahistorical, static and idyllic way. We observe this immobilty in the rigidity of public ceremony. Public matters, in principle, cannot be subject to a comic approach, though we certainly know very little about the presence of the comic, laughter or *ludus* in religious or secular ceremonies. The private sphere, on the other hand, does lend itself to, and even associates itself with, these jokes, by means of pictures which reflect intimate milieux with the lowness of vulgar language (popular proverbs, coarseness, obscenities), not in the least stylized, a language which – through the law of decorum – prevents the people who use it from being taken seriously in their actions, at least in their moments of privacy.

Performances

In the public sphere, we need to begin by attempting to differentiate, in the novel, between the reflection of courtly or liturgical performances of the period and the possible original creation of scripts or scenarios for performance. What is certain is that, if we examine in detail the scenes represented, we realize that they all imply, to a greater or lesser extent, spectacles of the medieval nobility, royalty, city or, to a lesser degree, Church. In *Tirant lo Blanc*, therefore – as one would expect – there would be no strictly original representations. Nevertheless, in every scene there is beyond doubt such an integration of characters and dramatic action in the plot that it would be quite inaccurate to speak of a mere reflection or of a simple picture inserted from the reality which Martorell knew. In any case, it would be more to the point to speak of two extremes between which the novel's chief representations are situated: that of closest identification with the spectacles of the period and least literary distortion, and, at the opposite pole, the greater literary elaboration and also, as a consequence, the greater distance from medieval historical representations. The three examples we are about to see are situated at different points on this imaginary line. The 'rock' of the English feasts at the maximum degree of imitation of real referents, the episode of Arthur and Morgana at a point equidistant between imitation and the creation of a fresh script, and the plot invented by the Viuda Reposada at a point furthest from imitation and closest to creative imagination.[3]

The chief representations that appear in the work have to do with royal ceremony, and specifically with wedding celebrations or marriage petitions.[4] Grilli (1994) has shown very clearly the theatricality of two of these representations, the episode of Arthur and Morgana and that of the Viuda Reposada. The studies of Oleza (1992), Cocozella (1993) and Massip (1996) lead one to add at least one more spectacle: the 'rock' of the English feasts. We shall examine them following the order in which they appear in the novel.

The 'Rock' of the English Feasts

In the midst of the English feasts, the 'magnificences of the rock', a great allegorical celebration, are described (chapters 53–5). One must remember that, as happens with the next representation we shall discuss, it is only one of the many spectacles which go to make up the London feasts, which last for a year, and which take place as a way of celebrating the marriage of the English King to a daughter of the King of France. The detailed account that Diafebus gives, at the request of Guy of Warwick, on returning from these feasts, confines itself to Tirant's victories over his successive adversaries, the procession of the estates of the Church, the wedding mass in the meadow with the 'portable altar', the dances and banquets, fishing and hunting, and the rule for each day of the week (chapters 41–52), details which, taken together, recall well-known celebrations in a great many medieval kingdoms.

The architecture of the 'rock' and the staging of the assault on the castle constitute a more elaborate spectacle, but one that is described in the same way from the fourteenth century onwards, with some – though not all – of the details that appear in *Tirant lo Blanc*. In the first place, the 'rock' is plausibly announced as a very costly construction: 'a thing of great magnificence, the like of which I believe is not to be found elsewhere in the world' (chapter 53).[5] Its exterior is described thus:

---

[3] The comedy would be a borderline case of this second extreme, that is to say, the maximum literary elaboration of a scene or group of scenes that are scarcely performable (if not impossible to act) in reality, like the aforementioned famous chapter 436 of *Tirant lo Blanc*, which derives directly from the *Pamphilus*.

[4] The scheme for classifying royal ceremonies in fifteenth-century Castile developed by Nieto Soria (1993) also applies perfectly to the Crown of Aragon: ceremonies of access to power, of changes of life (births, baptisms, weddings), of cooperation (oaths, discourses, knightly investitures), of justice (court hearings, challenges and defiances), liturgical, funerary, of reception (royal entrances, reception of embassies, etc.) and of victory.

[5] 'Magnificence' has the meaning of 'value', rather than that of something admirable or marvellous. There is an insistence on the financial cost of the machine, when the hermit asks: 'What was this thing of so much worth?' And see shortly before this in chapter 41 the same sense.

> In the middle of that meadow we found a big rock so cunningly crafted that it made one continuous surface, and on the rock stood a high castle with mighty walls, guarded by five hundred men in shining armour (chapter 53).

But the representation is not only scenic. It implies the movement of actors. And, in fact, an attack on the rock is simulated, which is repelled by its defenders:

> Those guarding the walls fired catapults, muskets and cannon. They hurled bars that looked like iron but were made of black leather, just as the stones were of white leather . . . They were filled with sand, and if they hit a soldier they could fell him (chapter 53).

The text of the representation appears when they pass from the warlike game to the courtly allegory. The castle only surrenders when the Queen herself asks who is its lord and the 'God of Love' appears at a window. The Queen begs him to 'open the doors of your glorious dwelling to me . . . and receive me into your longed for glory' (chapter 54). Only then do the doors open 'with a great noise'. They all enter into a courtyard covered with precious hangings and with angels above playing various instruments. The God of Love speaks, and then disappears. And then, after the tapestries and hangings fall as the result of a tremendous noise and movement ('they began to move almost as if in an earthquake'), the space is transformed into four parts, each of which contains many rooms.

It is certain that artificial displays like these were prepared for great solemnities, as for example the coronation feasts of King Martin I in Saragossa in 1399, or those of Fernando de Antequera (1414) in the same city, or the feasts of Lille, in France, in 1454. Massip (1996) shows very clearly the close relationship between the display of 1414 and that described by Martorell: a mock battle with stones of leather, celestial and allegorical decorations, music and other sound effects, scenic illusions (the appearance and disappearance of elements and personages), and so on. We might add that the opening of the 'rock' described by Martorell – not easy to understand – is more like that of the 'fortress' of wood and cloth presented in the neighbouring Kingdom of Castile, in the feasts of Valladolid (1428), by Prince Enrique. The 'fortress' consisted of a tower with four turrets and a belfry, surrounded by a fence and a barrier, the latter with twelve more towers, with a 'well dressed lady' on each of them. And 'below, on the floor of the fortress, resting rooms for the Prince and stables and mangers for horses' (Carrillo 1946:20–1). These interior rooms correspond to the four parts of the rock in *Tirant lo Blanc*:

> The King and his retinue were lodged in one, the Queen and her compatriots in another, and in a third were all the foreigners ... (chapter 55)

Nevertheless, the architecture described by Martorell seems to exceed the limits of what was historically possible. The 'stables and mangers' described in the 'fortress' of 1428 are replaced by fountains in each of the rooms: that of the mature, naked woman whose breasts gushed water in the King's, that of the golden maiden whose sex delivered white wine in the Queen's, that of the bishop from whose mitre oil came in a third; that of the gilded lion from whose mouth honey poured in the last. In the courtyard which gave entrance to the four rooms, the statue of a grotesque dwarf who gushed fine red wine from his navel. Close by, finally, the statue of an old bearded hunchback provided them with bread, bearing on his back the weight of no fewer than 30,000 loaves. Behind the 'rock' which clearly could not be more than ephemeral, though static, architecture, a garden was prepared, which included the entrance to a genuine zoo. Though the narrator, after describing these statues, insists that they were not made 'by magic or the art of necromancy, but by artificial means' (chapter 55), and though we have precedents like the courtyard of the Aljafería of Saragossa where, in 1414, there was 'a fountain of wood painted to resemble marble, whence flowed in three directions water and red and white wine' (and Massip [1996:154] gives more examples), there is no doubt that Martorell was pushing verisimilitude to an extreme by multiplying the variety of liquids and the quantity of bread.

As Keen remarks, in general terms 'fifteenth-century chivalresque literature is truer to reality than is often thought' (1986:275). In this spectacle, specifically, there is an imitative fusion of pageantry elements taken from royalty, from the nobility and from the city. Nor must one dismiss the influence of religious spectacles, which we shall see more obviously in the subsequent representations.[6] The balance clearly inclines towards the maximum historical fidelity and the minimum literary distortion. The latter, nevertheless, exists. On the one hand, there is an attempt to create an ambiguity or uncertainty, by making the actors comply with a kind of representation:

> Certainly it was a most genteel battle, but at first we thought it real. Many of us dismounted, drew our swords, and hastened to aid the Duke, but then we realized it was only a masque (chapter 53).

On the other hand, though the luxury, sensuality and exoticism of these and other scenarios are effectively ambiguous and create a striking unease in the reader, there is no doubt that the latter would be perfectly aware that the

---

[6] Thus, Massip recalls the relationship of the 'rock' to the meaning it had in Catalan at the time: 'pageant wagon', with the representation of religious pieces in the Corpus procession, though also, clearly, of profane elements in royal entries.

limits of what was architecturally conceivable for a feast, however great, had been exceeded. As Oleza points out:

> At this stage, the account of the English feasts seems to depart from that of certain historical celebrations, however embellished, and become pure fiction. The scenic space initially limited by its materiality and by the scenic tradition familiar to its readers, broadens out, dissolving its limits and opening itself to all the possibilities of the imagination (1992:328).

The Episode of the Prophetic Barque

The second representation takes place in chapter 189, when Tirant finds himself once more in the midst of feasting, this time in the court of Constantinople, and it is announced that 'a ship is come into harbour with neither masts nor sails, all covered in black'. As in the previous case, one must remember that this is not the only one, but rather one of the several – though the most theatrical – representations that take place in the course of the feasting which the Emperor offers the ambassadors of the Sultan of Cairo, who bring a marriage petition from the Sultan to the Princess Carmesina.[7] We are now in a double ceremonial milieu of royalty: the petition of betrothal and the foreign embassy. The ceremonies, as occurred in the historical spectacles of the time, are located in internal acting spaces (like the palace and the galley) and in external ones (like the market place and the harbour), and are organized around five types of spectacle. Of these five, the first three are a courtly judgement presided over by the Sybil (chapter 189), the jousting of knights, related to this judgement, and a tournament, actions which take place in a sumptuously decorated marketplace. The two following ones are the episode of the ship's arrival, with the meeting between Arthur and Morgana (chapters 190–202) and the vows of the knights (chapters 202–7). The jousting, the tournament and the vows represent, not without originality (especially in the case of the third), the perfect triad common to every chivalresque spectacle in the Middle Ages (Keen 1986:265–88).

The representation of the Sybil is of special interest since I believe it combines echoes of both courtly and religious spectacle. The Sybil, richly dressed and seated on a revolving throne, presides over a courtly tribunal of justice:

> There was a platform covered with brocade in the centre of the lists, and upon it stood a splendid chair that could turn in all directions. There sat the wise Sybil, richly dressed, with great magnificence. And she gazed continually, now here, now there (chapter 189).

---

[7] See for these feasts as a whole Riquer 1992:141–8. The eight days' duration is not much, given the complex ceremonies with which royalty entertained the ambassadors.

Although the oracular role ascribed to the Sybil in the medieval theatre will here be transferred to Arthur and Morgana, nevertheless, both her superior position, the setting, costumes and accessories, and her own activity as judge can be closely related to liturgical representations.[8] But there is an intermediate ground, for which we have Hispanic witnesses, although later than *Tirant lo Blanc*. The Sybil of the *Farsa del juego de cañas* of Diego Sánchez de Badajoz, from a position very like that of *Tirant lo Blanc*, announces an allegorical and musical *juego de cañas*,[9] in which the seven deadly sins are to fight with the virtues. Not only that. There are witnesses who relate the liturgical, theatrical personage to the literature of chivalry, as is the case with the *Auto de la Sibila Casandra* of Gil Vicente (1513), where there appears a proud Sybil, who claims to be the one chosen to be the mother of Jesus Christ (Lida 1966:168–72). In this instance, it is a question of a personage who departs from the religious tradition of the *Ordo prophetarum* and, on the other hand, reflects the secularized tradition of chivalresque fiction – more specifically, its source has been traced to the *Guarino mezquino* of Andrea da Barberino. Thus the 'wise Sybil' of *Tirant lo Blanc* owes something to courtly spectacles, but probably also to a medieval liturgy which, all things considered, as Zumthor points out, was 'spectacular in its most intimate parts' (1989:313).

It is only with the fourth spectacle related to the feast of the Sultan's ambassadors that we find a true articulation of non-verbal elements of communication (from the temporary architecture and scenery to the movement of the actors) with other verbal ones, which allows us to speak openly of representation. Although the inspiration of the episode of the prophetic barque in the *Tirant* is textual, the most recent criticism refers to it as as an 'interlude' (*entremés*).[10] In contrast to the first spectacle, where Diafebus revealed the cardboard deception of the scenery, here Martorell, 'with the intention of plunging the reader into this refined and fantastic literary milieu, recounts

---

[8] I study this aspect and others referring to the Arthur – Morgana episode in greater detail in Beltrán (1997a).

[9] The *juego de cañas* was a mock tournament, in which sharpened stakes were used as weapons. (*Translator's note*)

[10] The chief source of the episode is in the *Faula* of Guillem de Torroella, as has been recognized, but the idea goes back previously to a kind of vision experienced by Giflet, at the end of the *Mort Artu*, amidst dense rain and from a distant hill: the arrival and departure of a ship full of ladies, among them Morgana, having called and picked up her brother Arthur. It is called an 'interlude' by Riquer (1990:150 and 154), Hauf (1990:15–21), Badia (1993b:121), Grilli (1994:100–3), Perujo (1995:181) and Massip (1996:155–6). What is certain is that Martorell does not call the piece which follows an *entremés*, although it is one, at least if we go by the first localized appearance of the term in Castilian and its use in the Catalan of the period. In the *Tirant*, the word *entremés* appears always with reference to amusing situations, though not only capable of representation, like this one, but also real.

these deeds without ever revealing the deceit, deliberately hiding the fact that it is all comic illusion' (Riquer 1992:147).

A theatrical spectacle? The fact is that the spectacle of the galleys is one of the first examples of mobile scenery in the Middle Ages, since it is documented in the medieval urban feast from the twelfth century onwards. There are records going back to 1274 of ships which proceed through cities of the Crown of Aragon, though we do not find 'interludes' with whales until 1474 (Riquer 1990a 152–3). The whale is associated with the sea dragon which, as occurred with the enchanted castle, appears on occasion filled with fireworks. But it is not only that. The theme of the ship which arrives at a court bearing prophetesses (Sybil, Morgana) will appear in other Castilian books of chivalry, specifically in *Amadís de Gaula* and the *Corónica de Adramón* (in the latter, what is more, as a ship-whale), and will contain more explicit scenographic elements than the *Tirant* itself: the terrifying appearance, the transformation of the setting of the ship, music, noise, smoke, the behaviour of the personages . . . , are theatrical ingredients that coincide with *Tirant lo Blanc*, and whose presence shows that the condition of representation of this episode within a book of chivalry is not unusual.

The folklore motif of the ship coming from the Beyond, the religious motif of Jonah and the whale, announcing hope in the Saviour, the chivalresque theme of the Arthurian literary tradition, the sentimental theme of the dark galley which suggests penitence for the sin of love. . . , all these textual traditions, along with those of secular and religious spectacles, feed into the episode of *Tirant lo Blanc*, though the latter, all things considered, as Hauf explains (1990:24), is essentially a divertimento. The form of the spectacle, in this case, seems to dominate over the background of revelation, though it is very difficult to separate clearly the two aspects. There is, let us not forget, a representation, not only before the personages, but also before the reader. And we find for the first time, as Massip recalls (1996:156), a scenic use in the Crown of Aragon of Arthurian providentialism, a detail which on no account must be left out of consideration.

The Episode of the Viuda Reposada

The Viuda Reposada, Carmesina's nurse, weaves a subtle intrigue in the face of the knight's logical refusal of her amorous overtures. She begins by telling Tirant that Carmesina is so dishonest and lustful as to exchange secret loves with a palace gardener named Lauseta, a black slave and a Moor (chapters 265–8). Naturally, Tirant does not believe her words. But in order to demonstrate the accuracy of her incredible accusations, the Widow, with the excuse that the Feast of Corpus is approaching, orders a painter to reproduce in a mask the face of Lauseta the Moor:

> ... a mask covered with black leather that will look like our gardener Lauseta's face. Some of his hair is black and some white (chapter 269).

The Widow persuades Tirant to go into a hut near the palace garden from which he will be able to observe unseen what is to happen.[11] She then suggests to Carmesina that she should go down to this garden to play with the Corpus masks and persuades Plaerdemavida to put on the mask (chapter 283). The latter, playing her part to perfection, caresses Carmesina's body in a daring fashion:

> The Princess laughed so hard that she forgot her weariness, while the damsel edged closer and felt beneath her mistress's skirt. Everyone was delighted by Plaerdemavida's pleasantries.

Tirant spies on the scene from his hiding place, thanks to a system of mirrors that reveal that Carmesina is pursuing dishonest love with Lauseta. In despair, after once again refusing the still clearer amorous suggestions of the Widow, who thought she now had a clear field, and after a period of reflection in his room, he seeks out Lauseta and kills him (chapters 284–7).

It is obvious that in the *Tirant*, as in the story of Dalinda in Canto V of the *Orlando Furioso* which derives from it, we are faced with something much more complex than the simple story of a man who watches how his wife or beloved deceives him.[12] We are present at the representation of a previously prepared deception, at a comedy of deceit. The theatricality of the episode has been sufficiently remarked by Grilli (1994), Romeu (1994) and Massip (1996). Renedo (1996), for his part, sets it within the theory and moralizing concerning the medieval *ludus*, emphasizing its ambiguity as between the *ludus turpis et inhonestus* and the *ludus humanae consolationis*. The theatrical possibilities of the episode seem beyond doubt. For my own part, I am interested in pointing out only two things. In the first place, that the presence of a whole series of evangelical references, like that to Holy Thursday (although quite a bit earlier: chapter 228), or to Tirant compared by the Widow to Jesus Christ (chapter 264), and of festive–religious allusions, specifically the various references to the Feast of Corpus, make one think that Martorell is trying to play with the sacred–profane parallel of a Tirant who is the victim of deep amorous suffering, a genuine Passion.[13]

---

[11] As Renedo (1996) suggests, the 'agreed house of a very ancient woman' could be a house of assignation, literally a *prostibulum*, the name given, according to St Isidore, to the theatre as a place where prostitutes came after the end of the performance.

[12] The scene as misunderstanding also has notable precedents in the story tradition (Hauf 1990). I suggest a few more within the chivalresque tradition in Beltrán, in press.

[13] Compare, in this sense, the ambiguous use of religious language – obviously for sexual purposes – by the Viuda Reposada, with almost the same words and with the same purpose, when Calisto addresses Melibea in the opening scene of the *Celestina* ('... the

In the second instance, related to the first, there are the implications that this other level of reading may have on Tirant the spectator. In my opinion, Martorell wants the reader to see Tirant having the opportunity to decide his future, to calculate the possibilities that offer themselves, and that at this moment are reduced to two: to triumph over Fortune (if he takes seriously the oracle of Arthur and Morgana) or to be defeated in the face of Love (if he allows himself to be carried away by his sexual appetite). Naturally, it is a false dilemma, since the solution is already foreseen. But it seems to me, in this sense, that, in Tirant's amorous career, the episode of the Viuda Reposada signifies a second scenification at which Tirant is obliged to assist, thus doubling his own actions. The first, of course, has been the episode of the prophetic barque.

These two representations hold up the linear development of the character in order to penetrate two moments of his biographical trajectory. As we said before, from a modern point of view, certain realities perceived partially or mistakenly by some of the characters are presented to us, and it is left to the reader to reconstruct a meaningful whole. The two representations dramatize, bring to light (or to the stage) as a therapeutic diversion, as an 'interlude', two stages in his life, so that Tirant, from a distance, or through his bewilderment, may recognize the blindness of the love he is suffering, and may attempt to cure and put an end to his sickness.

In the first phase of the cure, the narrator shows Tirant – always in a playful and honest way, as *eutrapelia* (Renedo 1996) – the dangers of the world and the prophecies of the Last Judgement. The feminine embassy, headed by the mythical Urganda, reminds him of his heroic mission. Arthurian providentialism accommodates itself to the courtly spectacle of a galley bearing omens of destruction (the signs of judgement) and revelations of restoration (the ship-whale).

Nevertheless, Tirant does not learn his lesson. In face of his persistent idleness, in this second representation there is applied with greater force another of the accustomed therapeutic remedies: the dishonouring of the beloved. In my opinion, Martorell is proposing an unexpected escape from the unbearable tension that underlies the play of relations between Carmesina and Tirant, having recourse to the Ovid of the *Remedia amoris* (vv. 299–310), where he advises the lover, as the best therapy against the negative effects of love, to imagine in a concentrated form, as if they were before his eyes, all possible defects of the beloved ('pone ante oculos omnia damna tuos'), especially the cruel supposition that a servant is obtaining at night the favours that are denied to himself. The Widow makes use of the magic of the

---

service, sacrifice, devotion and pious works which I have offered to God in order to reach this place . . .'): 'Oh brave knight, how often have I prayed and lit candles for your sake! How many alms and fasts have I offered, lacerating my body that yours might be preserved!' (chapter 286).

theatre, of the necromancy of mirrors, since the normal perception of facts would be insufficient to bring the lover to reason – to *her* reason, but also to objective reason. The Widow organizes the representation of a fantasy as necessary for Tirant's recovery of integrity (health) as it is convenient for the prolongation of the plot. Clearly, she involves herself in it in such a way that she destroys herself in the sacrifice. The Widow's fiction is, as Renedo says (1996), *ludus turpis*, but by means of the sieve that cleanses it as a spiritual joy (theatre of devotion) it is converted into *ludus consolationis*, into a curative or cathartic theatre (the *catharsis* culminates in Lauseta's death).

The defeat of the Widow represents the explicit failure of a narrative option for Tirant. Martorell is saying to us that he cannot – obviously because he does not wish to – channel Tirant's career in a straight line, despite having warned him. Tirant, who has to begin from scratch another path of ascent, loses, but the novel, which prolongs his adventures through many more pages, is the gainer.

The narrator has delegated his functions to a series of intratextual narrators, and through them he multiplies himself as oral narrator (Diafebus), reader/reciter (the 'elderly man' of chapter 273), but also as theatre director, which includes a conception of scenery and decor (the Emperor, who conceives the setting for the feast), an awareness of the power of illusionary magic in temporary, static or dynamic architecture (the 'rock' or the 'interlude' of Arthur and Morgana), and a knowledge of the value of directing actors (those organized by the Viuda Reposada). All these partial narrators raise the building of the novel with an architectural complexity it is not possible to reduce to the level of linear action. Many of the rooms of this building remain open to the pleasure of reading the novel, which should not limit its possibilities as artistic communication to what is strictly literal.

Translated by Arthur Terry

'Poets and Historians' in *Tirant lo Blanc*: Joanot Martorell's Models and the Cultural Space of Chivalresque Fiction[1]

JOSEP PUJOL

1. *Joanot Martorell's 'Glory of Knowledge'*

The growth in recent years of critical studies concerning the literary sources of *Tirant lo Blanc* allows one to map the literary culture of Joanot Martorell with increasing precision, and shows above all the extent to which the reworking of his multiple sources implies a patient and attentive dedication to the writing of a novel that resonates throughout with literal reminiscences of classical Latin literature, of contemporary Catalan writing and that of the Italian *trecento*.[2] The literary and cultural ambition implied by these methods of composition, and the high rhetoric which Martorell demonstrates as a result of the imitation and creative appropriation of his sources, can no longer be seen, then, with the Romantic prejudice which praised the 'glory of ignorance' of the uninhibited 'realistic' narrator and which attributed to the author of long rhetorical speeches the consequent 'burden of knowledge', but must be the starting point for crediting Martorell – apologetically, if need be – with the 'glory of knowledge' which is his due.[3]

To take into account the author's dealings with knowledge means assum-

---

[1] This study forms part of research project PB–94–0894–A of the DGICYT of the Spanish Ministry of Education and Culture.

[2] For the state of the question up to 1993, see Badia 1993a. Some later studies insist on the presence of Corella, amplify the importance of classical historiography, of the *Històries troianes* of Guido delle Colonne and the *Heroides* of Ovid, and present data concerning the use of the tragedies of Seneca, the *Scipió e Aníbal* of Antoni Canals and various works of Boccaccio (Cingolani 1995–96; Renedo 1995–96; Pujol 1995–96, 1997, 1998 and 1999; Annicchiarico 1996; Guia 1996b; Martínez 1998:155–98).

[3] The concepts referring to knowledge and ignorance come from a well-known letter of battle from Martorell to Joan de Monpalau in which, replying to the latter's malicious allusions to Martorell's use of scholastic terms, he refutes him with the accusation that 'you charge me with knowledge, keeping for yourself the glory of ignorance' (Riquer and Vargas Llosa 1972:75). The phrase passed literally into chapter 131 of *Tirant lo Blanc*, in one of Carmesina's reproaches to Tirant, and, a little before this, in chapter 127, Carmesina had praised 'the glory of knowledge which foreigners possess'.

ing that the *Tirant* projects and realizes certain literary objectives which depend on Martorell's idea of the available literary traditions and that are the result of an elementary reflection on the methods of literary composition and on the value of chivalresque fiction in relation to these traditions. To be sure, the instruments on which the author could rely were limited. Martorell was a knight who had acquired his literary education through vernacular texts, and who had no proper schooling or direct access to Latin culture. Nevertheless, in 1460 the cultural possibilities of the vernacular, though limited, were sufficient – I give only two examples – to inscribe the story of a Breton knight who fights with the Greeks within the schemes of the Trojan myth and to begin by invoking the power of bestowing fame possessed by 'historians' and 'poets', the two literary categories to which, in practice, the basic sources and models for the narrative and rhetorical structure of the *Tirant* are reduced. That is why, leaving aside the fact that the phrase 'poets and historians' to which I refer derives directly from the source of the dedication of the *Tirant*, the model combination of history and poetry, without distinction between the factual truth of the one and the fabulous fictionality of the other, which clashes scandalously with the antipoetic belligerence of an influential model such as Guido delle Colonne, can serve as a guideline in sketching an interpretation of *Tirant lo Blanc* which, by combining what we know of his chief sources with what Martorell states explicitly in the dedication and prologue of the novel – the only spaces he has reserved for the authorial voice – will bring out the literary and cultural assumptions that make it possible. Moreover, these assumptions can also be seen as instruments for justifying and legitimizing fiction at a time when the problem of the legitimization of literary creation in the vernacular takes on its full urgency. The finest creations of fifteenth-century Catalan literature derive, in my opinion, from the need and capacity to face up to this problem, and Joanot Martorell is no exception.[4]

2. *Strategies of the Prologue: History and Translation*

Although it is obvious that the main function of prologues is to establish a bridge between writer and reader in order to shape the perspective from which the latter must read the work that is being offered, one must remember that in a vernacular work composed in the middle of the fifteenth century the

---

[4] What follows is merely intended to indicate some lines of cultural interpretation without attempting to be complete. Consequently, I do not take into account all the literary sources of the *Tirant*, nor am I concerned with aspects that go beyond the justifications of historiography and classicizing rhetoric, as for instance the treatment of amorous passion which, apart from the question of sources, should be read in a theoretical context of the 'recreative' justification of literature on the lines of Olson 1982.

genre of the prologue, often adapted to academic categories, has the specific function of situating the text in a particular literary and cultural tradition and, by means of this situation, of establishing or vindicating the authority of the writer. Thus it becomes the vehicle of a particular concept of literature. However, with few exceptions (Hauf 1989; Badia 1993b:132–5; Limorti 1993), the prefatory texts of the *Tirant* have scarcely been read from this point of view, perhaps because of the fact that the dedication is plagiarized[5] and because of an unspoken prejudice to the effect that both the dedication and a prologue which quotes Cicero and St Luke and which displays a certain erudition in literary matters, could have nothing to do with recognized virtues of the *Tirant* such as narrative verisimilitude or the supposedly modern treatment of sexuality. If, on the other hand, we look at the novel from the coordinates of Martorell's literary culture, we must return to the dedication and prologue and take into account the exact terms in which the author thinks and authorizes his fiction.

The fact that prologues are strategies for establishing authority within the conventions of a particular tradition explains why, in the late Middle Ages, they adopt quite concrete formal configurations. Remaining with vernacular texts, one may choose between forms derived from the scholastic sermon (Juan Ruiz, *Libro de Buen Amor*; Antoni Canals, *Scipió e Aníbal*), academic formulae of the *accessus ad auctores* type (anonymous Catalan translation of the *Paradoxa*; Gutierre Díez de Games, *El Victorial*)), a laudatory history of translation (translation of the *Paradoxa* of Ferran Valentí) or of poetry (Marqués de Santillana, *Prohemio*; prologue of Juan Alfonso de Baena), or else the epistolographic formalization of the dedication, accompanied or not by a prologue, as in *Tirant lo Blanc* and its model, Enric de Villena's *Dotze treballs d'Hèrcules*. That Martorell should have opted for the latter model, and not for any of the others, may have to do with a conscious refusal of the more markedly scholastic models and with a decided option for rhetoric – the same rhetoric that guides his pen throughout the novel – but this does not mean that the content will differ noticeably from that of texts that conform to other models, for example the academic models which underlie the long prologue of Gutierre Díez de Games in the *Victorial*, where the author frames a biographical story within the prefatory norms of the *accessus* in their Aristotelian version (Beltrán 1997c).[6] In this way the Castilian author proceeds to establish the four *causae* of the work in order to register its authority (effi-

---

[5] 'The plagiarism is frankly scandalous' is Riquer's only commentary (1990a:278). Moreover, I am not aware that anyone has ever considered whether the prologue which follows the dedication is original to Martorell or not. In any case, like the dedication, it is a veritable cento of historiographical commonplaces which should be related to the appropriate referents. It should be added that, not surprisingly, a few linguistic formulae in this prologue seem to echo Antoni Canals's translation of Valerius Maximus, as I intend to show elsewhere.

[6] For this type of academic prologue, see Minnis (1988:28–9), who on pp. 160–5

cient cause) and its values: since the praise of a knight (formal cause) allows him to construct a discourse on chivalry (material cause), the work is directed towards the moral end of instructing the reader (final cause). These same values may be extracted, *mutatis mutandis*, from the dedication and prologue of the *Tirant*: the material cause underlies the statement that 'the aforesaid treatise contains at length the greater part of the code and order of arms and chivalry', the formal cause is explicit in the last paragraph of the prologue, which is concerned with the virtues of the 'military order', and the penultimate paragraph of the dedication, devoted to the chivalresque and moral benefits which will ensue from the reading, corresponds to the final cause. The comparison is merely intended to show how, despite the differences in procedure, when presenting the novel to his readers, Martorell, following Villena, assumes a learned perspective which derives from the scholarly need to make clear the advantages of the work and which is resolved in the approximation between the novel itself and various models of a historiographic type. To be sure, the *exemplum* of Guillem de Vàroic, the doctrine based on Llull, the minute description of the ritual and codification of chivalresque combat, the *lletres de batalla*, the military harangues, the ordering of land and sea battles, the sermons and discourses *de regimine principum* may be read from that didactic point of view, all the more so since the prologue contains reflections on the importance of military ordering comparable to those which begin the *De coniuratione Catalinae* of Sallust (I and II), the *De re militari* of Vegetius (Badia 1983–4:213–14) and practically all the prologues to the vernacular translations of ancient historiographic and epic works.[7] Nevertheless, this doctrinal objective is not self-sufficient – in the sense that the novel is not intended to be a 'doctrine for knights', as Hauf had suggested (1989:23) – but depends on the two arguments with which Martorell establishes his authority (translation) and presents his book (the fixing in writing of the deeds of an historic hero).

The first argument corresponds to a necessary change of strategy in relation to the dedication of Enric de Villena's *Dotze treballs d'Hèrcules* to mossèn Pere Pardo, which serves as his model. Not so much in order to oppose it or detach himself from it (Cátedra 1993:199–200), as from Martorell's awareness of the distance that separates him from a *compilator* and *commentator* who had 'sought out, collected, expounded and ordered' the

---

studies its use in fourteenth- and fifteenth-century English literature. For academic prologues in fifteenth-century Castilian literature, see Weiss 1990: 107–17.

[7] Probably the most accomplished Hispanic example of this military assimilation of classical historiography is Pero López de Ayala's prologue to his translation of Pierre Bersuire's French version of the *Decades* of Livy. See Wittlin's edition (1984:215–20) and also Lawrance (1986:67–9) and Gómez Moreno (1995:87–90), who also note the military interest in the Latin *Iliad* of Pier Candido Decembrio and in the *Aeneid* (concerning the latter, see the translation by Enric de Villena, ed. Cátedra [1989 I:31]).

labours of Hercules.[8] Villena's task makes sense in view of the material and the order to which he submits it, since his work is not a simple narration of the deeds of Hercules, but rather an ethico-political treatise which derives its pedagogical effectiveness from the allegorical, historical and tropological exegesis of the fictions of the poets and the historical truth they contain. Martorell, on the other hand, does not have to undertake any exegetical operations: his is a text confined to the biography of a hero in which the academic task of compilation would have no meaning. Hence, of Villena's four verbs, there remains only 'to expound', meaning 'to translate'. Martorell, therefore, is very alert to his appropriation of Villena's prefatory epistle: he recognizes the historiographic value of the work, which allows him a tacit identification between the deeds of Hercules and those of Tirant, he assumes the academic categories and the rhetoric which the model embodies and, above all, he takes over a generic model of the author: that of cultural mediator by means of translation. This is of paramount importance, since translating is not only the culturally necessary task referred to in the exordia of the French *romans* of the twelfth century, but has also acquired, as Ferran Valentí explains around 1450, the same intellectual and moral dignity possessed by the *auctores* (Badia 1994). In the context which Valentí's reflections presuppose – and in the epistolar and rhetorical context of Martorell – I do not think one can reduce Martorell's attitude to the simple mechanical repetition of a *topos* derived from the earliest Romance fictions, especially if we take into account the use of this *topos* in historical chronicles and biographies of knights which have strictly historical acts and personages as their basic material (Gaucher 1994:276–9). One need only notice the clear-sighted coherence with which he reworks the obligatory *captatio benevolentiae* of Villena's text: where the latter merely compares himself to 'others more sufficient than myself', Martorell converts the problems of a compiler into those of a translator who has trouble in 'turning the words well . . . because of the said English language', as medieval translators who work from Latin never cease to complain (Russell 1985:11–26; Badia 1991). The equivalence between Martorell and a fifteenth-century translator, then, is complete. That he and all those other authors who take refuge in the same commonplace should tell us truths, half-truths or lies is of no importance from this point of view, since it is always a question of establishing the authority of the author by displacing it on to an original source, an older book which inevitably contains a truth that must be 'recited'.[9] Martorell, in particular, belongs to the group of those who fall back on half-truths: on the one hand, he justifies his knowledge of English

---

[8] For these categories, see Parkes (1991:58–59).
[9] Without wishing to affirm that Martorell was using the academic category of the *recitatio*, it is worth pointing out the fundamental similarity to the role of *recitator* which many late medieval authors adopt. For English examples, see Minnis (1988:192–3).

with an argument (his stay in England) not unknown to other translators;[10] on the other, the initial narrative material – whether he read it in French or English, which I doubt – is English, and his hero wins his fame in the England conceived by the author of the prose *Guy of Warwick* as 'fontaine et miroer de toute proesse et chevalerie'(Conlon 1969:57).[11] Thus, to displace authority in no way means denying it: in the very act of translating, the author restores it through the linguistic appropriation of the source for which he becomes the one and only person responsible,[12] since in the end the accent falls, not on an ancient *auctor*, but on the recording of certain deeds which Joanot Martorell, naming himself in the text, tries to make accessible to Prince Fernando of Portugal and to the public of his 'nation' through the agency of his work.[13] The result of the operation is, on the one hand, that Martorell's 'translation' becomes an independent textual reality, similar to the way in which Ferran Valentí, breaking down the frontiers between literature and translation, foregrounds a number of Catalan translations (Badia 1994:174); on the other hand, the authority and intellectual dignity of the translator increase in proportion to the grandeur of the deeds of a more or less ancient hero – remember that Tirant belongs to the sphere of the 'knights of the past' – whom we shall see acting in a skilful synthesis of a fifteenth-century knight and a Roman leader.

Tirant is an ancient knight, and his actions are 'ancient deeds and histories' which Martorell 'translates' following an obligation of status – 'since by

---

[10] For example, the Fra Pere Busquets who translated Domenico Cavalca: 'And it had been translated from that language [Tuscan] into Catalan by the priest Pere Busquets ... who had been in Italy for more than fifteen years and knew that language quite sufficiently' (Gallina 1967 I:23).

[11] Since it has often been said that Martorell pretends to translate from a 'normal' language and not an 'exotic' one, I hasten to say that I do not know which of these two images of English a Catalan reader of the second half of the fifteenth century might have. One thing, nevertheless, is certain: the practical non-existence of medieval translations from English to Catalan or Castilian, with one intriguing exception: the Castilian translation, made by Juan de Cuenca, of John Gower's *Confessio amantis*, which according to the author was done on the basis of an existing Portuguese translation, recently discovered. That is to say, like the *Tirant*.

[12] As Rita Copeland has written referring to the replacement of the original text by translation: 'Like commentary, translation tends to represent itself as "service" to an authoritative source, but also like commentary, translation actually displaces the originary force of its models' (1991:4). Despite the fact that Copeland's book is more concerned with situating translations in the context of academic practice (for late medieval literary creation, see especially pp. 179–220), the result of Martorell's pretended operation is the same. For games with authority in French chivalresque biographies, see Gaucher (1994:285).

[13] In note 11 I have commented on the singularity of another instance of the trajectory English–Portuguese–Castilian. One should ask, moreover, whether Martorell knew that Enric de Villena had also made a double version of his text: Catalan for a Valencian audience, Castilian when his public career finally moved in the direction of Castile.

my order [i.e. of chivalry] I am obliged to show forth the virtuous deeds of the knights of the past' – which reappears in various biographies of knights (Gaucher 1994:94–5) and which supplies a justification *de persona* to add to the justifications *de historia* and *de materia* to be found everywhere in prefatory texts, thus reinforcing the links between text and author.[14] Such insistence on deeds places the fictitious biography of Tirant in a previous and recognizable literary category, which can count on its own elements of legitimization since history implies, first of all, the presumption of truth ('res verae quae factae sunt', according to Isidore), but also, and above all, because the writing of history has a specific function relative to the reality from which it derives: the perpetuation, and the subsequent actualization, of the memory of heroes. Isidore had also said: 'quidquid dignum memoria est litteris mandatur. Historiae autem ideo monumenta dicuntur, eo quod memoriam tribuant rerum gestarum' (*Etymologiae* I, xli,11). And the prologue of the *Tirant* begins precisely with the premise that writing makes up for the weakness of human memory – a genuine commonplace of historiographic writing:

> Since manifest experience shows the weakness of memory, which consigns to oblivion not only those deeds made old by time but also the fresh events of our own era, it has been appropriate, useful and expedient to record in writing the feats of strong and courageous men of old. Such men are the brightest of mirrors, examples and sources of righteous instruction, as we are told by that noble orator Tully.

Parallel examples could be multiplied, from the sentence with which Pero López de Ayala begins his *Crónicas* ('The memory of men is very weak, and cannot recall everything which happened in the past' [Martín 1991:3]) to Guido delle Colonne's prologue to the *Historia destructionis Troiae*: 'Licet cotidie uetera recentibus obruant . . .' (Griffin 1936:3). The sentence, therefore, implies that the book – more precisely, the chronicle and the history – has been conceived in order to perpetuate memory and to overcome oblivion: the chronicles, the translations of ancient historiography and other praises of writing repeat it systematically, and it is with this statement that Martorell ends the second paragraph of his prologue: 'And many deeds and innumerable ancient stories have been compiled so that they may not disappear from human thought through oblivion.'

We have already seen that in the dedication this task of memory is entrusted to 'poets and historians', who do not represent opposing categories,

---

[14] I take these categories, in so far as they are systematic, from the treatise *De historia* edited by Karl Halm in *Rhetores latini minores*: 'Principiorum ad historiam pertinentium species sunt tres: de historia, de persona, de materia. Aut enim historiae bonum generaliter commendamus, ut Cato, aut pro persona scribentis rationem eius quod hoc officium adsumpserit reddimus, ut Sallustius . . ., aut eam rem, quam relaturi sumus, dignam quae et scribatur et legatur ostendimus, ut Livius ab urbe condita' (*apud* Jaffe 1978:312).

rather the contrary, as shown by the examples Martorell gives in the second paragraph of the prologue. Guido delle Colonne, whom Martorell and his contemporaries knew and admired, maintained precisely the contrary, and his antipoetic militancy, together with the insistence on his supposed historical foundations in order to distance himself from the fictional abuses of the poets (Griffin 1936:3–5; Miquel i Planas 1916:6–7), revived and transmitted to the vernaculars the polemic about poetry which has a central place in *Curial e Güelfa*. Martorell remains on the margin. He has enough with Villena, whom he transcribes literally at this point, without worrying about Villena's further distinctions in a passage he suppresses ('you thought I had read the historians who have treated of this and the poets who have decorated it with their fictions') (Riquer 1990a: 276), perhaps because he had realized that in the *Dotze treballs d'Hèrcules* the distinction disappears the moment the poetic fictions are reduced euhemeristically to the same historical truth which is conveyed by the historians. (Moreover, it is worth pointing out that in this early work there are signs of the theories of the ideal chronicler, founded on rhetoric and poetry, which Villena was later to expound in the prologue to his commented translation of the *Aeneid* and which also make the poet into a kind of chronicler [Cátedra 1989 I:27–8,47–8,54–5]).[15] We shall see how, in practice, Martorell's is a poetry without fable. That is why, in the theoretical dimension of the prologue, the list of works, deeds and memorable authors which takes up the central part can seem apparently indiscriminate: the heroes of biblical and classical history, of hagiography, of Arthurian fiction and of fable are alive because the writing perpetuates their memory. Also, of course, that of Tirant. Martorell, then, conforms precisely to an obligatory *topos*, not only of classical and medieval historiographical literature from Cicero, Sallust and St Isidore onwards, but also of any text which comes to the defence of writing, such as the *Philobiblon* of Richard of Bury which Antoni Canals used as a prologue to one of his translations (Bofarull 1857), the sermons of Felip de Malla on the *gaia ciència* (where Sallust serves to authorize the laudatory function of literature from the classics to Dante [Pujol 1996:218–20]) or Juan Alfonso de Baena's *prologus* to his *Cancionero*, based on the prologue to the *Historia de España* of Alfonso X of Castile (Dutton and González Cuenca 1993:3–8). To adhere to a tradition composed of historians and poets thus implies the presumption of truth, but also means that Martorell himself could claim the ennobling value of writing and the moral and intellectual advantages that derive from it, sanctioned by a vague reference to 'that great orator Tully' which Riquer (1990b:7) related to *Pro Archia poeta* VI,14.[16] However, the lack of literal parallels and the rarity of this speech outside humanistic circles invites caution; perhaps it is simply a

---

[15] Boccaccio also, in his commentary on the *Divine Comedy*, attributes to poets, who are superior to historians, a historiographical mission. See Padoan (1994 I:278).

[16] 'Sed pleni omnes sunt libri, plenae sapientium voces, plena exemplorum vetustas;

memory of an anthology piece like *De oratore* II,9 ('Historia verum testis temporum, lux veritatis, vita memoriae, magistra vitae, nuntia vetustatis'), available in the *Speculum historiale* of Vincent of Beauvais (VI,xviii 1624:180) and constantly paraphrased in the vernacular (Guenée 1980:18–19). The effect, in any case, is that of the classical authority which gives free rein to Martorell's novel.

3. Historiography and Poetry: the 'Stratification' of Sources

Despite the list referred to above, in practice Martorell is not so indiscriminate. Faced with a diversity which includes battles of Greeks, Trojans and Romans, Arthurian adventures, poetic fables and saints' lives, Martorell's terrain is that of battles, and his literary practice one that intends to found itself on the historical model, which in his eyes is represented just as well by the poet Homer as by the historian Livy. Reacting to the prestige and the vernacular diffusion of classical historiography and treatises *de re militari*, and assuming their justification as examples for modern chivalry, Martorell intends to write a knightly fiction that will resemble the true stories of the knights of the past and that will correspond to the ethical and literary demands of this kind of story. It should be said that, in view of the *Tirant*'s sources, this past also includes more recent deeds, like the pseudohistorical actions of Guy of Warwick and the historical ones of Roger de Flor narrated by Ramon Muntaner, but it seems clear from what we have read in the prefatory texts that Martorell does not doubt the superiority of the ancients, to whom he has recourse by indirect means, like the *Dotzè* of Eiximenis, used in strategic matters (Riquer 1990a:204–9), and directly in searching for models concerning the art of warfare, to the extent that many episodes that critics have interpreted as 'realistic' and 'modern' are the result of the deliberate imitation of Valerius Maximus, Frontinus, Vegetius, Sallust or Livy.[17]

However, the superiority of the ancients is also a matter of rhetorical elevation, perfectly manageable for someone who, like Martorell, read versions of the classics in a Latinized Catalan which created the illusion of a style adequate to the grandeur of the events narrated in the novel. In this sense, it is worth remembering that one of the best-known classical formulations of the

---

quae iacerent in tenebris omnia, nisi litterarum lumen accederet. Quam multas nobis imagines non solum ad intuendum, verum etiam ad imitandum fortissimorum virorum expressas scriptores et Graeci et Latini relinquerunt'.

[17] See Badia (1993a:72–3) and Cingolani (1995–96). All the historians I have quoted were circulating in Catalan versions from the end of the fourteenth century. Although so far no one has proposed any for borrowings from Livy, the fact that a medieval Catalan version existed does not rule him out as a possible source for lessons of war. In this sense, it seems to me undeniable that the burning of a wooden bridge in chapter 141 of the *Tirant* depends directly on the the ruse by which the Romans conquer the Sabines in Book I,

value of eloquence in ennobling historical facts is chapter VIII of Sallust's *De coniuratione Catilinae*, which explains that, if the deeds of the Athenians, while inferior to those of the Romans, enjoy more fame, it is because they could rely on *scriptores* who were able to increase their worth.[18] This was not a text to be passed over lightly: it is Sallust who guides the compiler of the donation document of the library of Pere III to Poblet when he explains that the deeds of the Catalan kings lacked the subtle arts which would improve them, and when he demands for the king a writer sufficiently lucid to provide him with praise or criticism worth recording (Rubió i Balaguer 1987:447). Sallust also underlies the excuse of the author of the *Curial* for his hero's slight reputation: if he seems less worthy than the ancient heroes, he says, it is because these have had the benefit of Livys, Virgils and Statiuses who, even by feigning, have improved their actions (Aramon i Serra 1930–33 III:13–16). Martorell knows perfectly well that rhetorical elevation is the cornerstone of a historiographical discourse that will rival the ancients and endow his hero with a comparable fame. And he does not avoid the consequences. What the anonymous author of the *Curial* did not wish, or was unable, to do, Martorell decisively resolves, and his hero, unlike Curial, undoubtedly *was* 'a great captain, a great warrior and conqueror, as we might say Alexander, Caesar, Hannibal, Pyrrho and Scipio and many others' (Aramon i Serra 1930–33 III:13), since, while the *Curial* follows a chivalresque model derived from the medieval chronicle, Martorell adds to this model the ancient *militia* and classicizing rhetoric.

Martorell's recourse to classical historiography and to collections and manuals concerning the art of warfare is, then, essential when it comes to endowing his leader and the armies he commands with the ancient dimension referred to in the prologue. It is also certain, however, that some of the structural aspects of the novel derive from medieval historiography, and in particular from the chronicle of Ramon Muntaner. Thus, although fulfilling the historical requirements of the position adopted by Martorell, it only half fulfils them, since Muntaner, despite his novelesque tendencies, pursues a writing which is concerned with simple recitation and with the epic exaltation

---

chapter xxxv,37 of the first *Decade*. Moreover, the influence of Valerius Maximus (Cingolani 1995–96) must not be limited to military strategy, since Martorell also used Antoni Canals's translation of the Latin historian as a rhetorical model. One need only compare the speech of the King of Tremicen which begins 'O ciutat tirantina' (chapter 349) with Valerius's words against the 'ciutat tarentina' (i.e. Tarentum) (II I, 14, ed. Miquel i Planas 1914:91–2).

[18] 'Atheniensium res gestae sicuti ego aestimo, satis amplae magnificaeque fuere, verum aliquanto minores tamen quam fama feruntur. Sed quia provenere ibi scriptorum magna ingenia, per terrarum orbem Atheniensium facta pro maximis celebrantur. Ita eorum qui fecere virtus tanta habetur, quantum eam verbis potuere extollere praeclara ingenia.'

of warlike deeds, which is more or less what happens in the prose *roman* of Guy of Warwick: it is a text which pretends to be historical and which displays a style not essentially different from that which characterizes the Arthurian *romans* and vernacular historiography; the style which, despite the reduction to which it subjects the text, issues in Martorell's *Guillem de Varoic*. A comparison between the *Guillem* and the *Tirant* will make clear what I am trying to say. Between one work and the other, Martorell has discovered Corella (Hauf 1993; Cingolani 1995–96) and the classical *militia*, and, when he returns to the original sources (*Llibre de l'orde de cavalleria* and *Guy of Warwick*), he does not only take from them small details of slight relevance (Riquer 1990a:257–71). Quite otherwise, as Espadaler has noted (1993:263–7), the return to the *Guy of Warwick* implies the recuperation and redimensionalizing of a long episode which in the *Guillem*, concerned only with the exemplary skeleton of a text identified as a *tractat* ('treatise'), Martorell had suppressed: the emotional crisis that Felice undergoes on hearing that Guy is to become a penitent, which furnishes the material for chapters 3 and 4 of the *Tirant* and offers a first taste of the emotional climate and high rhetoric that are to preside over the more 'discursive' aspects of the love relationships. Love, then, enters the novel by way of the *Guy of Warwick*, but redimensionalized by the Latinizing rhetoric. In other words, the adaptation of a medieval model to the narrative intrigue of the *Tirant* implies its systematic rewriting.

Martorell, however, had access to another *soi-disant* historiographical text which satisfied the double necessity of 'ancient deeds and stories' and of the amorous material which the laws of the medieval narrative genre demanded: the fourteenth-century Catalan translation of the *Historia destructionis Troiae* of Guido delle Colonne, known as *Històries troianes*. Martorell took from this all kinds of material, and the Guidian origin of battle schemes, amorous situations, descriptions and speeches makes the work of the Sicilian writer one of the literary keys of the *Tirant*. In the following section I shall deal in more detail with the literary and cultural importance of the *Històries troianes*. Before doing so, however, I would emphasize a paradoxical phenomenon: what Guido presents as true history is for the Valencian novelist the means of access to poetry, in the sense that Ovid's *Heroides*, the *Tragedies* of Seneca and the prose works of Corella, all texts more or less connected with the Trojan myth, are, as it were, the 'specialized sources' that complete and give a fuller rhetorical dimension to the episodes – chiefly amorous – narrated by Guido. In a sense, one could claim that Martorell's models act as strata which fall into place one on top of the other: Guido on the schemes of Muntaner, classical and neoclassical poetry on Guido. As I have shown elsewhere (Pujol 1995–96 and 1997), in chapter 125 of *Tirant lo Blanc* a scene from Guido's episode of Jason and Medea (Book II) is adapted to a narrative scheme that derives from chapter 213 of Muntaner's chronicle; in chapter 118, which explains how Tirant falls in love – and which is indirectly dependent on Muntaner and *Guy of Warwick* – some borrowings from Books VII and XXIII of the *Històries troianes* are completed by recourse to the epistles of Paris and Helen in Ovid's *Heroides*; and in chapter 119, these same epistles provide the text of a narrative scheme that derives from Corella's *Història de Jason i Medea*. These are not the only instances, and the *Heroides* – and modern derivations like the *Bursario* of Juan Rodríguez del Padrón – continue to supply words for all kinds of previous narrative schemes. The same, more or less, happens with Seneca, and the mere fact that the death of Tirant is assimilated to the catastrophe implied by the fall of Troy leads Martorell inevitably to combine borrowings from Seneca's *Troades* and Corella's *Plany de la reina Hècuba* in order to give the appropriate tragic dimension to the end of the novel.

4. Poetry, History and Translations: a New Space for Chivalresque Fiction

That poetry and history should mutually complete one another in the service of a chivalresque novel, without breaks between the two components, depends on an essentially rhetorical approach to the poetry of the ancients offered by Corella's rewritings of Ovidian themes, and which is perfectly compatible with the rhetoric displayed in the Catalan version of Guido delle Colonne or with the mastery of military eloquence which the treatises recommend and historiography exemplifies. Read avoiding the *fabula* component, poetry is reduced to 'stories' – generally amorous – which interest Martorell on account of the eloquence of their personages. And his way of reading the *Històries troianes* is scarcely different. Guido's work, as I have noted, is the literary key to *Tirant lo Blanc*, the model in which Martorell mirrored himself in order to create a novelesque fiction that would give itself a classicizing appearance. This value as a model can be explained for two reasons. The first is the place which Guido's *Historia* occupies in the cultural panorama of the late Middle Ages. As is well known, Guido delle Colonne had translated the *Roman de Troie* without admitting it, and pretended that he was working from the supposedly historical sources that Benoît de Saint-Maure had used, that is to say, Dictys and Dares. Leaving aside the extent to which the *Historia* is a conscious falsification, Guido's operation had enormous implications, above all because it presupposed a reworking of the facts narrated in the *Roman* on another cultural, ideological and rhetorical plane: Latin – *grammatica* – implied a true history uncontaminated by the fictions of the poets or the vernacular, and also implied a reinterpretation of history in the antiheroic and antierotic terms of a moralist (Dionisotti 1965; Bruni 1990:143–5 and 1991:50–6). This particular Guidian reinvention of the classical world in Latin prose rendered the *Roman de Troie* unserviceable, and became a mine of themes and models – as shown by Boccaccio, Chaucer or

Corella – provided one injected into the new text a good dose of Ovidian poetry and the 'ampliores metaphoras et colores . . . et transgressiones occurrentes' which Guido did not include in his own *Historia* (Griffin 1936:276). The second reason for Guido's importance depends on the first. The model character of the Latin text gives rise to a rash of translations and adaptations to the vernaculars which demonstrate the pressure exerted by a secular world which wishes to provide itself with the standard text, crowned with the prestige of the learned language, on the war of Troy (Marcos Casquero 1996:59–69). In this context, the Catalan translation of the *Històries troianes* begun by Jaume Conesa in 1367 is of capital importance, since it transfers to the horizon of cultural reference of the layman not only the cultural and ideological values of the Latin text, but also a Latinized linguistic model (Wittlin 1989) which was to favour Martorell's efforts to raise his individual style to what he believed was the style of the classics.

Evidently, these same statements could be applied to the translations of classical Latin poets into Catalan, whose stylistic results are in perfect harmony with the classicizing stylistic solutions of Boccaccio's tales or Corella's prose. The reason is simple enough once one realizes that the translation of ancient materials into the vernacular implies the transformation – in fact, the reinvention – of the works translated, beginning with the prose to which the verse texts are reduced, and ending with the confusion of text and glosses which characterize, for example, the translation of Seneca's tragedies (Martínez 1995). The immediate consequence is the lack of generic distinction and the abolition of the frontiers that separate not only learned Latin culture from vernacular culture, but also prose from verse, history from poetry and 'truth' from 'fiction'. Under these conditions, Martorell could read and admire the *Històries troianes*, which claimed to be history, just as he read and admired Seneca's tragedies, Ovid's *Heroides*, Boccaccio's narratives or Corella's prose, which are, or wish to be, poetry.[19] Once the distance between 'historians' and 'poets' is removed, the rhetoric they have in common imposes itself.

In its turn, this rhetorical reading of the classical tradition is explained by the kind of cultural consciousness we can suppose in Martorell, and which the comparison with *Curial e Güelfa* can help to illustrate. If the *Curial* is a 'poeticized chronicle' (Turró i Torrent 1991), the result of a difficult balance between chronicle and poetry raised to the level of debate within the novel, it is because the anonymous author is fully conscious of the cultural fracture between two worlds. For that reason, from his own lay and vernacular world, he vindicates the appropriation of part of what is alien to him, the learned Latin universe of the *reverenda letradura*. Its author competes in full con-

---

[19] The case of Boccaccio is a little different, though we should not lose sight of the fact that the *Filocolo* is explicitly placed within the orbit of poetry, and that the *Fiammetta* is basically Ovid plus Seneca.

sciousness, and this competition between the modern layman and the ancient and modern sages explains the words referring to Curial's reputation I have already quoted. For Martorell, on the other hand, there is no fracture. His cultural world is single, not dual, in the sense that he has assumed quite unproblematically the cultural limitations inherent in his status as layman, and all that these limitations imply: a literary work executed on the basis of an exclusively vernacular culture in which historians and poets, vernacular and Latin, finally belong to an identical world to which the entry is vernacular prose, and which excludes the exegetical aspects of poetic fiction which belong to the academic dimension. His poets, like his historians, are those he could read in Catalan, reduced to a rhetorical and historical dimension, and are confined in practice to Seneca and Ovid and to the modern writers Boccaccio and Corella. With all these instruments to hand, the literary result would inevitably be a *letteratura mezzana* in which the weight of the Romance tradition and that of the classical and pseudoclassical tradition balance one another. But the application of this concept which Francesco Bruni coined by way of defining the narrative of Boccaccio from the *Filocolo* onwards (Bruni 1990) and which can be extended to the literary project of *Curial e Güelfa* (Cingolani 1994), needs an important qualification since, unlike the latter, Martorell constructs his writing on the basis of a culture which is already *mezzana* and which, consequently, does not involve the author in any dilemma between separate cultural worlds.

This *mezzana* culture of Martorell's allows him to go beyond other existing narrative models, for example, the 'adventures of Lancelot and other knights' referred to in the prologue of the *Tirant*. In fact, despite their late-medieval diffusion, in French or in translation, the Arthurian novels have only a slight literary impact in Catalonia. They are read and admired, but not imitated, stifled by the increasing secular discovery of new literary models, from classical historiography to Guido delle Colonne or Boccaccio, which impose different narrative rules and nourish vernacular literature with ingredients deriving from Latin culture. To assume such models as guidelines for a new kind of chivalresque fiction is not an innocent act; it presupposes a desire to elevate and legitimize chivalresque fiction in the vernacular by means of a double ethical and cultural strategy which the dedication and prologue of the *Tirant* offer as a programme. Martorell is not the first or the only one to do this. A good part of the transformations of Catalan literature between the fourteenth and fifteenth centuries has to do with attributing cultural justification and prestige to non-Latin literary practice. It is on the basis of this interpretative key that one must read the conversion of poetry into a *gaia ciència* in Toulouse and Barcelona (Pujol 1994, 1996) or the *laudatio* of translations and learned literature in the vernacular by Ferran Valentí (Badia 1994), not to mention the *Curial e Güelfa* or the poetry of Ausiàs March. In the case of Martorell, his recourse to history, to antiquity and to poetry as guidelines could be a way of liberating chivalresque narrative from the cul-de-sac of useless and gratuitous fiction to which clergy and moralists had consigned it, insisting on the false and fictitious nature of certain Arthurian texts which Antoni Canals, Alonso de Cartagena or Jean Gerson had not hesitated to call 'fables' in the most derogatory sense of the word. The term appears explicitly, together with the adjective 'poetic', in a sermon of Gerson (Badel 1980:448) and in Canals' prologue to the *Carta de sant Bernat a sa germana* (Bofarull 1857:421) to define respectively the *romans* in French and 'vain books' like those of Lancelot and Tristan; significantly, Eiximenis adds 'romances' to the list of readings forbidden to the clergy he extracts from the *Decretum graciani* (*Primer del Crestià* chapter 31; Biblioteca de Catalunya ms.456,f.29), and the whole of chapter 9 of Alonso de Cartagena's *Epistula* to the Count of Haro is based on the irreconcilable opposition between the 'true things' of history and the *ficte compositae* of the books of Tristan, Lancelot and Amadís (Lawrance 1979:53–4).[20] One gathers, in the case of Cartagena, that knights should read chronicles: 'Cronice quoque militaribus viris perutiles sunt', because they are true stories which incorporate didacticism.

From Martorell's cultural perspective, then, to accomodate fiction to history means bringing it into an area of writing that is not affected by clerical prejudice since it fulfils the double function of glorifying its heroes and, through their virtue, of constituting an example of moral and military virtue. If, moreover, this novel with an appearance of historiography admitted sermons, debates, letters, expositions of Christian faith, speeches *de regimine principum*, discussions about fortune, quotations from *auctoritates* and so on, and adorned itself with a Latinizing rhetoric suited to the reputation of the heroes and appropriate to the prestigious tradition of the Latin classics – although tremendously mediated – the resulting text was freed from the promiscuity of Tristans, Lancelots and Amadíses, and placed itself automatically in the dimension of the 'ancient deeds and histories' entrusted to the 'poets and historians'. That, moreover, the heroes' deeds should continue in the bedroom is no longer a matter for 'historians'.

Translated by Arthur Terry

---

[20] It is also worth noting that in a letter addressed to the *consellers* of Barcelona in 1398, the Cardinal of Valencia, James of Aragon, praises the moral usefulness of Valerius Maximus as opposed to the unworthy 'romances' (Miquel i Planas 1914:3). The same point of view appears in Boccaccio's commentary on Canto V of the *Inferno* in which, from the learned position of the *commentator*, he states that the 'French romances' are 'composed more for pleasure than for truth' (Padoan 1994 I:323). On Boccaccio's intellectual position in this commentary, see Bruni (1990:465–77).

Tirant lo Blanc: Rehistoricizing the 'Other' Reconquista[1]

MONTSERRAT PIERA

The Catalan chivalry novel *Tirant lo Blanc*, written by Joanot Martorell between 1460 and 1464 and published in Valencia in 1490, might not have become known among hispanomedievalists if it were not for Miguel de Cervantes. In chapter six of his *Don Quixote* we find the most famous reference to *Tirant lo Blanc* in what has been labelled 'the most obscure passage in the *Quixote*'. In this passage Pero Pérez is carrying out the 'great and pleasant scrutiny' of Don Quixote's library and, surprisingly, he saves *Tirant lo Blanc* from the fire:

> 'Good heavens!' exclaimed the priest in a loud voice, 'Is *Tirant lo Blanc* here? Give it to me, friend, for to my mind the book is a rare treasure of delight and a mine of entertainment. Here is Don Kyrieleison of Montalbán, a valiant knight, and his brother Thomas of Montalbán and the knight Fonseca, and the fight the valiant Tirant had with the great mastiff, and the witticisms of the maiden Plaerdemavida, with the amours and tricks of the Viuda Reposada, and the Lady Empress in love with her squire Hipòlit. Really, my friend, for its style it is the best book in the world. Here the knights eat and sleep and die in their beds, and make their wills before they die, and other things as well that are left out of all other books of the kind. On that account, the author is a deserving fellow. For he did not commit all those follies deliberately, which might have sent him to the galleys for the

---

[1] 'Rehistoric*ize*' is used here in the sense expressed by Linda Hutcheon: 'My second reason for using the "ize" form of each of these terms is to underline the concept of *process* that is at the heart of postmodernism . . . it is the process of negotiating the postmodern contradictions that is brought to the fore, not any satisfactorily completed and closed product that results from their resolution' (1988:xi). I do not intend to suggest that *Tirant lo Blanc* should be considered a postmodernist novel like those studied by Hutcheon – even though there are some aspects of Martorell's text, like the self-conscious erasure of the boundaries between fiction and history, which make it comparable to what Hutcheon calls 'historiographic metafiction' (105); instead, the more relevant aspect of her formulation for the purpose of this essay is the concept of *process*. As we shall see, the reading of *Tirant lo Blanc* demands the active participation of the reader, who needs to negotiate the meaning of the text through a process of matching fictional narrative and historical episodes.

rest of his life. Take him home and read him, and you will see that all I have said of him is true' (Cervantes 1950:60, slightly modified).

I will not try here to propose yet another interpretation of this contradictory passage. Whether the priest's opinion is, in fact, Cervantes's true estimation of the Catalan novel is not what this essay is trying to decipher. Daniel Eisenberg, among others, has convincingly argued that if we take into account the personality of the character that expresses *Tirant lo Blanc*'s praise, then we must conclude that Pero Pérez's comments are, in fact, damaging to Martorell's novel (Eisenberg 1982). Even though I believe Eisenberg's views are for the most part accurate, I cannot help wondering why it seems so important to undermine a character's credibility as literary critic only in the case of *Tirant lo Blanc* while this credibility is not challenged with reference to *Amadís de Gaula*. None of the critics, including Eisenberg, takes issue with the barber's comment about the Castilian chivalry novel ('. . . for I have heard that it is the best of all the books of this kind ever written. So, as it is unequalled in its accomplishment, it ought to be pardoned' [Cervantes 1950:57]) and the priest's acceptance of the barber's verdict, which will actually save the *Amadís* from the fire. If we must conclude that the priest and the barber are not reliable literary critics then we should also disregard their praise of *Amadís*. I think it is very symptomatic that the critics have readily agreed on and accepted the characters' praise of the Castilian novel without discussion while they have devoted at least fifteen articles and several studies to the question of Cervantes's approval or disapproval of the *Tirant*. On the other hand, other critics strongly believe that Cervantes truly considered *Tirant lo Blanc* 'the best book in the world' (for example Mario Vargas Llosa who labels this text a 'total novel' [1969]).

What interests me here, however, is to highlight the priest's or in this case, Cervantes's misreading of *Tirant lo Blanc*. I am certainly not trying to undermine Cervantes as a writer or as a reader. It is my contention, though, that while Cervantes's reference to the *Tirant* might have saved the text from oblivion[2] it also consecrated a literary perception of the novel that has con-

---

[2] That is, oblivion in Castilian circles, since the novel was well known in Valencia by Martorell's contemporaries. Joan Fuster reproduces a few verses of *Lo Somni de Joan Joan* written by the Valencian Jaume Gassull in 1497 where there is a reference to the *Tirant* (Fuster 1994:267). Furthermore, Fuster affirms that *Tirant lo Blanc* was a long-awaited novel within the intellectual circles of Valencia. From the time Martorell died, in 1464, to 1490, when the novel was finally published, people knew of it and were interested in its contents. Fuster advances the idea of a 'pre-typographical reputation of the *Tirant*' (265). The book was not only famous in Valencia; the second edition of the work in Barcelona in 1497 'fulfilled another demand: a demand on the part of readers who had heard tell of the *Tirant* and might not have been able to purchase it at their usual bookshop' (274).

tributed to a false or incomplete understanding of Martorell's textual design. For what Cervantes does is unintentionally to dehistoricize *Tirant lo Blanc*.

First, he does it by simplifying what constitutes the substance of the novel. I disagree with E.T. Aylward when he asserts that:

> the priest's praise is, in effect, a compilation of the most striking aspects of Martorell's and Galba's book. With the single exception of the knight Fonseca (a man who exists only in name and who takes no part in the action), Pero Pérez indicates in his review almost all the main characters and plots of the Valencian novel.... Moreover, the priest's praise... is an index of the positive elements of the *Tirant*, literary virtues which Cervantes would later have to suppress in the summary (Aylward 1993:23–4).

On the contrary, Pero Pérez's remarks refer only to secondary elements of the plot of *Tirant lo Blanc* that can hardly be used as examples of literary competence or originality. For example, the characters Kyrieleison of Montalbán and his brother are very brave indeed, but their appearances are very brief (seven chapters out of 484). Furthermore, Kyrieleison of Montalbán does not have much time to prove his chivalric worth: overwhelmed with grief over his dead king 'he choked on his own bile' (chapter 80). As for the reference to Fonseca, which occupies only one line in the text, his character is totally irrelevant to the novel; he is just a banner bearer: 'First came the Emperor's banner, borne by a warrior named Fonseca on a splendid white charger' (chapter 82). And while prominent characters like Plaerdemavida and the Viuda Reposada are mentioned by the priest, he does not allude to Tirant or Carmesina, who are the main characters.

The other passages applauded by the priest in the novel are those that are full of humour and erotic innuendo which are also the ones that are more appealing to modern readers and some critics of *Tirant lo Blanc*.[3] Moreover, the adulterous and almost incestuous relationship between the Empress and Hipòlit hardly deserves special mention by a priest. As for the last remarks, they stress and praise the verisimilitude (or the much debated 'realism') of the Catalan text in which the knights sleep, eat and even die like normal people; however, we will see that Tirant's death cannot be considered realistic within the frame of the chivalry romance.

Secondly, Cervantes made a dehistoricized reading of the text because he only knew and read the 1511 Castilian translation of *Tirant lo Blanc*, printed

---

[3] The priest's comments about some of these erotic episodes coincide with the attitudes of some critics who praise Martorell's novel for its supposedly uninhibited approach to sex and eroticism. For a detailed analysis of this misleading interpretation of *Tirant lo Blanc* see my article ' "Com Tirant vençé la batalla e per força d'armes entrà lo castell": Rape and Conquest in the Chivalry Novel *Tirant lo Blanc*', in *Actes del IX Col.loqui de la North American Catalan Society* (Barcelona, Publicacions de l'Abadia de Montserrat) 1995: 259–80.

in Valladolid by Diego de Gumiel. The author of the *Quixote* was unaware of the fact that the original had been written more than fifty years earlier, in Catalan, by a subject of the Crown of Aragon:

> For Cervantes, naturally, Martorell's work was Castilian; the 1511 translation nowhere indicates the language of the original, not even that it was a translation. Likewise, the authors of the work are not mentioned; in the commentaries on the *Tirant* in *Don Quixote* I,6, he can only refer to the author as 'he who composed it'. Clemencín only knew the *Tirant* in its Italian translation (Eisenberg 1982:134, n. 6).[4]

Therefore, it is understandable that Cervantes misses the political implications of Joanot Martorell's design.

It is no mere coincidence that the fifteenth century produces two chivalry novels within the domain of the Crown of Aragon, *Tirant lo Blanc* and *Curial e Güelfa*, which share some of the same themes and narrative strategies: they both make ample use of historical events and references, they include 'realistic elements', both heroes endure a long captivity in North Africa where they eventually engage in a very effective missionizing campaign of converting the infidels to Christianity and, finally, both Curial and Tirant defeat the Turks in Constantinople. It is no coincidence, either, that these two Catalan novels are so different from their sixteenth-century Castilian counterparts that a different generic term has been created to classify them: according to Martí de Riquer, the two Catalan novels should be called 'chivalresque novels' to set them apart from the 'books of chivalry' produced in the sixteenth century and modelled after the works of Chrétien de Troyes and the *Amadís de Gaula* (Riquer 1968: II, 578).[5]

Moreover, it is in the fifteenth century (1453) that Constantinople is forever lost to the Turks and it is the same century which marks the irreversible political decline of the Crown of Aragon. It is within this context that these two 'different' and outstanding Catalan romances were conceived and composed.

The importance of the fall of Constantinople in 1453 cannot be overemphasized. It caused a tremendous impact on Christian society; after four centuries of crusades the Christians lost, and the Muslim threat was now more present than ever:

---

[4] See Riquer's introduction to the Castilian edition of *Tirant lo Blanc* for further information about the translation published in Valladolid by Gumiel and its omissions.

[5] I cannot discuss here the question of the generic classification of these works. I am not trying to imply, though, that the Catalan texts are unique and independent. *Tirant lo Blanc* and *Curial e Güelfa* present some elements that differentiate them from other texts within the genre of the Arthurian romance or the chivalry romance. Nevertheless, both texts clearly belong to the genre of the romance and they should be referred to as such instead of as novels.

No event since the fall of Acre caused as much dismay in the West as the news of Mehmed II's capture of Constantinople. To distress at the slaughter and enslavement of the Greeks, and the loss of the fourth, and last, eastern patriarchate to Islam, the voices of lament added two other themes, the destruction of Greek culture, so dear to the humanists of Italy, and the accretion of Ottoman power, which enormously added to the danger the Turks posed to the West (Housely 1992:99).

In September 1453 Nicholas V issued the Bull 'Etsi ecclesia Christi' which was meant to inspire the Christian rulers to launch a Crusade. The most enthusiastic reaction came from the court of Burgundy. Philippe le Bon organized in 1454 the banquet known as the Feast of the Pheasant, an example of the Burgundian penchant for chivalric display and extravagance. Joan Oleza gives a detailed description of this celebration while comparing it to the tension between fiction and history clearly discernable in *Tirant lo Blanc* and in other chivalry romances of the late Middle Ages:

> In the Burgundian court . . . there is expressed over and over again the fantasy of an impossible 'reconquest' of the Holy Places, and gestures multiply after 1453 and the fall of Constantinople. The most famous of the Burgundian feasts, that organized by Duke Philippe le Bon in the city of Lille from the 31st January 1454, had this historical referent. Various banquets of the nobility prepared that which crowned the series, held in the ducal palace, and which began with the knightly challenge of Adolphe de Ravenstein to all those present at the banquet. The fabulous interludes which graced it, or the episode of the Lamentation of Holy Church, embodied in no one less than Olivier de la Marche mounted on a camel and watched over by a giant who represented the power of the Turk, were only the foretaste of the climactic moment, that in which the King of Arms, Toison d'Or, entered the hall with a live pheasant on which the Duke solemnly swore to reconquer Constantinople . . . Needless to say, these celebrated feasts led to no crusade, but precisely in the fiction created by desire there is best expressed the sense in which the feasting represents a sublimation of the dreams which reality dooms to failure (Oleza Simó 1992:333).

In the Iberian Peninsula the reaction to the fall of Constantinople differed from one kingdom to the other. In Castile, constantly engaged in fighting the Muslims in its own domain, Constantinople was a distant city. For the Castilians, the only Crusade that counted was their own *Reconquista* which aimed at the expulsion of the Muslims from the Peninsula, and in the middle of the fifteenth century they were very close to their victorious end.

The *Reconquista* had very different degrees of success throughout the Middle Ages. The most substantial gains of the three principal Christian kingdoms in the Peninsula were obtained mainly after the defeat of the Almohads at Las Navas de Tolosa in 1212. Sancho II and Alfonso III of Portugal completed the Portuguese *Reconquista* by extending their lands to the coast of Algarve. Jaume I of Aragon conquered the Balearic Isles (1229–35) and Valencia (1232–45). And Fernando III annexed to his territories Extremadura, Murcia and extensive parts of Andalusia, including Córdoba (1236) and Seville (1248).[6] Exerting effective control over the newly conquered lands proved to be very difficult, especially for the Castilians. Consequently, even though there was a renewed interest in the crusading endeavour during the thirteenth and fourteenth centuries, the Castilians' military efforts concentrated on preserving and consolidating what the previous campaigns had achieved (Housley 1992:267–8). Despite the fact that the Castilian rulers showed interest in participating in the Crusade to recover Constantinople – even as late as 1480 Fernando of Aragon promised the Papal Curia assistance against the Turks but only after Granada was won – by the end of the fifteenth century the Castilians were too close to the conquest of Granada, the last Muslim bastion in the Peninsula; therefore, Castile could not be expected to participate in an anti-Turkish Crusade.

In the lands of the Crown of Aragon, however, the effect of the fall of Constantinople was more devastating. The Aragonese King, Alfonso V, el Magnànim (1416–58),[7] who was in an ideal position to fight the Turks after his attainment of the Kingdom of Naples in 1443 and in whom the Popes had their greatest hope, even tried to organize another crusade in order to regain control of the Byzantine capital, but he died, after many unfulfilled promises, before he could carry out his plans (Housley 1992:294).

For the Catalan-Aragonese the fall of Constantinople meant, to some extent, the end of their *Reconquista*. The concept of *Reconquista* which has been defined as a solely Castilian phenomenon which supposedly contributed to the configuration of a singular Castilian national identity is, in fact, a much wider phenomenon:

> The Reconquest is not, as the majority of historians have assumed up to now, merely a movement of an awakening Spain in search of its (almost lost) identity, but also forms part of the general expansion of Christian Europe from the eleventh century onwards (Dressendörfer 1989:33).

The ambitions of the Crown of Aragon responded to this desire of expansion common to all the European nations of the period. Even though, as we have seen, Aragon actively participated in the military campaigns to reconquer Iberian soil from the Muslims, very early on its interests also took other

---

[6] For more information about these events and their historical background see Hillgarth 1976 (especially chapter two) and Riu Riu 1989 (especially the chapter entitled 'Los reinos cristianos de la España occidental después de las Navas').

[7] For more information about Alfonso V and his crusading interests see Sobrequés Vidal 1952:232–52.

directions outside the boundaries of the Peninsula, namely the north of Africa, Sicily and the eastern Mediterranean.[8]

This 'other' Catalan-Aragonese Reconquest had been laid out in the historical chronicles of the thirteenth and fourteenth centuries and was founded on Mediterranean commercial and political expansion and the eradication of the Muslim 'heresy' through preaching and conversion. The historian T.N. Bisson sees in the extant monuments of Catalonia a trace of this national inclination towards the east:

> For the castles, churches, tombs and trading-houses ... are the vestiges of a proud and expansive Mediterranean civilization. They evoke the ambitions of counts of Barcelona who were kings of Aragon by dynastic descent; the energies of knights and merchants who followed the count-kings in overseas conquest and settlement, spreading Catalan speech throughout the Mediterranean (Bisson 1986:1).[9]

The four chronicles (*Llibre dels Feyts*, *Crònica de Bernat Desclot* [1282–88], *Crònica de Ramon Muntaner* [1325–28] and the *Crònica de Pere III*) confirm Bisson's accurate description of the Crown of Aragon. These texts are held in great esteem by scholars and lay people of Catalonia alike. For the former they are historical documents which attest to the creativity and dynamism of the best centuries of the Crown of Aragon. For modern Catalans, the chronicles are tangible remnants of a bygone era of nationalistic pride and political and linguistic independence. For Martorell these chronicles were a source of inspiration as well as pride. They repeatedly furnish him with the historical (or pseudo-historical) material[10] which he will use in his fictionalized history of the Catalan 'Reconquest'.

Roberto González-Casanova has studied extensively the connection between Muntaner's *Crònica* and Martorell's *Tirant lo Blanc*. Having applied 'the methods of cultural historicism (as practised by Greenblatt and Montrose, as well as by Said) and of the rhetorical and mythopoetic analysis of historical literature as propaganda (as established by Hampton, Stierle and White) (1994:211), González-Casanova concludes that:

---

[8] These interests were predominantly economic and commercial. Early Catalan trade was firmly established in Tunis, Bougie and Sicily in the thirteenth century, and new charters studied by Bensch demonstrate that by 1281 a Catalan consul had been appointed to Byzantium, 'which implies the presence of a Catalan community at Constantinople' (Bensch 1995:138).

[9] Even though the Catalan-Aragonese expansion in the Mediterranean is a proven fact, it is still debated whether or not we can properly speak of a 'Catalan Mediterranean Empire'. For a thoughtful and unprejudiced analysis of the subject see Hillgarth 1975.

[10] All the historical references and characters present in *Tirant lo Blanc* have been comprehensively studied by Riquer (1964; 1990a).

> As heroic legend and modern history, these Catalan works should be read in the West as mythical stories, propagandistic tracts, and exemplary lessons on Christendom's own survival and gradual transformation in a new age of world powers that are struggling for empire and hegemony.
> (González-Casanova 1994:225)

It is true that both texts can be read as historical narratives about ages of Western expansion and conquest. Nevertheless, there is one considerable disparity between these two accounts of the Catalan-Aragonese expansion that González-Casanova overlooks: Muntaner's narrative is written when Catalan-Aragonese expansion is at its peak and there is a conscious effort, eagerly promoted by the rulers of the House of Aragon, to record in written form the noteworthy exploits of the dynasty and their subjects. King Jaume I even authored his own historical chronicle, the *Libre dels Feyts*. On the other hand, Martorell composes his fictional account more than a century later under very different historical circumstances; this fact alone should alert us to the necessity to read the two texts with different expectations, regardless of how valuable a comparison between the two might be. Both texts glorify the past but their audiences, their tone and their intent are not equivalent.

A review of the historical events that are described in both narratives is required at this juncture. During the years of the expansion (1276–1330) the Balearic Islands, Valencia, Sardinia, Corsica and Sicily were conquered or annexed by the Kings of Aragon. At the same time, the Aragonese kings had promoted military and commercial interests in the north of Africa. In fact, on some occasions the Count-King became virtually the protector of Christians in the post-crusade Levant. On other occasions, conquest of north African territories would entail active preaching to bring about conversion of the infidels. The forthright theologian Ramon Llull and the Kings of Aragon often concurred with this combination of military or commercial crusading and religious missionizing (Kedar 1984:189–203).

Moreover, in 1302 an army of Catalan mercenaries (called *almogàvers*) led by Roger de Flor sold their services to the Emperor Andronicus of Byzantium who was being assailed by the Turks. The chronicler Ramon Muntaner took part in the expedition and proudly, albeit not totally reliably, told the story as a feat of the Catalan-Aragonese dynasty. In the summer of 1303 Roger de Flor married the Byzantine princess Maria and took the title of Megaduc (Megas Dux). Subsequently, the Catalans defeated the Turks in a series of astounding and daring campaigns. Nevertheless, the Greeks who had employed the Catalan Company, and specifically the co-emperor Michael, became increasingly distrustful of the mercenaries. The Byzantines devised a plot to attract Roger de Flor to Adrianopolis, where he and his companions were treacherously assassinated by their hosts (Laiou 1972:145–6; Lowe 1972:63).

However, if the Byzantines thought that the massacre would subdue the Catalans and force them to leave the Empire, the ensuing events certainly proved them wrong. The Catalan Company proceeded to exact their bloody revenge from the Greeks, sacking every town and leaving a trail of destruction. After the 'Catalan vengeance' (Laiou 1972:226; Lowe 1972:127), the Catalan Company still remained in the east, where they were again employed as mercenaries and again defrauded by their employer, Walter de Brienne, Duke of Athens (Laiou 1972:226; Lowe 1972:127). The Catalans then went on to attack the Duchy of Athens. Against all odds they defeated Walter de Brienne and his army: 'The Catalans used the treacherous terrain to their advantage, and the flower of Frankish chivalry fell there, on Monday, March 15, 1311' (Laiou 1972:227). After this victory the survivors of the Catalan Company established themselves in the Duchy of Athens where they ruled until 1387.

All of these conquests and deeds are dramatized in *Tirant lo Blanc*. In the pages of this book we encounter again all those Catalan heroes who conquered the Mediterranean, the Christian warriors who fought against the spread of Islam. The fiction not only reverses the historical events about the fall of Constantinople but also erases within the textual stage the threat of the demise of two proud Empires: the Byzantine and the Catalan-Aragonese, which act in the text as a reflection of each other. In short, the fictional narrative undoes history. In this sense, *Tirant lo Blanc*'s design corresponds to other medieval texts 'that self-consciously and deliberately override this basic distinction between the factual and the fabulous, history and romance, for their own strategic purposes' (Patterson 1987:200–201, n. 7).

Martorell revives, within the narrative frame of Tirant's chivalric pilgrimage, the past history of Catalonia and superimposes it on contemporary events. Tirant begins his story as an aspiring young knight who learns the laws and ways of chivalry from a retired knight, Guillem de Vàroic, who had fought in Constantinople. He travels to the court of England and there he practises his newly acquired knowledge. After proving his chivalric worth in the episodes that take place in England, Tirant abandons the court and continues on his journey of discovery. Now that he is an accomplished knight, he transports himself to another milieu, the Mediterranean Sea, so dear to Martorell's contemporaries. The sea will become the stage for Tirant's greatest victories but also for his worst misfortunes: the shipwreck, the separation from his beloved Carmesina, the slavery in Africa . . . His first Mediterranean adventure is the liberation of the island of Rhodes from the Turks – one of the real attacks on Rhodes took place in 1444 – then he rapidly goes to Constantinople to assist the Emperor against the infidel. Tirant, naturally, annuls the Turkish threat.

In Constantinople he meets Carmesina, who is the heiress to the Byzantine Empire, and falls helplessly in love. Later, after several misfortunes, Tirant ends up in north Africa as a slave. But not for long. Soon he will be asked to help his captor, the King of Tremicen, against a mightier enemy, the King of Ethiopia. After crushing the enemy army he becomes captain of the north

African kingdoms and while there engages in a missionary campaign; he manages to convert everyone to Christianity. (Curiously, this massive conversion was the dream of another subject from the Crown of Aragon, the aforementioned Ramon Llull, philosopher and visionary, who died from the injuries inflicted on him by angry north African Muslims when he was trying to convert them.) After the successful conversion, his task completed, it is time for Tirant to return to Constantinople because the Empire is being threatened again. Needless to say, Tirant destroys, once and for all, the Turkish enemy, marries the Princess and becomes Caesar of the Empire. Then, during an excursion to survey the territories, he falls ill, writes a will and dies in Adrianopolis, the same city where Roger de Flor was treacherously assassinated.

The end of the story, with the death of the only hero capable of maintaining order and peace, the death of Carmesina, heiress of the Empire and the death of the Emperor himself, foreshadows the ultimate fall of Constantinople and the demise of the Byzantine Empire. This unexpected denouement revokes the earlier erasure effected so carefully by the author. Now the reader comprehends that Constantinople will never be reconquered again and that the Crown of Aragon will not reconquer the Mediterranean either. Earlier Martorell undid history, now he undoes fiction. Tirant, the embodiment of strength, valour and hope, fades and with him the hope of recovering Constantinople, preserving the past and upholding the chivalric values the aristocrat Martorell values so dearly also fades.

Throughout the novel the author has skilfully depicted the maturation of a perfect knight: gradually we see Tirant becoming a perfect knight errant, a perfect naval commander, a perfect diplomat, a perfect lover, a perfect Christian and missionary and, eventually, he will become the Emperor of the Greek Empire of Byzantium, the most prestigious title in Christendom. The entire narrative conforms to the unwritten generic rules of the Arthurian or chivalry romance. Except in one instance: the hero has a very unheroic death.

This prosaic death is not intended to show Martorell's inclination towards realism. On the contrary, this death is highly idealized because it is a metaphor of the end of Martorell's world. Tirant's successors are also unheroic: an adulterous, almost incestuous, old Empress and her young lover and inexpert commander, Hipòlit. The latter is even portrayed in the text as a cynical opportunist after Tirant's death:

> Do not think Hipòlit was overly distressed, since as soon as Tirant died he realized that he would be emperor, and still more after His Majesty and Carmesina passed away. He was certain that the enamoured empress would set aside her shame and take him as her husband and son, for old ladies usually wish to marry their sons to repair and atone for the sins of their youth (chapter 479).

More importantly, this succession – which is highly irregular not only in the socio-historical context but also in the textual frame where the narrator has insisted on elevating Tirant and Carmesina's exemplary relationship above the rest of the couples – will break the dynastic continuity, because when the Empress dies three years later, Hipòlit will marry an English princess and their children will become the heirs of the Empire.

Even in this case history offers a fascinating parallel. The dynastic continuity – so highly praised by Muntaner but also by other writers like Ramon Llull, Bernat Desclot and the troubadour Cerverí de Girona (Hillgarth 1976:7–8) – had also been broken in Aragon when the last Catalan king from the House of Barcelona, Martí I, died and in 1412 the crown passed to a Castilian dynasty, the Trastámaras, in the person of Fernando de Antequera. His father was King Juan I of Castile and his mother was Leonor, daughter of King Pere IV of Aragon and III of Catalonia, also called 'el Cerimoniós'. The problems this disputed succession originated were to be instrumental in the decline of the once powerful Crown of Aragon. After the death of Martí I, representatives from the kingdoms – three from Valencia, three from Aragon and three from Catalonia – were appointed to choose among the five pretenders to the throne of Aragon:

> The nine delegates having met at the castle of Caspe (1412), St Vicente Ferrer, the most outstanding of those present, declared himself in favour of Fernando de Antequera, at that time Regent of Castile. Five of the delegates supported this proposal, with one blank vote and two against. The decision, read out after a sermon by the famous Dominican theologian and preacher, was received with pleasure in Aragon, though not so much in Valencia and still less in Catalonia (Riu Riu 1989:378).

Of all the setbacks suffered by the Catalans in the fifteenth century, this is the one which prevailed in the popular mind since the election of a Castilian king was seen as an unlawful dispossession.

That Martorell was knowledgeable and concerned about the dynastic conflicts of his age can be attested in yet another passage of *Tirant lo Blanc*: its dedication. Martorell dedicates his novel to 'the most serene Prince Don Fernando of Portugal', referring to him as 'Rei spectant' (expectant King). It is an astonishing dedication if we take into account that the lawful king of Aragon at the time was Juan II. It is noteworthy that this dedication did not appear in the 1511 Castilian translation of the novel. Therefore, Cervantes could not have been aware of Martorell's dynastic preferences and their significance in the text.

This puzzling passage has been persuasively analysed by Martí de Riquer (1990a:279–84). This critic believes that Martorell considered Don Fernando to be the possible successor to Pedro el Condestable of Portugal as King of Aragon (282) and, therefore, was opposed to the Castilian dynasty then in power. Pedro of Portugal was 'King of the Catalans' from 1461, when Catalonia rebelled against Juan II and offered the crown to the Condestable, until his death in 1465, when he was defeated by Juan II's son, the future Fernando el Católico (Riu Riu 1989:381). After a thorough examination of several Portuguese and Aragonese historical documents, Riquer summarizes his findings concerning the meaning of *Tirant lo Blanc*'s dedication:

> My conclusions assume that Martorell believed in the rights of Pedro el Condestable to be king of the realms which constituted the Crown of Aragon. To be sure, the Portuguese Condestable had few supporters in the Kingdom of Valencia, but we have already had reason to record that two leading Valencians, Gaspar and Joan de Valeriola, were in 1464 in relations with Pedro el Condestable and his cousin Prince Fernando. It is obvious that Martorell, writing in Valencia while the Catalan civil war was going on, could not name Prince Fernando of Portugal so as to make it clear that he considered him the heir of the 'King of the Catalans', and for that reason he called him by the unusual and scarcely cancellerial term of 'rei spectant' (expectant King). His Valencian contemporaries, most of them supporters of Juan II, would not find anything reprehensible in this unusual title, and, if it came to it, most of them must have had little idea of which kingdom it was that the Portuguese prince was 'expecting' (1990:283-4).

Considering this, I have to disagree with González-Casanova's appraisal of the effects of the dynastic changes in Aragon: 'For Martorell's contemporaries it [the end of Alfonso V's reign] represents an age of renewed power for the House of Aragon, climaxing with the dynastic union with Castile in 1479 to create Spain as one of the strongest nation-states in Europe, that contrasts with the rapid decline and demise of the millenarian empire of Byzantium' (1994:222). The real union[11] between Castile and Aragon took place much earlier, in 1412, when the kings who ruled both kingdoms belonged to the same Castilian family. Henceforth we witness not a renewed power of the House of Aragon but an irreversible decline in the social, political and linguistic conditions of the Kingdom of Aragon. It is true that the fifteenth is a century of brilliant literary and cultural achievements in the Crown of Aragon, especially in Valencia. Nevertheless, as the century progresses it becomes evident that Aragon is losing its pre-eminence. Politically, Aragon ceases to be a maritime power and linguistically, Catalan begins to be subtly persecuted, especially after the establishment of the Inquisition in Valencia and Catalonia in the 1480s by the Catholic Monarchs (Ventura 1978; Kamen

---

[11] Paradoxically, it is not accurate to speak of a real union between the two kingdoms either in 1412 or in 1469: 'It was hardly likely that a royal marriage in 1469 between the heirs of Castile and Aragon could unite peoples which had possessed for centuries "their own character, their own language, and their mission to achieve"' (Hillgarth 1976:15).

1993). The decline of Byzantium, then, can be seen as a reflection of Aragon's decline.

In the light of all these facts, it is hard to believe that the ending of *Tirant lo Blanc* can be interpreted as a return to society's harmony and also as a textual closure, that is, as a happy ending. What this ending signifies is the impossibility of social and political harmony after the hero's disappearance and also the impossibility of a textual closure. The story is not finished; it will finish when fiction catches up with history, when Constantinople, under the rule of one of Hipòlit's descendants, finally succumbs to the Turks. Or perhaps we should say instead that the story finished at the precise moment Tirant died and an acute sense of loss and despair started to infiltrate the Court of Constantinople and, undoubtedly, the contemporary reader:

> Oh unjust Death . . . in slaying Tirant you have killed the Emperor of Constantinople . . . And you, Princes of Darkness, laugh . . . since he through whom the Holy Christian religion each day increased is dead. Finally, let all the hostile nations rejoice, for that invincible Tirant, whom the ferocity and united forces of all the infidels could not overcome, now conquered and vanquished by death, his dying causes you great pleasure . . . Everyone, sad and wretched, takes great comfort in our tears and lamentations, and we can truly say the pillar of chivalry is dead (chapters 472 and 474).

A comparison with other texts that belong to the genre of the medieval romance can offer some insight into this new tragic sense of hopelessness that permeates *Tirant lo Blanc* and which suggests a dismal view of the chivalry world. The *Mort Artu*, which is the last romance of the 'Vulgate Cycle', displays a tragic element to the story that was only latently present in twelfth-century Arthurian romances. When King Arthur dies, the Round Table is destroyed and with it the harmonious society of chivalry. The causes of such a denouement further underscore the tragedy of this society's destiny: Arthur and his knights were unable to renounce the courtly values in order to succeed in the quest of the Grail. When they most needed to uphold the virtues of chivalry they faltered and their imperfection brought about the demise of their world.

The implicit criticism of chivalry or, instead, of the failure of chivalry is found in another Catalan text of the Middle Ages, *La Faula* of Guillem de Torroella. This text, which is a metafictional continuation of the *Mort Artu*, is actually plagiarized by Martorell in his novel (chapters 189 to 202). In *La Faula* an incredulous narrator who has read about King Arthur's death in the *Mort Artu* has a meeting with the real Arthur, who has been supposedly cured of his mortal wounds by his sister Morgana. Arthur complains about the deterioration chivalric values have suffered since his death and orders Guillem to return to his land where he is to speak to his contemporaries about what he has seen and urge them to modify their behaviour so that chivalry can be reborn again. *La Faula*, despite its pessimistic message, concludes with the possibility of redressing an inauspicious predicament. *Tirant lo Blanc*'s ending, on the other hand, does not allow for any possibility of redress.

Tirant lo Blanc is a twofold tribute: on the one hand, to a nostalgic historical past and, on the other, to the joy and brilliance of the chivalric world in which Martorell felt so comfortable. But the text also reveals the inevitable transmutation of this world. This revelation begins when the reader rehistoricizes the fictional discourse. What the text tells us then is different from what the text told Pero Pérez and Cervantes. They probably enjoyed the romance since they saved it from the fire, but their reading was incomplete in the sense that their horizon of expectations, as defined by Jauss, had nothing in common with the *Tirant*'s implied reader's expectations. Martorell's implied reader[12] would have had to be acquainted with the historical past of the Crown of Aragon and would have had to know Muntaner's *Crònica* in order to exact meaning from the text. I subscribe to Patterson's argument that 'there is no such thing as an objectively determined, self-evident, original context that can reveal the original meaning of the text' (1987:44), therefore, interpretative correctness may be a fallacy. Nevertheless, by the process of rehistoricizing *Tirant lo Blanc* new elements emerge that can enrich our reading experience.

Tirant lo Blanc is a great romance and I agree with Pero Pérez in this, but I do not concur with his literary appraisal of the work. There are many chivalrous heroes in the novel, but Fonseca is not one of them. Tirant succeeds in many battles and defeats many enemies but his highest military achievement is not a battle with a dog. It is true that the novel has many humourous moments, but the marriage of the Empress and Hipòlit is not meant to be amusing. Also, *Tirant lo Blanc* has some realistic moments, but the fact that Tirant dies of illness – presumaby a heart attack – is not meant to be mimetic but highly symbolic.

Consequently, Pero Pérez (and possibly Cervantes) might have enjoyed the 'pasatiempos' of the novel but he probably overlooked some or many of the political and social overtones that emerge when we rehistoricize the fictional world which is so intertwined with the history of the Crown of Aragon. And then again, maybe the priest was not interested in it and just selected what he enjoyed most. And it is a good thing he did because now each one of us can read it too and try, very humbly, to reconquer their distant world.

---

[12] I use the concept of implied reader as defined by Wolfgang Iser in *The Act of Reading: A Theory of Aesthetic Response* (Baltimore: Johns Hopkins University Press, 1974) and *The Implied Reader: Patterns of Communication in Prose Fiction from Bunyan to Beckett* (London: Longman, 1974). The implied reader is the hypothetical reader of a text who embodies all those predispositions necessary for a literary work to exercise its effect.

Tirant lo Blanc and the Muslim World in the Fifteenth Century

MARÍA JESÚS RUBIERA Y MATA

Islam is a character in *Tirant lo Blanc* and could hardly fail to be, since the protagonist is a knight and, according to Ramon Llull, whom Martorell paraphrases in chapters 33 and 34, the office of a knight is to defend the Holy Church with his arms in the face of the infidel. In the Hispanic world of the fifteenth century, infidelity, by definition, means Islam. This is why Joanot Martorell converts the Danes who attack England in the poem of Guy of Warwick, which serves as his source, into Muslims, 'Moors', from the Canaries. The infidelity of the Danes, Normans or Vikings had been forgotten in the Peninsula after their distant and bloody attacks in the early Middle Ages, and they are made into Moors. This was an old tradition among the Hispanic peoples after a centuries-long confrontation with Islam, but in the fifteenth century it had been brought up to date with the conquest of Constantinople in 1453. The infidels, the Muslims, had taken possession of the most important Christian city in the east, and the function of chivalry, as stated in the chapters of the *Tirant* already mentioned, was the restoration to Christendom of the cathedral of Constantinople, converted into a stable by the Turks.

The Muslims are to be characters in the novel, the enemies in war, and have to be characterized as such. But as Martí de Riquer pointed out in masterly fashion, *Tirant lo Blanc* is not a *book of chivalry*, based on the Arthurian or Breton novels, on the deeds of the knights of the Round Table, but a *chivalresque novel*, inspired by the knights of its own time (Riquer 1990a). In the same way, Tirant's enemies are not the enormous blackamoors of the *books of chivalry*, but fifteenth-century Muslims. It was precisely through the characterization of these Muslim personages that we discovered that in one part of the *Tirant* there were obvious discrepancies with the rest, and that a different pen from that of the original author has changed the novel. This change is internal and ideological and does not affect the style or the form, which are liable to have been varied by the editor.

Joanot Martorell's Muslims

The *Tirant* reflects fairly precisely the names of the Muslims of the eastern Mediterranean, or at least that part which was known in fifteenth-century Valencia, which received reliable information especially through the merchants of the Crown of Aragon. Thus we know that the adventurer Jaume de Vilaragut, a personal friend of Joanot Martorell (Riquer 1990a:127–9), was the prisoner of a *caraman* or lord of the Turcoman kingdom of Caraman which would give its name to the character of the Gran Caramany in the *Tirant*. So also, despite the leading role of the Ottoman Turks, the conquerors of Constantinople, Joanot Martorell shows himself more familiar with the Mameluke dynasty of Egypt and Syria, in accordance surely with the commercial and military relations of the Crown of Aragon. Thus he refers to them by name – *mamelluts* (Mamelukes) – in chapter 99, and alludes to the fact that they were captive children, instructed in the military arts and brought up in Islam (chapter 107). Perhaps this greater knowledge was based on coincidences between the knights of both ends of the Mediterranean, since the Mamelukes preferred the ancient office of chivalry to the use of modern weapons and were as fond as the Christians of books of chivalry in Arabic versions (Rubiera y Mata 1990:267–74).

Among these characters there stands out Aben Amar or Abenamar, King of Egypt, who is in love with the daughter of the Grand Turk – the Ottoman – just as Tirant is in love with Carmesina, and both women are praised to the skies in the letters of battle which both knights interchange (chapters 159 and 152). This character is contrasted with his literary double, the Sultan of Babylon, the title of the Sultan of Egypt, a loud-mouthed bully who tries to pull the Greek Emperor's beard, to make Carmesina a chambermaid and the Empress a cook, and to erect a statue of gold to himself when he conquers Constantinople. However, this character is not a normal Muslim but a renegade (chapter 178), a personal situation quite frequent in the Mediterranean. Martorell makes this personage write a letter which he copied from the Catalan translation of a genuine letter discovered by Gili y Gaya (1947–48:138–9), in which *Jacomach, Great Sultan of Babylon* – that is to say, az-Zahir Chakmak, Mameluke Sultan of Egypt (1438–53) – addresses the King of Cyprus. The anonymous translator, reproduced by Martorell, has taken the liberty of freely interpreting one of the titles of the Egyptian Sultan, *Sahib al-Haramani* or Lord of the Two Sacred Places (Mecca and Medina) as 'Lord of Two Temples, that is to say, of the Holy Temple of Solomon in the city of Jerusalem and of the Holy Temple of Mecca'.

Martorell had documented himself with those eastern names known to the international politics of his time, but it appears that he himself was never in the Middle East, nor did he know any Arabic literary sources (Rubiera y Mata 1993:27–37), so that in order to characterize these personages with oriental names he used data gleaned from those Muslims he knew perfectly well: the *mudéjares* or Muslims subject to the Crown of Aragon who peopled the Kingdom of Valencia in great numbers. Martorell himself was lord over two settlements, Murla and Benibrafim in the valley of Xaló, mostly populated by Muslims. But still further: according to the most recent documentary discoveries, Joanot Martorell captained a band of 'Moors' – as the Muslims were called – with which he attacked a number of travellers (Chiner and Villalmanzo 1992: Document 566). He consequently knew Muslims sufficiently well not to commit major errors in his literary characterization, except in supposing that the way of life of the Valencian Muslims was the same as that of their oriental brethren. Thus, for example, Martorell knows that the Muslims make their solemn prayer (*çalà*) on Fridays and that Muslim women receive their dowry in jewels, a resource which acts as a guarantee should they be repudiated or left widows:

> A Turk said: 'I saw the Gran Caramany's daughter one Friday after prayers (*çalà*), and she wore a jubbah embroidered with pearls said to be worth a whole city. There are twenty five betrothed damsels, each of whom has a dowry, each of them destined for a great lord' (chapter 163).

The author also knows that the Moors swear while looking to the south (*alquibla*), in the direction of Mecca:

> '. . . you will say to the Sultan and the Grand Turk that I will on no account grant them peace nor truce, if they do not swear it facing south [*alquibla*]'
> (chapter 138).

Martorell knows that the *mudéjares*, the Hispanic Muslims, celebrate the feast of St John or the summer solstice, just like the Christians and the Jews (chapter 276), and that they also wear festive or luxury clothes on this day. Thus the Moorish King of the Canaries writes to the King of England: 'And on the day of the great St John, you will wear some clothes of mine which I shall hand on to you' (chapter 13), after which, 'on St John's Day, the Moorish King, to make his people happy, came with all his might before the city of Warwick' (chapter 5).

Martorell is not mistaken, for the Muslims of the Peninsula celebrated this feast with the name of *Ansara* and they commemorated it with festive clothes and tournaments as the *kharja* of the Blind Man of Tudela (twelfth century) says:

> Bright day, this day
> truly the day of *Ansara*,
> I shall wear my brocaded clothes
> and we shall break lances.

In this same sense, Martorell knows that the *mudéjares* eat couscous (*cuscuso*), the dish of steamed semolina with vegetables and lamb's meat, of north African origin, which was known in al-Andalus from the thirteenth century and which is included in the menu Tirant offers the ambassadors of the Sultan of Babylon, without realizing that this dish was – and still is – unknown in the Arab Middle East, where even its name, couscous, produces hilarity because of its homophony with an intimate part of the female anatomy:

> Tirant seated the emissaries at one table, his prisoners at another, and his dukes and lords at a third. And they were well served with chickens, capons, pheasants, rice, couscous and many other dishes and fine wines
> (chapter 137).

Martí Joan de Galba's Muslims

After what I have said about the characterization of Muslims in the *Tirant*, it is surprising that, from chapter 301 onwards, there begin to appear strange errors concerning the beliefs and customs of the Muslims. The most serious is the confusion of considering the prophet of Islam, Mohammed, as the 'god' of the Muslims:'but I pray you, do not deny me your name, for I swear by Mohammed, my God, that I shall have you as a son' (chapter 301).

In the 300 previous chapters, the name of Mohammed had always appeared just as the Muslims consider him, that is to say, as a prophet (chapters 107, 113, 135, 150, 178), but this is not an isolated mistake since in a series of chapters, starting with 300, the prophet of Islam is granted divine attributes such as omnipotence or the power to forgive sins as if he were Allah (chapters 302, 303, 305, 308, 321, 347, 349).

As well as these theological errors, we find other inaccuracies concerning the behaviour of the Muslims. Thus the author believes that they make use of images, as when King Menador – whose name could be a deformation of *mamandar*, the Turkish word for a public office, employed in the Mameluke court – says to his brother, the King of Lesser India, when he sees the St Christopher with the child Jesus which Tirant is wearing:

> 'An image of his Mohammed hangs from his neck: a bearded man crossing a river with a child on his shoulder, and I believe that that child must be the son of his Mohammed' (chapter 334).

And the King of Tunis wore an image of Mohammed on his helmet: 'the King of Tunis bore an image of Mohammed on his helmet, which was all of gold' (chapter 334).

As it happens, the Muslims of this part of the *Tirant* do not eat couscous (chapter 309), when they are precisely from Maghreb, where the dish originated, and their women, like Maragdina, daughter of the King of Tremicen, do not wear the jubbah (*aljuba*) and *alquinal* or veil, items of clothing which Plaerdemavida had put on before chapter 301 in order to appear a Muslim (chapter 299).

These elements, so different from the rest of the novel before chapter 300, might lead us to suppose that Joanot Martorell had lost his memory and had forgotten what he knew about the Muslims in the earlier chapters, but recovering it later, as we shall see. It seems more logical to revert to the hypothesis that there exists in the *Tirant* at least one other author, as the well known colophon of the book suggests:

> ... Sir Joanot Martorell, who because of his death could only manage to translate three parts. The fourth part, which is the end of the book, was translated ... by the magnificent knight Sir Martí Joan de Galba.

The incoherencies of the *Tirant* with regard to the Muslims begin in chapter 300, which corresponds to the third part of the Castilian translation of 1511, which is the only edition divided into parts, but which does not necessarily correspond with a possible original division, where this chapter might begin the fourth part mentioned in the colophon. But the literary characterization of the Muslims creates a new problem, since the author who knows about the Muslims, that is to say, Martorell, reappears in chapter 350, after the change has been announced at the end of the previous one. ('Now the book makes an incision to relate the doings of Plaerdemavida.')

With the reappearance of the genial Plaerdemavida, there reappear those elements that characterize the Muslims more or less adequately, together with Arabisms. Thus Plaerdemavida dresses as a Moor and paints her eyes with alcohol:

> That day Plaerdemavida dressed like a Moor, very honourably, and disguised her eyes with alcohol so that she would not be known, and took twenty well dressed maidens to accompany her (chapter 350).

Immediately after this, the Arabism *algemia* is used to denote a non-Arabic language: 'By my faith, my Lord, there is a fair damsel among those Moorish maidens who speaks *algemia* very well, and with much grace' (chapter 350). The veil or *alquinal* reappears: 'Tirant had lifted her veil (*alquinal*) and she remained bareheaded' (chapter 366) and Mohammed appears once more as prophet and not as god: 'which is built in the place of our holy prophet Mohammed' (chapter 362), and with this information regarding the Muslims there reappears an element which had also been lacking in the forty-nine previous chapters: eroticism.

An Ideological Interpolation

By means of the characterization of the Muslims we have reached the conclusion that an author other than Joanot Martorell interpolated the part corresponding to chapters 300–49. The actual plot structure of the novel facilitated the interpolation since this is the north African episode, which begins with Tirant and Plaerdemavida being shipwrecked on the coast of north Africa in a story inspired by one of Boccaccio's tales, the history of Martuccio and Constanza, as Farinelli pointed out (Riquer 1990a:190).

Both the *Tirant* and its model relate the adventures of the castaways with a technique common in the Byzantine novel, in which the vicissitudes of the protagonists are not told alternately but, after the initial situation, follow one of the characters, to take up the other's adventures only when the anagnorisis and re-encounter of them both is about to occur. In this way, after leaving Plaerdemavida, who has taken refuge in the house of the old Moor, the novel follows the adventures of Tirant. When the latter has triumphed, Plaerdemavida's story is resumed. The interpolator changed Tirant's adventures, leaving the story of Plaerdemavida in the house of a great Moorish lady identical to Martorell's original, since its happening did not concern his plans.

We can suppose that the interpolator was Martí Joan de Galba if we take the colophon seriously, together with the new fact that the latter was of Catalan origin (Renau 1991:48) and could have been less familiar with the *mudéjares* than a Valencian. Whoever he may have been, his ideology differed from Martorell's. In the Prologue / Dedication of the *Tirant*, Martorell sums up the actions which his hero is to perform:

> Tirant lo Blanc, who through his courage subdued many kingdoms and provinces, offering them to others and desiring only the simple honour of his victories, and later he conquered the entire Greek Empire, winning it back from the Turks who had brought the Christians under their yoke.

Here nothing is said of the mass conversion of the Muslims to Christianity which takes place in the forty-nine interpolated chapters. But once interpolated, it now figures in the knight's curriculum: 'Tirant lo Blanc, who through his very great chivalry and ingenuity conquered many kingdoms and brought infinite peoples in Barbary and Greece to the Holy Catholic religion' (chapter 466).

From an ideological point of view, it is a different approach, one which disfigures the chivalresque ideal, whose mission is not the conversion of infidels but the armed defence of Christendom, as Martorell, paraphrasing Ramon Llull, had explained. But chivalry had failed in its most important mission, the reconquest of Constantinople, after the death of John Hunyadi on 11 August 1456 – a natural death, like that of his literary counterpart Tirant – and the end of Calixtus III's Crusade. Some intellectuals of the

Church, like Juan de Segovia and Nicholas of Cusa, had put forward the idea of a peaceful crusade, *per viam pacis et dotrinae*, convincing the new Pope of Rome, Pius II, the intellectual Enea Silvio Piccolomini, who sent a letter to the Ottoman Sultan Muhammed II, the conqueror of Constantinople, to persuade him to convert to Christianity and thus become the Christian Emperor of the East (Hocks 1942). From force of arms, one has passed to attempting the conversion of the Muslims, and this was the doctrine spread by the preachers sent by Pius II to advocate the new crusade (Delumeau 1989:409). Given that this Pope died in 1464, one year before Martorell, this ideology could scarcely have been reflected in the *Tirant* as written by the Valencian author, who had pledged the original to Martí Joan de Galba at the beginning of 1464 (Chiner and Villalmanzo 1992:85). Between this date and 1490, when it went to press, Galba had plenty of time to introduce into the work the new ideology of the 'conversion' of the Muslims instead of the conquest of the lands of the infidels.

The Last Part of the Tirant

From chapter 350 onwards, Galba respected Martorell's original, merely introducing some adjustments to make it cohere with the new interpolated narrative. But some things escaped him, like the double presentation of King Escariano. Thus in chapter 330 there appears his description, written, in our opinion, by Galba:

> King Escariano, a powerful black much taller than other men, who was a King very powerful in himself, with many men and riches, sent his entire power against him, and many kings came to his assistance. . . . This King Escariano's realm bordered that of Tremicen (chapter 301).

Later, the description taken from 'the book' (*lo llibre*) – a reference which in chapter 349 had indicated a return to Martorell's original work – is repeated:

> King Escariano, a tall, handsome black and a most valiant warrior, ruled the inhabitants of Ethiopia, who called him King Jamjam. . . . And his kingdom was so big that it bordered not only on Tremicen but on Prester John of the Indies' lands, through which the River Tigris runs (chapter 404).

King Escariano – Eskender or Alexander was a name used by the Neguses of Ethiopia – who was called Jamjam, the name of a mythical King of the Yemen, whose skull or *jamjam* came back to life, according to the Muslims, through a miracle of the prophet Jesus (Epalza 1987) – was King of the blacks of Ethiopia. The Valencians knew the Ethiopians were Christians, since some Ethiopian ambassadors had even come to Valencia in the time of

Alfons the Magnanimous (Mascarino 1953–54:189–94). We suspect that the personage of the King of Ethiopia in Martorell's original – to which the second description corresponds – was a Christian and that his function was to be an ally and companion in arms to Tirant, thus fulfilling one of the Utopian dreams of Christians in the Late Middle Ages, the hope of encountering an Asian or African sovereign, Christian or at least not Muslim, who would be their ally, like Tamburlaine or Prester John (Riquer 1990a:142, note 2). If this is true, then possibly the oath that Escariano swears to Tirant (chapter 330) may correspond to Martorell's materials, used by Galba in his interpolation, which made the King of Ethiopia a Muslim so that he might be converted by the intervention of Tirant, the knight-turned-missionary.

Something similar happens with Maragdina, the Queen of Ethiopia and, before that, of Tremicen and Tunis. Galba, in his interpolation of chapters 300 to 349, presents her as the daughter of the King of Tremicen, married to the son of the Bey of Beys, in love with Tirant, a widow, an orphan, and therefore Queen of Tremicen – another misinterpretation of Islamic customs, since it is not possible for there to be queens – and then, married to Escariano and converted to Christianity, although she continues to propose marriage to Tirant.

But in chapter 348 there appears a King of Tremicen other than Escariano, who forms part of the coalition against Tirant. Until chapter 385 there is no explanation of his personality: he had been elected on the death of the previous King, Maragdina's father, and was his nephew (chapter 380). Thus Maragdina had not been Queen of Tremicen, and she and her husband had mysteriously remained without a north African kingdom until finally Tirant conquered and gave them that of Tunis, a fact which is mentioned in chapter 390. And from that point onwards, Escariano and Maragdina are presented as Kings of Ethiopia and Tunis. Later, in chapter 463, the Queen appears again and, apart from speaking Latin to Carmesina and being clothed with great elegance and crowned with jewels, she is accompanied by duennas and maidens, white and black like Tunisians and Ethiopians. It is also confirmed that she had asked Tirant to marry her:

> To all the courtiers this queen seemed of inestimable beauty, and they spoke severally among themselves, saying that Tirant was very virtuous to have spurned such a fair lady, for they were all certain that the queen had asked him to be her husband and lord of the kingdom of Tunis and of the whole of Barbary, and that, for love of the Princess, he had renounced it all.
> (chapter 463)

Thus we can infer that Maragdina's request of marriage to Tirant took place in Martorell's original, but that it did not occur in Tremicen, as in Galba's interpolation, but in Tunis. Perhaps it was an allusion to the story of Dido, which also inspired the Tunisian episode of *Curial e Güelfa* (Espadaler 1984:129).

Other elements help us to discover Martorell's original in the last part of the *Tirant*, such as the episode of the knight Espercius in which Tirant's deeds are mentioned without reference to the mass conversion of the Muslims (chapter 406), or the reappearance of the Grand Turk and the Sultan of Babylon, who once again use the language of genuine Muslims in the letter of credence, which refers to *alcaides* (generals) and *alcadis* (judges) and the month of Ramadan or fasting (chapter 455).

Martorell also seems responsible for the reappearance of Diafebus, Duke of Macedonia, who had been a prisoner, and who wore 'a yellow burnous and a blue turban on his head' (chapter 459), since the blue towel worn as a turban was a defamatory item of clothing which the *mudéjares* of Valencia were forced to wear in order to indicate their status as Moors.

Galba introduces several interpolations in accordance with his ideology, such as the appearance and sermon of Brother Joan Ferrer, of the Order of Mercy, a Catalan from the city of Lleida, who speaks Arabic well (chapter 402), and who represents intolerance in dealing with Muslims, a mentality which fully corresponds to the last quarter of the fifteenth century, and which is to lead to the Inquisition, the expulsion of the Jews and the forced conversion of the *mudéjares*. His sermon (chapter 404) and the description of the baptism (chapter 404) are certainly the work of Galba, as is the enumeration of the 'missionary' activities of Tirant (chapter 466).

Our methodology, which has enabled us to discover the double vision of the Muslims in the *Tirant*, does not allow us to say which of the two authors brought Tirant's life to an end and made Hipòlit, the Empress's lover, heir to himself and to the Byzantine Empire (Alemany 1994:13–26). If we suppose Martorell to have used as a historical model John Hunyadi, conqueror of the Turks at the Battle of Belgrade, who died of the plague before consolidating his victory, Tirant's death would be the work of Martorell, as would be the transformation of the hair-raising history of Hunyadi's successors, Laszo and Matias, who murdered Ulrich of Cilli, the former's father-in-law, and were cruelly punished (Reynaud 1988:187–92), into a bedroom adventure, something which corresponds to Martorell's strange sense of humour, which, to judge from his interpolations, is not shared by Martí Joan de Galba.

Translated by Arthur Terry

The Eschatological Framework of Tirant's African Adventure

ALBERT HAUF

In a true work of art, any fragmentary analysis of one of its constituent elements, even of only a single chapter, inevitably points to a theoretical unity or superior harmony of the whole. If we start from the premiss that the *Tirant*, such as it was received and assimilated by fifteenth-century readers and later by Cervantes and eventually by the modern reader, is an artistic creation of considerable ambition, an essentially homogeneous text beneath its obvious heterogeneity, the only justifiable literary criticism is that which derives from a wish for overall understanding which does not evade or distort the meaning of its individual parts.

It is on the basis of this supposition that I want to concentrate in the first place on one of the chapters – 300 – to attempt to explain its function and to see if we can detect some clear lines of thematic convergence, both with regard to the context of the African campaign in which it is inserted and to its relation to the book as a whole. What I am basically interested in bringing out is the impact on a contemporary reader of Martorell of the prophecy which the *Tirant* contains, paying special attention to the eschatological framework and the social crisis which determined it. That is to say, a type of beliefs and expectations very much alive in fifteenth-century Valencian society, and which must be considered crucial, both for the creative process and for the reading of the great Valencian novel.

1.1. Meaning of the lunar prophecy: Tirant, an anti-Mohammed?

If we analyse the novel as it has come down to us, we cannot ignore one of the cruxes which, potentially, reveals a great deal concerning the author's intentions: the enormously long parenthesis of Tirant's north African adventure. An episode which follows on a triple crisis caused by Carmesina's seeming degradation, apparently given over to a blackamoor 'hostile to our holy faith' (chapter 283), and the defeat and fall of Bellpuig and of a good number of Tirant's friends at the hands of the Turks (chapter 288). Both disasters affect the double axis – amorous and military – of the novel and lead, at a real and symbolic level, to Tirant's breaking his leg again, thus emphasizing the hero's breakdown or spiritual crisis, placed as he is by the author at death's door in one of the more extreme calamities of his career (chapter 291).

His prayers before the crucifix anticipate the scene of his final passing in chapters 467–8, so that, strictly speaking, this would be a convenient place to end the novel with a final catastrophe if the author had wanted to offer us a kind of fictionalized justification *a posteriori* of the fall of Constantinople, instead of reserving a much more transcendental mission for his hero.

Since this extraordinary mission required the continuity of the narrative, the author brings his protagonist back to life, not miraculously, but in an extraordinarily expeditious manner (chapter 292). A wise Jewess, using in her medical practice the well-known theoretical principle that shame is at the root of chivalry, makes Tirant believe that the Turks are at the gates of the city. He 'decides rather to die than to bear shame' and immediately gets up from his bed. By means of this picturesque and partly humorous ruse, the author not only confirms Tirant's excellence, but finds a quick way of throwing him into the next fictional action, which is nothing less than the conquest and subsequent conversion to the Christian faith of the entire geographical space of north Africa!

One can hardly call superfluous this long sequence of events (chapters 297–413) which presupposes a sudden change of decor and actors. The author brings about this change with masterly rapidity in chapter 299, initially borrowing descriptive matter from Boccaccio (*Decamerone* V,2), and combining themes and motives from the ancient Byzantine novel with Shakespearean or Romantic scenic effects *avant la lettre*.

Tirant, who, as we have seen, has just got up from his deathbed thanks to his inherent chivalresque virtue, will now see himself immersed in a kind of cosmic cataclysm. The author arranges things so that the conflict of contradictory feelings within the soul of the disenchanted hero finds an objective correlative in the irresistible force of the winds and waves of an actual storm which casts Tirant's galley on the coasts of Barbary.

Fortune, or rather Providence (the theme of fortune recurs in chapters 304, 307, 310–1, 317–19, 345, 351, 353, 355, 366–7, 371–9. See chapter 299 and especially 301) thus situates Tirant in the appropriate place and moment to give a new twist to his existence. As he is reborn from his material and spiritual wreck, he is given an opportunity to reconstruct and even to reinvent his identity (chapters 301 and 397) in a rapid process of adaptation which involves his change of name. It will be through overcoming adversity that his virtue will remake and demonstrate itself, by means of the harsh catharsis of slavery and exile.

Thus the author of the *Tirant* appears to emphasize some of the theses of the book, such as the subordination of fate to free will and to a superior divine Providence (chapter 376) which is far above human designs and which often permits evil so that good may come of it. (We remember the famous and paradoxical episode of the lady of Rhodes, where God uses the sin of the knight and a prostitute in order to save the religion of St John, or the problematic ending of the book which so preoccupied Vaeth [Hauf 1994:79–118; Perujo 1995:229–58].) The other thesis, which also recurs, is that in reality what elevates the knight is not the blood he inherits, but virtue and his own deeds. In the present case, Tirant escapes once again, completely naked, from a death he has already accepted. His nakedness signifies total vulnerability, but also his natural aptitude (chapter 299), which will help him to reconquer power and glory.

A mysterious prophecy announces the transcendance of this new stage. When Tirant falls exhausted on the beach, the Moors think he is dead. But the hero reacts, proving his quickness of wit and the extraordinary theoretical preparation which allow him to find on the spot the appropriate reply, transforming a bad omen into a glorious prophecy.

In reality, Tirant is simply putting into practice a classic strategy which Eiximenis attributes to a wise emperor:

> ... who did whatever was in his power to avoid spells and by turning to good every sign which came to him: for if on entering the land he wished to conquer he fell to the ground, he said it was a sign that the land wished him to be its lord ... If the moon went into eclipse, he said it was a sign that the moon shielded them ... So that all the spells others took to be evil, he turned to good ... (Eiximenis 1484: *Dotzèn*, chapter 247).[1]

The obvious ingenuity of the hero and of the author of the novel are clear from the adaptation of this source, since the lunar eclipse of Eiximenis's text is replaced by the full moon which, 'above' the hero's head, surrounds him with gleaming light. Apart from this, Tirant relates the intense brightness of the moon – the emblem of Islam – to his own lineage, which he now says is his 'true name' (chapter 301) and which, while continuing to point to the maternal line of the mythical descent of the hero (chapters 29 and 222), is well adapted to his person. The Bey acknowledges this in an oriental-type encomium: 'Blessed be the mother who named you in accord with your perfection' (chapter 301). The name in question is a Germanic etymon, *Blanc*, meaning 'brilliant, clean, resplendent', which is related to 'stripped, naked':[2] 'My name is Blanc, and the moon is *clear, white* and *fair*, now at this hour when I fell' (chapter 301).

Notice that the two main adjectives also coincide with the description of one of the signs which Eiximenis himself recommends military leaders to

---

[1] See Riquer 1973:334–5, where he relates the advice to Frontinus, *Strategemata* I, XII, 1.

[2] I translate these usages from Herman Paul, *Deutsches Wörterbuch*, edited by A. Schimmer (Halle 1961:98): ' "glänzend"; daraus "rein", "geputzt"; ferner "unverdeckt", "bloss" '. See also Joan Coromines, *Diccionari Etimològic i Complementari de la Llengua Catalana* I (Barcelona: Curial, 1980).

bear in mind 'after God' when they begin their campaigns, a comet which 'is called the Silvery One (*argentre*), since its rays are *clear* and *white*, like pure silver, and for that reason no man can gaze long at it . . .' (Eiximenis 1483–84: *Primer*, chapter 288).

Martorell seems to associate this star metonymically with the moon, which 'was at the full, for it shed great clarity, so that it seemed to be day' (chapter 301). Thus the star of night, which was related to silver and to another element much esteemed by Muslims, i.e. water, accumulates references to other evil signs of popular superstition.

The recourse to the moon also serves to emphasize emblematically the anti-Mohammedan character of the Christian hero, who, with his arms extended, superimposes the sign of the Cross on the earth which is dominated by the moon. And when he states that the latter has placed itself above him, he appears to emulate one of the miracles attributed to Mohammed, since, according to a little-known legend also reported by Eiximenis, the Muslims carried the moon on their banners for the following reason:

> Thus they make a sign of the moon, for they have reason to, so they say. And the reason is that they claim that the moon was friendly to Mohammed, insofar as it bowed to him on earth to pay him honour . . . (Eiximenis 1483: *Primer*, chapter 100).

I cannot detect any possible basis for this symbolism in the *Koran*, apart from 54.2: 'The hour of Doom is drawing near and the moon is cleft in two', a verse which refers to the battle of Badr, in which the chiefs of the Arabs who rebelled against Mohammed perished. A textual note which I cannot resist copying[3] gives us interpretative clues that suggest how familiar this kind of prophetico-symbolic language was in the Muslim milieu. Not in vain does Plaerdemavida, whose function throughout this episode is to redirect Tirant's energies towards Constantinople (chapter 357), say, in parallel and not without irony, to a confused Tirant: 'I speak with the spirit of prophecy . . . And I, who am a Moor, speak to you in riddles' (chapter 355).

Tirant's improvised prophecy, then, is an intelligent artistic creation which provides the new episode with a memorable and appropriate entry to the providential mission which Tirant announces, to some somewhat sceptical

---

[3] See *El Sagrado Corán* (Bungay: Islam International Publications, 1988), 1212, n. 2896: 'But the most plausible explanation, which also has a deep spiritual significance, is the fact that the moon was the national emblem of the Arabs and the symbol of their political power, just as the sun was that of the Persians. When Safiyyah, the daughter of Huyay ibn Ajtab, the leader of the Jews of Jaibar, told her father that she had dreamed that the moon had fallen into her lap, the latter struck her, saying that she wished to marry the chief of the Arabs. After the fall of Jaibar, the dream was fulfilled . . . In the same way, Aisha had seen in dreams that three moons had fallen on her dwelling, which took place when the Holy Prophet, Abu Bakr and Omar were buried there one after the other . . . .'

Moors, that he will accomplish 'with the aid of the Divine Power', and which is none other than the conquest 'of the whole of Barbary' (chapter 301) which the author proposed to describe.

Evidently the prophecy remained engraved on the impressionable mind of the Bey: 'For he had often pondered our knight's words after his fall, how he would conquer that land' (chapter 302), and, because of the arrogance it implies, it will be one of the causes of Tirant's rapid promotion: 'Your words when you fell convinced me when you said that, with the help of your God, you would conquer the whole of this land' (chapter 303). The Bey himself, who considers Tirant a mere instrument of his own ambition, hypocritically raises the omen to the status of a prophecy in order to flatter the hero and rouse him to action:

> And I see clearly the signs which your prophecy showed forth, for I remember how, when you fell, they heard you say you were to conquer the whole of this land. And since I see the beginnings are good, I cannot but think the end will be much better. And I pray you to carry out my wishes with diligence, that is, to bring the conquest quickly to an end . . .
> (chapter 315).

But it is Tirant who takes maximum advantage of the situation and little by little transforms the prophecy into a reality in which his mediocre protector will soon play no part.

Martorell not only confirms once more the chivalresque qualities and the subtlety of his hero, but endows him with a new dimension. He makes him into the military leader who Machiavellianly puts into practice one of the most insistent predictions of apocalyptic messianism: the destruction of the Mohammedan sect and the conversion of the infidels in a stage prior to the imminent coming of the Antichrist. With the curious detail that Tirant himself is the subtle prophet of his own action.

In this way, the novel touches on one of the themes which, as we shall see, was of burning actuality at the time of writing. The conquest and swift annihilation of an enemy present *ante portas* was a fascinating literary theme. Still more so, if one was to avoid sacrificing costly Christian armies, as was demanded by the standards of the traditional chronicles of Joinville, Rui de Pina, Muntaner or Froissart, to a crusading idea which had proved fairly ineffective, without, however, abandoning the objectives outlined by projects like those of Llull and Haithon of Gorigos, or that which Alfons the Magnanimous feigned to have and which Calixtus III fought stubbornly and vainly to put into practice. It was a question, in short, of crushing Moorish power beneath the combined energies of two convergent allied forces, one's own and those of possible allies whom some claimed to seek in the mythical Prester John or in the collaboration of the Tartars (Atiya 1970/2; Hauf 1996:111–54).

The attraction of the programme that Martorell offers in his fiction comes from the fact that it is based on the courage and ingenuity of a superhero whose individual actions feed to a great extent on the resources of the countries he conquers. The key to his strategy, in which the mysterious King Escariano, a possible literary version of Prester John or of the Tartars themselves, plays a decisive part, consists of his profiting by the internal divisions of the enemy in order to build alliances and finally to become the arbiter of the material and spiritual destiny of countless kingdoms. Kingdoms which, once they are controlled and Christianized, will provide the necessary forces to wrest the Greek Empire from the hands of the Turks and to bring the novel back to the framework of the Byzantine Empire.

Martorell continues to link the progress of his crusading project to a new double plot – both military and emotional – whose basic axis is the conflict between the King of Tremicen and the King of Ethiopia, Escariano, the ally of the King of Tunis and claimant to the hand of Maragdina, a daughter of the King of Tremicen married to the son of the Bey, Tirant's master.

From being the Bey's slave and prisoner, Tirant will go on to become the efficient collaborator of the King of Tremicen. The latter, like the Bey and his son, dies in the course of the war with Escariano. When Escariano achieves his desire to marry Maragdina, now Queen of Tremicen, they both are Christians, thanks to the direct action of Tirant, who becomes brother in arms to the Ethiopian and transforms himself into the indisputable leader and active propagator of the Christian religion (chapters 325–30), which rapidly extends itself through the combined energies of armed force, the example of the governing classes and even the influence of Maragdina's love for a Tirant always faithful to his distant Carmesina (chapters 322–3).

The campaign soon reaches Fez and Bugia and ends with the conquest of Caramen (chapters 350–87) and the subsequent organization in Tunis and Constantine of an army of 250,000 men destined to bring an end to the reconquest, still pending, of the ancient empire of Justinian. Catalan friars, well versed in Arabic, arrive to collaborate in the unstoppable process of evangelizing the whole of Barbary. The spirit of this process is summed up in the sermon of the Mercedarian from Lleida, Fra Joan Ferrer, who, despite referring to 'that vile pig, your leader Mohammed', has the extraordinary effect, since for his listeners it is a blasphemous speech, of bringing about the conversion of 334,000 Muslims in three days (chapters 401–7)! This sermon, a boring hotchpotch of topics from manuals, deals with a theme that is too serious – and above all, too risky – to be considered a parody, and may be regarded as the climax of the African episode and perhaps of the novel as a whole.[4] It represents the victory and the official public proclamation of the superiority of the Catholic faith over Muslim belief as the result of Tirant's

---

[4] I indicate the possible theological and scholastic sources of this sermon in Albert Hauf, 'Sinó per la fe de Jhesucrist', *BSCC* (in press).

chivalry. As such, it not only implies the fulfilment of Tirant's prophecy, but also the theoretical justification for the African episode and, one must suppose, of a whole book which can be understood much better by knowing some of the theoretical assumptions which the Valencian readers of the time would take for granted.

It is perhaps worth attempting to document this now practically forgotten contextual reference.

2.1 Prophesying as a Social Constant: From the Western Schism to the Fall of Constantinople

Already throughout the fourteenth century, in the territories of the Crown of Aragon which owed obedience to the Aragonese Pope Benedict XIII, people related the terrible chaos brought about by the Western Schism to the apocalyptic signs which announced the end of the world and the expected coming of Antichrist. The insistent preaching of St Vicent Ferrer infused the sensibility of Valencian society from top to bottom, combined with the residue of ancient predictions of Byzantine origin transmitted by the Franciscan Spirituals and assimilated by Arnau de Vilanova and Francesc Eiximenis (Lee 1989; Reeves 1992; Guadalajara 1996; Pou 1996:9–112). Both Vicent Ferrer and Eiximenis fully agree on the need for a total reform of society.

Both friars denounced the injustice of 'effeminate and sensual princes who allow themselves to be ruled by women' (*LA* III, chapter 14),[5] the bad example of simoniac prelates and ecclesiastics and corrupt priests; the decadence of chivalry ('... knights do not live in a manly fashion but like women, and on account of evil women go through streets and squares singing vile songs. They are so effeminate that they have no care for orphans, widows, the commons of the city, town or village, nor for what they should do for the good of the state' [*TSM* 272]); the shamelessness of women ('Women ... of whatever class and condition, have not a bit of shame, of honesty, modesty or maturity, but all is "vanity of vanities" ' [ibid.]; the lack of truth and charity, and popular vices, especially pride, avarice and lust (*LA* III, chapters 13 and 15; *TSM* 272–4), which are those which Martorell, through the mouth of the Albanian, attributes to the King of Tremicen when it comes to justifying the defeat he has suffered.

---

[5] The quotations given here are taken from the following works: Francesc Eiximenis, *Llibre dels Àngels* (Barcelona: Publicacions de L'Abadia de Montserrat, 1494) = *LA*; Albert G. Hauf, 'El *De Triplici Statu Mundi* de Fr. Francesc Eiximenis, O.F.M', *Miscel.lània Aramon i Serra* I (Barcelona: 1979), 265–83 = *TSM*; Sant Vicent Ferrer, *Sermons*, ed. J. Sanchis Sivera and G. Schib, 6 vols. (Barcelona: 1932–88) = *S.*, See also Mensa 1998.

While the holy Dominican assures his listeners that 'this world will come to an end quickly, soon and in a short space of time; (*S* I,197–208), and even states that 'Antichrist . . . was born thirteen years ago' (*S* I,208), the Franciscan announces future catastrophes similar to those which Martorell predicts in chapter 330 for Valencia.

Notice that Eiximenis, when he relates the abominable coexistence with Muslims to these future punishments, repeatedly prophesies the end of the Mohammedan sect as the prelude to the temporal establishment of a universal Christian empire which is to precede the end of the world:

> . . . great invasions and disturbances on the part of the Moors which they themselves [the princes] suffer . . . until an end be made to that cursed people, which in every respect must be broken of their Mohammedan sect for ever . . . and then the mysteries will be fulfilled . . . in the opening of the sixth seal (*LA* V,chapter 38).

As we can see, the disaster of the Schism and the general corruption had encouraged the conviction of having touched bottom and that a positive reaction was imminent, which implied the conversion of the Muslims 'in the hundred years which followed, of which we have already had seventy or seventy five':

> . . . until an end be made to this evil sect, the which we shortly hope for . . . about which there have been diverse prophecies, and the Saracens themselves say they have had prophecies to the same end which agree with us . . . according to this prophecy, within this century, which is the fourteenth counting from the birth of Jesus Christ, the Saracen sect is to come to an end, and thus everything will finish . . . (Eiximenis 1483: *Primer*, chapter 102).

> . . .We still hope, beyond all doubt . . . to arrive at the swift destruction of the Mohammedan sect. And we know from the sayings of the saints that the whole of Christianity must now especially flourish . . . We still hope for a great conversion of the infidels . . . (*Primer*, chapter 208)

And not only this: Eiximenis and others pointed out that the King of Aragon, represented by the bat which still figures in the Valencian coat of arms, was destined to play an extremely important part in the campaign against Islam:

> . . .A learned man says here that this bat signifies the King of Aragon . . . The latter says he will conquer Africa, which at the present time is inhabited by Saracens. And he will bring low the head of the beast. After which there will appear the son of perdition, which is Antichrist, not the final one, but he who is the figure and precursor of that one . . . (*Primer*, chapter 102).

Of this House [of Aragon] it is prophesied that it will achieve monarchy over almost the whole of the world . . . We hope that, by a special prophecy we have had, so some say, that a Prince of this House will shortly go into Africa and destroy the entire sect of Mohammed . . . (*Primer*, chapter 247).

As we can see, the moralizing discourse of some of the most representative Valencian authors of the fourteenth and fifteenth centuries has an eschatological side which can be related to our theme, since it paved the way, not only for a great many new prophecies, but also for any work of literary fiction which would reflect in one way or another the feeling of an entire epoch.

2.2. The Valencian Economic and Social Crisis in the Time of Alfons the Magnanimous

In contrast with the preceding period, the Neapolitan court of Alfons the Magnanimous (1396–1458) is rightly considered a landmark of courtesy, in which splendour and munificence were placed at the service of a critical thought and of a culture represented by the magnificent royal library. Panormita proclaimed Alfons to be an ideal prince: '. . . without doubt, he is the greatest of all the kings of our age in fortitude and wisdom'. And his translator, Jordi de Centelles, will add a further encomium worthy of a novelesque hero like Tirant himself: 'greater than Alexander in calm and temperance, equal to Caesar in clemency and chivalresque diligence' (Panormita 1990:73–4).

What one tends to forget when one reads a book like the *Tirant*, so rich in extravagance, is that this proverbial magnificence and that associated with the courts of Alfons and the Borgia Popes was actually in complete contrast to the sad reality experienced in the Hispanic territories of the Crown of Aragon and in particular in the Kingdom of Valencia during the prolonged absence of the monarch.

A discreet sampling of the abundant official correspondence of the Valencian *jurats* (city councillors) in the crucial years which see the gestation, and perhaps the writing, of the *Tirant*, confirms how acute the sensation of disaster was in Valencia.[6] According to these writings, the chief causes of this situation were:

1. On the one hand the plague, which regularly laid waste the country. In 1450, the mortality rate was 150 victims a day:

---

[6] These *Lletres Missives* (*LM*) are preserved in the Ajuntament of Valencia. The volumes I have used bear the signatures g–3/21 (1449–53), 22 (1453–6) and 23 (1456–61). Another important source is Sanchis Sivera 1932.

> Throughout the city you will only see communions and the burying of corpses, for there is a shortage of priests . . . this city, with this misfortune and others is on the point of perishing . . . (*LM* to Manuel Suau, 18–VII–1450);

> . . . of the three parts of the people, two have left and absented themselves from this city, and we believe scarcely one part remains . . . The only office or rite is that of extreme unction and to bury corpses . . . with the strange poverty which exists among the people, the most extreme ever seen . . . And there is no human heart, however evil and reprobate, which does not break and have great grief and compassion . . . (*LM* to the the King of Navarre, 9–VIII–1450).

2. The ruin of the merchants, which involves that of pension schemes (*censals*), the basis of the economy. The *jurats* provide a logical, and frightening, summary of the causes of the deplorable economic situation:

> . . . we well believe that your Majesty is convinced that merchants are said to be the equalizers of the world. And where there is trading, the earth is increased and made prosperous, and where there is not, it is deserted and destroyed, since your Majesty, in this city and kingdom, by reason of the wars which have gone on for a long time, trading has completely ceased . . . When trading ceases, rights also cease; when rights cease, the payment of the city's pensions, which are its purse and soul, cease also, without which one cannot live . . . and the people will perish . . . Kindly think, your Majesty, how or with what the pensions, which are the soul of this city, are to be paid . . . we, your Majesty, see no way or remedy in the world, but are heading towards complete dejection and perdition . . . (*LM* to the King of Navarre, 9–VII–1450).

3. The piracy of the Moorish corsairs and of the actual galleys designed to protect the city:

> . . . for people dare in vain to go by the sea routes without being attacked, captured and robbed and put into galleys . . . May God give them better work to do, for between the Moorish and the Christian galleys, the ones at Dénia and the others at Peníscola, they are besieging our city. (*LM* to the local governor and the procurators of Tortosa respectively, 11–VII–1450; 30–IV–1457.)

4. Hunger, due to the chronic lack of wheat, caused by a strict prohibition on loading foreign ships:

> . . . we cannot find anyone prepared to insure wheat anywhere on the sea . . . if we do not assure them that the sailors who bring wheat to this city may load their ships and return with the cargo (*LM* to Francesc Mascó, 16–VII–1454).

5. The feeling of danger from the constant presence of a Muslim population capable of being used by the Moors of Granada, which will lead to an attack on the Moorish quarter. According to the *jurats*, the Moors of Valencia:

> ... are too presumptuous and hold their heads too high ... they firmly believe they are at a time when they desire and think to take over this kingdom which is before their eyes, and have it as an article of faith that the Christians own it unrightfully ... Our enemies are very favoured at home ... (*LM* to the King of Navarre, 26–I–1451).

> It does not seem to us tolerable that the Moors should go in the open with crossbows ... (*LM* to Jofre de Blanes, 8–X–1456).

6. The neglect caused by the absence of the chief authorities. In the first place, King Alfons the Magnanimous:

> ... We attest to your long absence from your lands and kingdoms this side of the sea, and see ourselves as sheep without a shepherd ... and we see prepared before our eyes such and so many dangers, evils and inconveniences ... that if your Majesty does not quickly provide due remedies, we are destined to sheer ruin and desolation ... (*LM* to the King of Navarre, 26–I–1451).

But also that to the Cardinal Bishop Alfonso Borgia, requesting money and reminding him that he has been Bishop of the City for twenty-five years:

> that you have not resided there, or very little, and have received each year for you ministry more than XXM florins ... (*LM* 8–III–1453).

7. A major emigration to Rome and Naples:

> ... with those who have left the city for this reason, and those who shortly afterwards have gone to Rome and Naples to join the King and others, this city remains today bereft of people (*LA* to the King of Navarre, *loc. cit.*).

The *Dietari* (Sanchis 1932:198) also notes that:

> 'most of them have returned in debt and in considerable affliction'.

8. The vices and sins of society. The *jurats* attempt to control the moral life of the city, moved by an exemplary concern for the common good. A letter addressed to Alfons the Magnanimous (*LM* 9–VIII–1450) is especially explicit. Here, they complain at the imposition of burdensome taxes on

> ... hospitals, confraternities and pious works of this city. If this continues ... the poor will be lost, naked, despoiled and bereft of such benefits, they will sleep in the streets ... they will perish from hunger and cold. Many children who are fed and brought up there will be killed by their mothers,

since the hospitals, thus deserted, will not be able to receive them. We do not and cannot believe, nor can we presume of your Majesty, that you will not assume this burden in some way, for we are sure that you know from ourselves that our entire faith is founded on charity, and if charity, your Majesty, which sustains the world, is lost, what is to become of us?

It is not only a lesson of Christian ethics that they are offering the luxury-loving monarch, pointing out *sotto voce* the all-too-obvious contrast between his own way of life and the poverty of the country which served as the economic platform for his imperial ambitions:

Consider, your Majesty . . . all these things which with infinite benefits are brought to pass in this city: the Lord God visits us with pestilence and mortality and in such a way, how much more, your Majesty, if the contrary is done? And in your favour, your Majesty, the hospitals, confraternities and pious works, the poor and the new born, those who live and the souls of those who are dead, the which have been received, welcomed and fed in these, sire, will pray to our Lord for you . . .

The zeal of the Valencian *jurats* allows us to survey some of the actual sins of that society: lack of virtue on the part of the clergy, with precise notes 'on the very dishonest and relaxed life of Brother Bernat Català', in charge of the monastery of the Mercè in Valencia (*LM* to the General of the Mercedarians, 16–XI–1453); the immoral behaviour of certain hermits of Puçol, 'so that not long ago some of them were executed . . . by burning . . .' (*LM* to the Queen, 12–II–1455, and to the Bishop Cardinal, 18–III–1455); references to Dominicans who leave the convent by day and night in order to frequent women of bad reputation ('visitantes persepe mulieres non bone fame' [*LM* to Brother Pere Queralt, Vicar General of the Dominicans, 7–IX–1454]); or to 'an unusual and admirable case which occurred in the monastery of Porta Celi' (13–X–1455); and especially

the murders, thefts and abominable crimes committed by some who claimed to be tonsured . . . perpetrators of murders, premeditated or for money, others public go-betweens, others frequenters of brothels and taverns, and in very short and dishonest lay garments, living very dissolutely and immorally . . . (*LM* to the Cardinal Bishop, 13–XI–1454, and to Pere Climent, 25–X–1454).

Among the secular sins, apart from murders and swindling, there stand out the continuous faction warfare and quarrels (*LM* to the King of Navarre, 22–VI and 2–VII–1453), the forging of money, lawsuits and actions, blasphemies, procuring, rapes and bestiality.

2.3 An Extraordinary Conjuncture: the Literary Fulfilment of the Prophecy

It is in this more or less dark and pessimistic panorama that one must situate, in 1453, the striking news of the fall of Constantinople at the hands of the Turks, which seemed to confirm the worst prophecies. We find its effects and the evidence of the oral accounts which the survivors were circulating throughout the Christian world in a letter to the Queen (*LM* 8–I–1455), concerning the presence in Valencia of Joan Cèsar, a relative of the Emperor of Constantinople 'who found himself by chance in the prison of the said city'. The narration, full of horrifying details concerning fathers flayed alive, brothers impaled or burnt, sons sodomized and daughters taken prisoner and violated, must have made a strong impact on the popular imagination and confirmed the most pessimistic complaints and portents.

But shortly afterwards there came the news of a providential event: the election to the Pontificate of the Cardinal Bishop of Valencia, Alfonso Borgia, which arrived together with that of the 'solemn and most singular vow he immediately made to exterminate and destroy the Turks' (*LM* to Manuel Suau, 14–V–1455), whereby Calixtus III announced his plan to change the course of history and to shed his own blood in 'the recovery of Constantinople and the rooting out of the diabolical Mohammedan sect'. This vow, and the Pope's enthusiasm, must have caused an enormous reaction, as is evident from the letter which the *jurats* sent to the Pontiff, in which the secretary, showing off his best Latin, expresses his natural satisfaction at this extraordinary event which he attributes to the inscrutable providence of a God who from all eternity had destined Calixtus III to be his vicar. I shall translate a fragment of this congratulatory letter, in which the *jurats* consider that Christ has shown His mercy by ensuring that the cruel 'plague of the Eastern coast or Levant' should be cured by 'a strong leader and a most holy shepherd' arisen from the other, ill named, Levant, or

> ... the Western coast of Spain, who will be the restorer of the great Constantinople now lost, the destroyer and scatterer of the most infidel Turk, the shameless enemy of Christ. Oh, how is shown in this the divine beatitude, merit, glory and honour, which are most clearly evident in this admirable portent: that Your Holiness, sybillinely inspired by the Holy Spirit, should have assumed the apostolic crown at the same time as he bound himself to such a work with a solemn vow, the fruit of a marvellous and extraordinary devotion ... (*LM* to Calixtus III, 14–V–1455).

The letter and the vow summarize quite accurately the obsessive idea which guided the brief Pontificate of this Borgia Pope, and the hopes which the Valencians must have entertained in the face of an extraordinary conjuncture created by the existence of a Valencian Pope and a King of the Crown of

Aragon who, with Naples and Sicily, held virtual control over the Mediterranean.

How can one forget that Alfons aspired to the glory of the Greek imperial crown, held the title of King of Jerusalem, and extended his protection to the most important leaders of the anti-Turkish resistance: the Hungarian John Hunyadi or the 'White Count' of the *Dietari* (Sanchis 1932:196) and the Albanian George Castriota or Scanderbeg (Marinescu 1994)? It seemed that the bat or *vespertilium* would soon extend its wings in order to restore Christendom. But the deaths in 1458 of the possible protagonists of the prophecy, the Pope and the King, must have caused a sudden awakening to the crude and naked reality of the Catalan civil war of 1458–60, and imposed on the country the sad lesson of the futility of human projects and glories, leaving it more than ever in need of the balsam of hope, that is to say, of new and more portentous prophecies (Duran 1997; Guadalajara 1996:375–463).

And in this sense Joanot Martorell's novel, which aims to be a fictitious, though plausible, biography, seems constructed in accordance with, not only the author's personal disenchantment in the face of his own vital and family breakdown, but also with the continuing local crisis which he was forced to live through and which he perhaps tried to avoid but could not help reflecting (Chiner 1993:19–131). Who knows whether it was from resentment of his own monarch that he decided that the 'head of the secular power, sword and dagger in defence of the sacred Christian religion' (chapter 327), that is to say, the hero destined to elude, replace and transform reality in accordance with the intensely felt hopes of his fellow citizens, should be a Breton of Arthurian descent, a member of the grandiose Order of the Garter and an enthusiastic fan of the King of England ('For just as the moon outshines the stars, so this King excels in virtues all the other kings of Christendom' [chapter 317].). It seems, in fact, that he meant to link to an Arthurian inheritance, increasingly discredited and basically impossible to recover, the role of anti-Mohammed which Eiximenis and others reserved for the House of Aragon.

Be that as it may, the massive conversion of the Moors brought about by Martorell in the long episode of Tirant's African adventure, satisfied the very real expectations of his readers at the precise moment when Mohammed II seemed to be carrying them out in a contrary sense!

Despite the realistic and disenchanted ending and the touches of demythifying humour in the preceding episodes which prevent Tirant from turning into a pure *deus ex machina*, Martorell nonetheless creates in his story a marvellous psychological war which transforms the conquered into a conqueror. His hero, now become a prophet, avoids, in the memorable pages of his novel, the great disaster which history could not prevent, and offers his readers the substitute of a longed for, but imaginary, reality.

Translated by Arthur Terry

Language and Intimacy in *Tirant lo Blanc*

THOMAS R. HART

Nearly a half century ago Dámaso Alonso made an eloquent case for *Tirant lo Blanc* as a modern novel (Alonso 1961). For Alonso, modern novel means realistic novel; he praises *Tirant* for its realism, insisting that 'Martorell sees minutely and clearly the particular' (208) and that 'we find everywhere the expected, most natural detail, often not essential to the verisimilitude of the story' (222).

An important element in the realism Alonso attributes to *Tirant* is its language: 'What astonishes in this art . . . is the reproduction of the spoken word in brief phrases of the most natural everyday language' (231). He concedes, however, that much, indeed most, of *Tirant* is written in a quite different style that modern readers, including Alonso himself, find boring:

> two techniques converge most strikingly in the form of *Tirant*. One, so new, that it seems to issue from Martorell's own hands: lively, agile, free, unconcerned, swift . . . ; in a word, 'modern'; another, traditional, confined, reasoned, paralyzed, all procedure, exceedingly slow; for the modern reader tiresome and a bore (252).

More recently, Martí de Riquer, while agreeing that two distinct styles are found in *Tirant*, has argued that both are realistic. Martorell's rhetorical style reflects the usage of aristocratic society in contemporary Valencia:

> It is likely that high Valencian society of the time took pleasure in speaking, or in trying to speak, in this solemn, pompous manner, as is shown by certain letters of challenge [*lletres de batalla*] of Valencian knights of that century (Riquer 1990:238).

Albert Haufa makes a similar point:

> These speeches, which even a well-disposed reader now finds tiresome, also fulfilled the didactic function of imparting refined models of a clearly affected way of expressing oneself which cannot have been easy to master with a modicum of naturalness, and which, for that very reason, demanded an apprenticeship which a reading of the novel could facilitate'
> (Hauf 1993b:384).

For Alonso and, of course, for most readers today, only one of the two styles in *Tirant* has positive aesthetic value. Alonso does not attempt an analysis of Martorell's rhetorical style, which he sees merely as a reflection of the taste of the time. Rolf Eberenz's excellent study of Martorell's style in *Tirant lo Blanc* is likewise concerned primarily with Martorell's use of colloquial speech. We need not agree with him that 'the decadence of chivalry, the degradation of its myths and norms of conduct are demonstrated in the person of Tirant', nor that

> we must interpret the antagonism between the two styles of the dialogues as a faithful translation of the tension between two social conceptions, between idealism and materialism, a tension which is one of the basic elements of the book (Eberenz 1982:66).

I do not believe that Tirant represents the decadence of chivalry nor that Martorell was conscious of any 'antagonism' between the two styles he uses in his book. In *Don Quixote*, Cervantes makes the curate praise *Tirant*, in the Castilian translation of 1511, precisely for its style: 'for its style, this is the best book in the world' (Cervantes 1978:I, 117). We should not be too quick to assume that he means the colloquial style favoured by most modern readers. Erich Auerbach notes that 'Cervantes is very fond of . . . rhythmically and pictorially rich . . . beautifully articulated and musical bravura pieces of chivalric rhetoric . . . And he is a master in this field' (Auerbach 1953:341).

Cervantes's innovation in *Don Quixote* is to use several different styles and to allow both the narrator and the characters to choose one or the other in particular circumstances, sometimes skillfully, like Don Quixote or Dorotea, sometimes clumsily, like Sancho. There is nothing comparable in *Tirant lo Blanc*. Although some characters, for example Plaerdemavida, tend to favour the popular style while others, like Carmesina or Tirant, favour the rhetorical one, Martorell's narrator and his characters speak essentially the same language throughout the book. Rolf Eberenz rightly emphasizes that in *Tirant lo Blanc* 'public space and private sphere do not appear to be separated as rigorously as we might expect. Tirant's and Carmesina's erotic games are carried on in the presence and with the complicity of all the Princess's ladies' and that 'the protagonists, and especially Tirant and Carmesina, resort to the rhetorical register even when they are alone' (Eberenz 1982:57–8).

Martorell's rhetorical style in *Tirant lo Blanc* has none of the charm of the elaborately literary and pseudo-archaizing style of Max Beerbohm's delightful comic fantasy *Zuleika Dobson*. For Martorell, as for his characters, there is nothing funny or absurd about chivalric rhetoric. I find it difficult to agree with David Rosenthal, whose excellent translation abridges many of the speeches Martorell assigns to his characters, that Martorell would have removed many of the 'redundancies' if he had lived to complete his work

(Martorell 1984:xxiii).[1] I think it can be argued, nevertheless, that *Tirant lo Blanc* makes much less use of rhetorical devices than another nearly contemporary work that most readers would hesitate to call boring: *La Celestina*.

Martorell is much less indebted than Fernando de Rojas to Latin models and it seems reasonable to accept the view of Riquer and Hauf that his characters speak much as their Valencian counterparts did, or at least believed they did, or tried to do, in real life. Rojas's Latinizing is apparent in the first scene of *La Celestina*, in which Calisto tells Melibea that he sees God's greatness

> en dar poder a natura que de tan perfeta hermosura te dotasse y fazer a mí, imérito, tanta merced que verte alcançasse, y en tan conveniente lugar que mi secreto dolor manifestarte pudiesse (Rojas 1991:211).

Rojas here introduces the Latinism *imérito* (from *immeritus* 'unworthy') and imitates Latin syntax by placing the finite verbs that govern his three infinitives at the end of their respective clauses. All three verbs are imperfect subjunctives, thus constituting the rhetorical figure homoioteleuton or *similiter desinens*. Rojas follows the practice of Latin comedy by having Calisto address Melibea as *tú*, something his real-life counterpart would not have dared to do at this stage in their relationship. None of these devices is characteristic of Martorell's style in *Tirant lo Blanc*. Nor would it be easy to find a passage in *Tirant* that exploits rhetorical figures so openly as this quite typical passage from the *Tragicomedia*, in which Celestina combines antithesis (*sobí . . . decender*) and anadiplosis, the repetition of a word that ends a phrase to begin the next, when she tells Lucrecia that 'bien sé que *sobí* para *decender*, *florescí* para *secarme*, *gozé* para *entristecerme*, *nascí* para *bivir*, *biví* para *crecer*, *crecí* para *envejecer*, *envejecí* para morirme' (Rojas 1991: 418; my emphasis).

If Martorell's style is so much less rhetorical than Rojas's, why does *Tirant* affect us so differently from *La Celestina*? The short answer, of course, is simply that Rojas was a better writer. Martorell is much less skilful in deciding what is relevant to his subject. The more elaborate speeches in *Tirant lo Blanc* produce much the same effect as the speeches and state papers of the Count-Duke of Olivares a century and a half later:

> Their arguments were forcefully marshalled, their phraseology occasionally enlivened by some surprising colloquialism or popular proverb, but they also convey an impression of prolixity and diffuseness.... It remains unclear to what extent the overblown sentences and the tendency to digress reflect the influence of contemporary models, and how far they simply derive from a lack of mental discipline (Elliott 1986:17).

---

[1] I refer to the author of *Tirant* as Martorell purely for convenience; it is impossible to determine Galba's share in the creation of the text.

In his 'Carta de batalla por *Tirant lo Blanc*', Mario Vargas Llosa asserts that Martorell is

> a disinterested novelist: he is not trying to demonstrate anything, he only wishes to show. Which means that, although he is everywhere in the total reality he is describing, his presence is (almost) invisible.

Vargas Llosa contends that Martorell created 'the disappearance of the narrator from the world of the narrated', an innovation he considers wrongly attributed to Flaubert (Vargas Llosa 1991:30). But, as Wayne Booth has shown, 'though the author can to some extent choose his disguises, he can never choose to disappear' (Booth 1983:20). Martorell's occasional interventions do not make *Tirant* less 'modern' than, say, *Madame Bovary*; Booth observes that

> the author's presence will be obvious on every occasion when he moves into or out of a character's mind . . . . Flaubert tells us that Emma's little attentions to Charles were 'never, as he believed, for his sake . . . but for her own, out of exasperated vanity' (ibid.:17).

It is easy to demonstrate Martorell's presence in many passages of *Tirant lo blanc*.

Often Martorell merely says explicitly what the reader would easily infer from the context. Thus, in chapter 147, he comments that 'the Viuda Reposada, *moved more by love than pity*, was also constantly at [Tirant's] side' (my emphasis). Sometimes he contrasts what his characters are thinking with the mistaken interpretation of their words or actions given by other characters. In chapter 81, for example, Thomas of Montalbán thought Tirant was frightened, as did many others, but they were mistaken, for the Breton only wished to atone for his adversaries' deaths'. Similarly, in chapter 124, Martorell tells us that 'the Emperor was pleased by these precautions and by Tirant's punctuality, though this was more to see the princess than for His Majesty's sake'.

Again, in chapter 125, the Emperor is puzzled by Tirant's behaviour, saying ' "I wonder if this knight is tormented by some sorrow and regrets venturing so far from his friends and family, or perhaps he fears the Turks" '. No one familiar with the poetry of the troubadours would be puzzled by Tirant's behaviour on this and other similar occasions. D.R. Sutherland observes that 'the convention of courtly love rests on a paradox: only the truly *cortes* can be *fin aman*, yet *fin'Amors* renders its devotees incapable of observing some of the essential rules of *cortezia*'. The lover 'must at all times be guided by *mezura* – yet when he becomes a *fin aman* he will be led into extravagance of feeling and behaviour' (Sutherland 1961:165).

Although Martorell often tells us what one of his characters is thinking, he usually does so very briefly and does not show the character's thought as it actually develops. This is one cause of the ambiguity that several critics have noted in *Tirant*. Alan Yates suggests that

> we are obliged to respond to the main characters and their reactions in a way analogous to how we interpret characters and situations in real life. . . . Ambiguity . . . has a crucial function in making and sustaining this fiction (Yates 1980:185).

Arthur Terry concurs:

> certain kinds of action . . . throw light on character; what is distinctive about the *Tirant* is that these actions can often be taken in more than one way, and that the ambiguity this creates may be emphasized, rather than resolved, by the actual discourse of other characters (Terry 1982:193).

Some of the ambiguity Yates and Terry see in *Tirant* does not, however, exist for the reader but solely for the characters, who have no direct access to other people's thoughts and must infer these from their words and actions.

Martorell's most ambitious attempt to enter the mind of one of his characters is perhaps his account in chapter 416 of the Viuda Reposada's thoughts when she decides to kill herself. David Rosenthal's translation, although abridged, keeps the essential points:

> Tirant's approach dismayed the Viuda Reposada, who said her heart ailed her and retired to her chamber, where she wept and beat her breast, considering herself as good as dead, for she knew that Plaerdemavida had unmasked her treachery. She trembled to think of facing Carmesina once her wickedness was revealed, and on the other hand, her love for Tirant augmented her despair.
>
> She spent the whole night imagining things and battling within herself, uncertain of what to do or whom to ask for advice, but finally she acted in the manner of most women, whose fickleness makes them err when their need is greatest. She decided to poison herself so subtly that no one would detect her deed, since otherwise they might burn her body or feed it to the dogs.

One cannot help feeling that Martorell has thrown away a magnificent opportunity for monologue. A striking difference between *Tirant lo Blanc* and *La Celestina* is the absence in Martorell's work of the monologues that Peter Russell considers 'one of the great innovative triumphs' of Rojas's masterpiece (Russell 1991:139). In *La Celestina*, as María Rosa Lida de Malkiel notes,

> the monologues . . . are invaluable for the depiction of character because of the light they throw on the intimacy of individual souls, who in no way

reveal themselves with equal frankness in dialogue (Lida de Malkiel 1962:124).

Rojas would surely have allowed us to see the Widow's mind at work, not merely summarized her thoughts as Martorell does. And of course he would not have interposed his own views; if it is just possible that the Widow might now think her actions constituted a 'most evil crime' she would hardly have seen her present desperate situation as an example of 'feminine nature, frivolous and variable'. It is tempting to believe that these false notes were inserted by Martí Joan de Galba, though I can think of no reason for concluding that they were.

Umberto Eco remarks that 'every text . . . is a lazy machine asking the reader to do some of its work', that is, to interpret it in the light of other more or less similar texts (Eco 1994:3).[2] Problems arise, however, when a text does not obviously belong to any of the established genres. I have suggested elsewhere that 'what is unsettling about *Tirant* is not that it combines elements of epic and of chivalric romance, but that it includes others that do not fit comfortably into either tradition' (Hart 1993:65). The most important of these other elements is Martorell's incorporation of comic motifs in a fundamentally serious and even tragic story.

Like Cervantes's curate, who suspects that the author of *Tirant* 'did not commit so many stupidities on purpose', many readers have laughed at the book with the uneasy feeling that perhaps they are not meant to. Martorell's reluctance to enter the minds of his characters is perhaps partially responsible for their doubts. He never shows his characters laughing at each other's follies, as Cervantes shows his characters laughing at Don Quixote or Sancho, sometimes at incidents that seem anything but funny to most modern readers (Russell 1969:320). Nor does Martorell often tell us how his characters react to events, unlike Cervantes, who says repeatedly that his characters feel *admiración* at something they see or hear, thus giving a hint that the reader, too, is expected to find it astonishing.

Like Fernando de Rojas, Martorell is fond of making his characters cite 'sentencias y dichos de philósophos'. In *Tirant lo Blanc*, however, the choice of a *sententia* does not usually reveal anything about the person who cites it, while in *La Celestina*, as Peter Russell notes,

> very often the *sententia* . . . is placed in the mouth of a personage whose character and intentions are completely contrary to the doctrine contained in what he is saying . . . . This an original and very important feature of the work (Rojas 1991:123).

---

[2] I discuss this point further in my Kate Elder Lecture *The Reader's Role in 'The Lusiads'* (London: Queen Mary and Westfield College,1995).

Although Martorell, unlike Rojas, does not use maxims and proverbs as keys to the individual personalities of his characters, he achieves a similar effect by using what we may call indirect narration. Arthur Terry remarks that

> characterization in the *Tirant* . . . hardly seems to be assisted either by direct self-revelation or by the intervention of an omniscient narrator. What *does* assist it – and this is one of the great achievements of the novel – is Martorell's ability to exploit less direct forms of disclosure: dream narrations, actions and gestures, and certain less formal kinds of discourse.
>
> (Terry 1982:189)

These 'less direct forms of disclosure' are examined by Cesare Segre in a fine study. Segre notes that often an action that has already been narrated is repeated in the form of a story told by one character to another, as Plaerdemavida, disguised and unrecognized, tells Tirant about his past to persuade him that he should return to Constantinople to help the Emperor (chapters 351, 355, 357): 'here, the evocation of the past does not have an informative function but rather a persuasive, that is to say, a pragmatic, one' (Segre 1993:581).

Segre observes that Carmesina's letter to Tirant in chapter 398 gives a distorted account of what has actually happened:

> Literary taste comes into play here, as if the writer wished to transform her farewell and her nostalgia into a *Heroides* of Ovid. And thus she emphasizes the pathetic tone, she presents herself as an abandoned and heartbroken woman, with attitudes and exclamations to which the novel has certainly not referred. Once again, the characters feel themselves introduced into a book, they recite instead of living (Segre 1993:583).

Embedded narratives like that found in Carmesina's letter are often deliberately slanted to persuade or deceive. Carmesina's letter, however, does not fit comfortably into either category. It seems rather an example of self-dramatization that borders on self-deception, though it is hard to be certain about this, since Martorell may be following a convention that accepts the existence of words not found in the text. Peter Russell suggests that the authors of *La Celestina* may have considered that their dialogue offers no more than a summary of the words 'actually' spoken on a given occasion (Rojas 1991:138).

A more clear-cut example of an embedded narrative that is intended to deceive is the Empress's account of her dream, which she offers to prevent the Emperor and the other members of the court from discovering that she has just spent the night with Hipòlit (chapter 262). The dream may not be wholly imaginary. It perhaps reveals more about her feelings for Hipòlit than she intends it to, while at the same time, given her awareness of her husband's stupidity and her resentment at his interest in the younger women of the court, it suggests that she is no more than half unwilling to confess what she has done. Here again, as with Carmesina's letter, the Empress's motives are sufficiently ambiguous to make the reader wonder just how conscious she is of what she is saying.

The novelist and essayist Milan Kundera has written that

> I understand and share Hermann Broch's insistence in repeating: The sole *raison d'être* of a novel is to discover what only the novel can discover: a novel that does not discover a hitherto unknown segment of existence is immoral (Kundera 1988:5–6).

This 'unknown segment of existence' is often the access to another person's consciousness through a presentation of his or her unspoken thoughts, which Dorrit Cohn calls psycho-narration (Cohn 1978). The long *parlaments* that fill so many pages of *Tirant lo Blanc* are almost always addressed to another character and intended to influence his or her behaviour. Because of this element of persuasion, and therefore of deliberate intention on the part of the speaker, they cannot be considered examples of psycho-narration. The 'comunicación indirecta' noted by Terry and Segre helps to compensate for its absence.

Vargas Llosa calls Martorell's novel 'eminently theatrical' (Vargas Llosa 1993:595). One sees his point, but there are some crucial differences between Martorell's characters and actors on a stage. Martorell's actors speak lines they themselves have created, or have at least chosen from a repertory of appropriate remarks. More importantly, they do not see their role-playing as something apart from the rest of their lives: the whole world is their theatre. Part of the fascination of *Tirant lo Blanc* lies in the opportunities Martorell gives to look directly into the consciousness of characters who seem to be almost always on show and to see things they do not.

Death in *Tirant lo Blanc*

JEREMY LAWRANCE

After prodigies of courage and endurance, Tirant is promised a princess and an empire (chapter 452). That is a proper end to romance, which tells of such perilous quests and their deserts, but it is not the end of *Tirant lo Blanc*, which is not a proper romance. For one thing, Tirant has long since 'won the battle and forced his way into Carmesina's castle' with the lance of love (chapter 436), so the Emperor's belated offer of his daughter's hand is less a reward than a bargain for the rescue of the empire from the Turks (chapters 454–66).[1] Tirant undertakes the task, but before he wins the prize he falls mortally ill from a 'sharp pain in his side' during a morning stroll (chapter 467). The penultimate chapters of the book are devoted to a lengthy account of the hero's deathbed, and to equally punctilious relations of the decease from grief of Carmesina and the Emperor (chapters 468–78).

Even this is not the end. In a coda which seems a burlesque reprise of what has gone before, Tirant's heir Hipòlit – his grief assuaged by the prospect of inheritance (chapter 479) – is persuaded to wed *his* lover, the aged Empress. This Machiavellian plan is acceptable to everyone, for as Diafebus says in the imperial council, 'knowing that Hipòlit and Her Majesty are old friends I see nothing else we can do but marry them and make him emperor . . . so he, being our relative, will confirm our new titles' (chapter 480). After a further night of fornication spent 'with very little heed of those who lay upon biers awaiting honourable burial' (chapter 481), the Empress with maidenly reluctance gives her consent (chapter 483). The adulterous couple hold a marriage-feast, stow the bodies of Tirant and Carmesina in a box for transportation to far-off Brittany (chapter 485–6), and make peace with the Turkish sultan. The Empress dies of old age and Hipòlit lives happily ever after (chapter 487).

An ending so full of surprises puts the reader in a quandary. The untimely deaths of Tirant and Carmesina at the moment before they achieve their reward, and the consequent collapse of the Greek imperial succession, seem

---

[1] By medieval notions of 'silent' or clandestine marriage (*bodes sordes, uerba de praesenti*), Tirant's and Carmesina's 'true betrothal' in chapter 271 was already a valid ceremony of matrimony – though, like the girl's deflowering, unbeknown to the Emperor. See Beltrán 1990.

like a tragedy – though an unnecessary and illogical tragedy. On the other hand, the flouting of romance tradition – the unheroic timing and manner of the hero's death, and its travesty in the happy fate of the adulterers – suggests scepticism, or even disgruntled sarcasm, about the chivalric ideal. This ambiguity of tone is already present in the sententious apostrophe which introduces Tirant's death (chapter 467):

> Among so many other travails I cannot avoid this one: my weary hand may not shrink from delineating on white paper man's ignorance of Fortune. For though the memory of Tirant's glorious deeds never fails to give me pain since he never received his reward, let it serve as an example to posterity never to trust in Fortune by risking life and soul for great pleasures or prosperity. Those who act in this way fall into deceptive and dangerous paths through their folly and violent ambition; from which it may happen that the vain and pompous men who spend their whole time in search of vainglory end up wasting the useless span of their wretched lives.

The reference to Fortune serves to locate Tirant's demise in what fifteenth-century writers regarded as the characteristic ambit of tragedy, the fall of princes. But the 'example to posterity' suggests a more desolate lesson: that Tirant's quest for love and fame – 'great pleasures or prosperity' – was at best a wild-goose chase, and at worst a vain and pompous folly. The same moral is latent in the second of the two epitaphs sculpted in letters of gold on the lovers' mausoleum (chapter 485):

> Cruel love united them while living
> and with wretched woe caused them to lose their lives;
> after death, let it close them in one grave.

The heart-rending verses are quoted verbatim from Joan Roís de Corella's tragic *History of Hero and Leander*, but, as Riquer points out, the claim that the hero died for love, while literally true in the earlier story, is here a contradiction of the truth' since Tirant died of natural causes. This disturbs the decorum of the sentiment, and drives us to conclude that the expression 'lose their lives' (*perdre lo viure*) may admit a second interpretation, 'waste their lives', for Love's causation of Tirant's death is explicable only in moralistic terms, even if his 'sharp pain in the side' was often associated in popular parlance with love malady.[2] The last line of the epitaph suggests a pun on *l'amor* 'love' and *la mort* 'death', and this picks up a connection between the two

---

[2] Riquer 1990a:298–301. Beltrán (1997b), while convincingly demonstrating the point about *mal de costat*, insists that Tirant's death must be a moral, not a clinical, outcome of an erotic mania which he had by then suffered with comical timidity for some ten years (see, for example, how Carmesina deals with him when he 'brings out his artillery and tries to storm the castle' in chapters 280–1).

words which has prepared us for this outcome from the moment when Tirant, wounded by Venus's dart on seeing the heavenly crystalline apples of Carmesina's breasts in the chamber tapestried with stories of Love's martyrs, exclaimed to Diafebus:

> Never have I suffered an illness like this, which will either bring me to a cruel death [*a mort*] or sovereign bliss . . . for the end of all these things is pain through that love [*amor*] which is bitter (chapter 118).[3]

A palpable ambivalence thus hangs over the narrative of Tirant's and Carmesina's deaths. The peculiar sense of mingled tragedy and disenchantment is underlined by comparing *Tirant lo Blanc*'s ending with those of other chivalric romances. One kind, which we may call the fairy-tale type, concludes within the hero's triumph, excluding death altogether; a notable example is the Catalan *Curial e Güelfa*, which closes with the pure and joyous fantasy of the eponymous hero and heroine's marriage. This ending follows a touching scene in which the virginal Güelfa is visited in a dream-vision by Fortune. The magnificently attired goddess informs the damsel that she has persecuted Curial with trials and tribulations solely 'to please the false old woman I have beneath my skirts' – that is, the horrid hag Envy – and that the moment has come at last to 'spare him from the clutches of Atropos' and return him to high estate, favour and renown. So saying, Fortune opens her mantle to reveal Cupid, 'a shining young lad dressed in golden feathers with great wings and a cloth before his eyes, and face, feet and hands as red as fire', who shoots a golden arrow through Güelfa's left side and into her heart, to dancing and rejoicing by all the court of Love. By contrast, the other kind of romance tends rather to the sublime resolution of epic and tragedy. Such, for example, are the tales of Lancelot and Guinevere and the *Morte Arthur*, Tristan and Isolt, and the quest for the Grail. These end with the death of the hero, but represent it as allegory or symbolic apotheosis – as in Malory's account of the dissolution of the Round Table, the return of Excalibur to the Lady of the Lake, and the vision of Arthur's funeral barque drawn into the westering sun by the queens of Avalon after the battle of Camlac.[4] By comparison with either of these kinds of ending, one can see why critics have been perplexed by the conflicting signals at the close of *Tirant lo Blanc*, which are certainly not what we were led to expect by Martorell's ringing proem to the effect that Tirant 'bravely subdued many kingdoms and provinces, offering them to others, . . . and later conquered the entire Greek

---

[3] Barberà 1997, especially 265–67. The word *mort* occurs 440 times in the book, and Barberà shows that the idea of death and its connection with love is also represented in many other less direct ways.

[4] For these passages see Waley 1982:284–7 and 273–7, and Malory 1971:714–15.

empire, winning it back from the Turks' (Dedication to Don Fernando of Portugal).

There is, however, a medieval narrative form which provides a closer model for the death scenes in *Tirant lo Blanc*. These are the chivalric biographies – romanticized lives of knights based to a greater or lesser degree on historical circumstance and written to glorify chivalry and noble lineages – which relate either real lives, like Gutierre Díaz de Games's *El Victorial* on the Castilian Pedro Niño (1378–1453) and the *Faits* of the Burgundian Jacques de Lalaing (1422–54), or fictional lives with an apparatus of verisimilar historical detail and names, like Antoine de la Sale's *Le petit Jehan de Saintré* and the Anglo-Norman *Guy de Warwick*. When such works include the hero's death, they give an idealized but realistic account whose purpose is to demonstrate that the knight, though 'not ontologically different from any ordinary man', conforms to the exemplary and panegyric patterns of the genre.[5] The following, for example, is the ending of *Le petit Jehan de Saintré*:

> And now I will make an end of this book about this most valiant knight. . . . When it was God's pleasure to take his spirit to Him and Death which spares no man shut the door upon the light of his eyes, he was held the most valiant knight in the kingdom of France. He ended the days of his natural life in the town of Saint-Esprit on the Rhône, having received all the holy rites as befits every true Christian, and was buried in the said church, where for the sake of his valiant deeds I gladly sought out his tomb and learned by heart the letters on the slab, which say in Latin: 'Hic iasset dominus Johannes de Saintre miles, senescalus Andegauensis et Senomanensis camerariusque domini ducis Andegauensis, qui obiit anno Domini M CCC LXVIII, die XXV Octobris, cuius anima in pace requiescat, Amen.' . . . And I have heard other brave old knights and squires say that those who made his tomb found a little casket with a parchment which said: 'Here shall lie the body of the most valiant knight of his time in France and beyond.'[6]

There are interesting parallels here with Tirant's and Carmesina's deaths, notably in the emphasis on the Christian rituals of shriving (confession) and houselling (communion), and in the tomb and double set of epitaphs (cf. chapter 485). Suggestive correspondences occur also in the more circumstantial account of the hero's deathbed in an important Catalan example of the genre, the supposedly autobiographical *Book of Deeds* of King Jaume I of

---

[5] The phrase in quotation marks is Vargas Llosa's comment on Tirant's death (1991:27).

[6] Quoted with some amendments from La Sale 1931:321. According to Gray, the epitaph belongs to a real knight mentioned by Froissart; the reference to the duke of Anjou (*dux Andegauensis*) is a transparent compliment to La Sale's patron, Jean d'Anjou-Lorraine, later lieutenant of Catalonia.

Aragon (1208–76). On his last campaign against Muslim rebels near Xàtiva in the kingdom of Valencia, the king fell ill, like Tirant, from 'some indisposition' (*algun destemprament*).

> In full possession of our faculties we confessed our sins many times to bishops, preachers and friars, with great contrition for our sins and great lamentations, and afterwards, purged of worldly sins by the aforesaid confession, with great satisfaction received the body of our Lord Jesus Christ.

Knowing that his hour was near, Jaume then summoned his heir the Infant Pere and all his courtiers to the deathbed and delivered his benediction and testament, with detailed instructions on the burial of his body and the disposal of his kingdoms and inheritance.[7]

It is clear that for the authors of such chivalric biographies a good death was a moment for showing the Christian devotion of the hero at its greatest intensity. As Tirant takes his last communion, 'all those present in the room said he showed himself to be not a knight but a saintly monk by the many prayers he said before the Host' (chapter 468); and at Carmesina's last moments 'a shining light of angels was seen bearing her soul away with the soul of Tirant, which was standing nearby to greet her at her death' (chapter 478). The latter detail, which is a commonplace of saints' lives and passions, recalls the dream of the anchorite-bishop at the death of Lancelot in the hermitage of Joyous Garde in *Morte Arthur*:

> 'Truly,' sayd the bysshop, 'here was syr Launcelot with me, with mo angellis than ever I sawe men in one day. And I saw the angellys heve up syr Launcelot unto heven, and the yates of heven opened ayenst hym.'
>
> 'It is but dretchyng of swevens [*imagination of dreams*],' sayd syr Bors, 'for I doubte not syr Launcelot ayleth nothynge but good.'
>
> 'It may wel be,' sayd the bysshop. 'Goo ye to his bedde, and than shall ye preve the soth.'
>
> So when syr Bors and his felowes came to his bedde they founde hym starke dede; and he laye as he had smyled, and the swettest savour aboute hym that ever they felte. Than was there wepynge and wryngyng of handes, and the grettest dole they made that ever made men.[8]

In *Guy de Warwick* the motif of the angelic epiphany effects a slightly different, though still relevant, apotheosis: an angel informs the hero of his impending death so that he may have time to summon his wife to Guy's Cliff,

---

[7] Jaume I 1991:172–80, §560–66. For the *Llibre dels fets* as a chivalric biography – not, as it was formerly misnamed, a chronicle – see Pujol's excellent introduction.

[8] Malory 1971:724. Riquer cites as a hagiographic example the end of Joan Roís de Corella's *Life of St Anne*: 'her soul departed . . . accompanied by innumerable angels' (1992:224–5).

where she arrives just in time to steal a last kiss from the dying hermit's lips before herself falling dead with grief.[9]

What the deaths in these chivalric biographies and in *Tirant lo Blanc* have in common is their dependence on the medieval *mort gisant* ritual, or that 'craft of dying well' which the popular *artes bene moriendi* claimed to impart in six easy lessons (praise of death, the temptations of the deathbed, questions to put to the dying, the correct liturgy of prayers to be said by the dying, 'admonishments, encouragements and comforts' to be used *in articulo mortis*, and 'prayers to be said for the dying by bystanders at their passing').[10] A direct allusion to the title of the *Art de bé morir* appears in the epigraph of chapter 478 ('Words of dying well [*bé morir*] which the princess said at her end'), and sure enough the deaths in *Tirant lo Blanc* closely follow the time-honoured ceremony. When the hour came ('holding himself for dead', chapter 467, 'seeing that death draws nigh', chapter 470 – the technical term *l'hora de la mort* occurs in Tirant's will, chapter 469), the dying man lay down on his back (*gisant*) with face to heaven and eyes fixed on a Crucifix (chapter 477), the head towards Jerusalem and the hands crossed, and took leave of the world with a short ritual lament for family and friends (chapters 470, 473–4), pardons and benedictions to those gathered round the bed (chapter 477), and a last will and testament (chapters 469, 477). Then he turned to the business of shriving his own soul by reciting a contrite prayer of confession such as the *Mea culpa* or *Confiteor*, and commended his spirit to Christ with litanies known as the *Ordo commendationis animae* (chapters 467, 471, 476, 478). Finally he received absolution and the last rites of housel from a priest (chapters 468, 476). Hauf, who was the first to notice the 'total correspondence' of the deaths with the *ars moriendi*, points out in passing that the lovers' dying words, and notably Carmesina's speech in chapter 478, provide Catalan versions of the 'Proficiscere', 'Deus misericors', 'Libera Domine'. 'Commendamus tibi' and 'Delicta iuuentutis' prayers from the *Ordo commendationis animae*.[11] One might add that the accounts of ritual ululation, tearing of clothes and hair, face-scratching and formulaic laments

---

[9] This episode is lacking both in *Tirant lo Blanc*, where Tirant leaves the hermit alive ('From this point on the hermit is not mentioned', chapter 97), and in Martorell's MS *Guillem de Varoïc*, which is incomplete (Martorell and Galba 1982:1235–49; Riquer 1990a:257–71), but it must have been known to him.

[10] *Libro intitulado arte de bien morir* ([Saragossa: Hans Hurus, 1489–91]), Prólogo, fol.A2. For a MS Catalan *Art de bé morir* probably earlier than *Tirant lo Blanc* see García 1976; a printed edition was issued at Barcelona by Juan Rosenbach c.1493 (Haebler 1903–17:II, 13–14, §37.5), and five or six other versions were produced in Spain between c.1470 and 1505. The following account of the *mort-gisant* rite is based on the classic exposition in the first volume of Ariès 1977. The mentalities of death and the influence of the *ars moriendi* in fifteenth-century Iberia are discussed at further length, and with additional bibliography, in Lawrance 1998; Anthony Lappin, Carina Vitti and I are currently preparing an edition of all the Iberian texts of the *Ars moriendi* and *Danse macabre*.

[11] Hauf 1995:144–5,n.7.

(*planctus, planys*) which accompany the deaths in *Tirant lo Blanc* are by no means extreme by comparison with the documentary evidence for real behaviour at fifteenth-century Iberian funerals. It is at least possible, therefore, to argue that the actual narrative of these deaths – as opposed to their placement, tone and role in the book's grander design – seeks the effects of that particular verisimilitude, idealized and stylized but recognizably life-like and familiar, which we associate with the chivalric biographies.

Nevertheless, the ending of *Tirant lo Blanc* constantly draws us back to the ambiguity of tone which I mentioned before. Neither a tragic conviction of the omnipotence of Fortune and the culpability of adulterous love, nor a desire to chronicle as realistically as possible a good Christian dying, can satisfactorily explain the facetiously burlesque touches of tone and circumstance with which the narrator chose to portray Tirant's and Carmesina's deaths. When a hero is killed by a chill on the eve of his wedding, his future father-in-law dies by falling out of bed, and his betrothed expires of a self-inflicted nosebleed, it is hard to talk of fairy-tale romance, tragic apotheosis or intense devotion. The elements of bathos were not lost on the book's most attentive early reader, Miguel de Cervantes. In making his Curate exclaim that *Tirant lo Blanc* is 'in its own way' the best book in the world, because 'here the knights . . . die in their beds, and make their wills before their deaths, with these things which are wanting in other books of this kind' (*Don Quixote*, Part I, chapter 6), he was holding up Tirant's and Carmesina's deathbed antics as absurdities no less risible than the other episodes that he chose to list: the monstrously-named Kirieleison of Muntalbà (who dies by choking on his own bile, chapter 80) and his boastful brother Tomàs (who fails to die, and is ritually degraded, chapters 82–4), the knight Fonseca ('Dryfount', mentioned only once as a man who carries the Emperor's banner in chapter 132 – a circumstantial detail whose pointlessness is the point), Tirant's battle with a large dog (which he bites to death, chapter 68), the ribald witticisms of the incorrigible pander Plaerdemavida, the 'amours and artifices' of the Viuda Reposada, and the Empress's infatuation for a man young enough to be her son. These contraventions of romantic decorum, like the plodding verisimilitude of the deathbed scenes, were 'idiocies' for which, in the Curate's estimation, *Tirant lo Blanc*'s author deserved to sent to the galleys for life.

However, the idiocies also point – albeit in a darker key – toward the ethos and aesthetic of *Don Quixote* itself. To express it in broader terms, a bathetic reading of Tirant's humdrum death and its diverse consequences takes us down several notches from the enchanted postulates of high romance or didactic homily, to the low realism of comedy or the even lower absurdity of black humour, satire and parody.[12] If it is true, as Northrop Frye claimed, that

[12] That the deaths might be 'parodic' is suggested by Beltrán (1993:130). The felicitous adultery of Hipòlit and the Empress may also be a parody of the catastrophe of Lancelot and Guinevere (Badia 1993b:58,n.33).

European fiction 'has steadily moved its centre of gravity down the list' of five fictional modes – from myth and the romance of medieval knight-errantry to the high mimesis of epic and tragedy and the Renaissance 'cult of the prince and the courtier', and thence through the low mimetic realism of the novel to modern irony, then *Tirant lo Blanc*'s singular innovation is to blend all the modes simultaneously in ambiguous admixtures which at any given moment are impossible to disentangle.[13] So it is with the tragicomedy of its hero's and heroine's deaths. Cervantes's gentle humour at *Tirant lo Blanc*'s expense – best of books, most incompetent of romances – conceals a precocious insight into the innovative features of narrative, tone and form which distinguish *Tirant lo Blanc* from classic romance. It is now commonplace to describe the book as a proto-novel, as an imaginary chronicle with features of romance, or as an ironic romance (in Frye's definition of irony).

The episodes of Tirant's and Carmesina's deaths evidently hold a key to the ironic modulation of genre and ethos, but until recently they received surprisingly little study. This was perhaps due to the claim that, owing to Joanot Martorell's own demise, the translation of 'the fourth part which is the end of the book' was finished by Martí Joan de Galba at the behest of Isabel de Lloris (colophon of the 1490 edition). By any calculation, this fourth part ought to include the death-scenes, but this has proved a hard nut to swallow for critics weaned on Romantic notions of the individual talent and decades of imprudent hero-worship of Martorell at the expense of the less well-known Galba. Menéndez Pelayo reckoned that the final scenes in Constantinople must be by Martorell because, besides being 'tender and pathetic', they are 'essential to the plan and purpose of the novel'; others have asserted that they must be by Galba for the opposite reason.[14] Such literary arguments are a tautology, based on a naive notion of literary unity as a providential hypostasis of authorial intention rather than a function empirically derived from the structure of actual texts. From the infinite range of possible endings, each of which would have produced a different book with its own unity and meaning, it is impossible to conjecture at this distance which of them might have occurred to Martorell, and which to Galba. The dispute about dual authorship can be resolved, if at all, only by quantitative stylometric analysis.[15]

We are left with our ending, and with the task of trying to make sense of it.

---

[13] Frye 1957:33–4. In *myth* the hero is divine, 'superior in *kind* both to other men and to the environment', in *romance* he is human but marvellous, 'superior in *degree*'; *high mimesis* has a hero superior to us in authority and passion but 'subject both to social criticism and to the order of nature'; *low mimesis*, a hero superior neither to us nor to his environment; and *irony*, a hero inferior to us, 'so that we have the sense of looking down on a scene of bondage, frustration, or absurdity'.

[14] Menéndez Pelayo 1943:I, 400–01, 396n.; cf. Coromines 1971:373–4.

[15] Riquer 1990a:285–97, abandoning his earlier hypothesis of Galba's sporadic

One approach might be to take Tirant's ironic death, not so much as a moral *exemplum* of the mutability of Fortune, as the narrator recommends, but as an elegiac swansong for the whole of late-medieval chivalry, and hence for the literary genre that was its representation. Beltrán's monograph on the anti-heroic elements in *Tirant lo Blanc* comes to just this conclusion.[16] The 'shame-faced' nature of Tirant's and Carmesina's sorry exit from the story and the cynical implication of the 'tired, sad ending' of Hipòlit's accession to the imperial throne subvert the ideals expounded by the mythical 'father of chivalry' William of Warwick at the outset of the book, and which Tirant aspires to imitate throughout his adventures. William's own end provides a telling contrast to Tirant's: at the age of fifty-five, having been 'moved by divine inspiration to retire from arms and make a pilgrimage to Jerusalem, as every good Christian should, to do penance and contrition for the many deaths he had caused as a young knight in wars and battles' (chapter 2), William feigns his own death and returns incognito to end his days as a hermit in anonymous and holy contemplation (chapter 27). According to the *artes moriendi*, the last and most dangerous temptation of Death, the one which 'most torments secular and carnal men', is 'the inordinate love of wife, family and friends' (*Libro intitulado arte de bien morir*, fol. B5); and it is abundantly clear that Tirant, despite his Christian comportment in other respects, fell gravely prey to the love of the first of these, proving himself an irredeemably carnal man (see the 'farewell note to the princess' which he dictates immediately after receiving the Eucharist and drawing up his will, chapter 470):

> and thus was brought to an end the final destruction of the whole lineage of the imperial house of Greece, which . . . should have won blessed repose if Fortune had permitted it; wherefore no man should put his trust in worldly prosperity, which smiles only to deceive (chapter 479).

The contrast between William's and Tirant's ends cannot fail to remind us of the very first sentence of the story (chapter 1):

> The knightly estate excels in such high degree that it ought to be highly

---

interpolation from chapter 326 or 349 and wholesale intervention from chapters 416–87, defends Martorell's sole authorship 'with light copy-editing by Galba'. His arguments are elegant, but remain a sentimental appeal to a fallacious postulate of unity. Well-attested medieval examples of finishing incomplete MSS, documentary evidence (Galba possessed Martorell's MS of 325 fols from the latter's death in 1465 until 1490, by which time he had 'another copy, all finished', used as copy-text for Spindeler's 388-folio edition – an increment of c. 20%) and stylistic data lend credence to the colophon's circumstantial account (Ferrando 1995).

[16] Beltrán 1983:152–57.

revered, if knights kept its rules according to the ends for which it was created.

For Beltrán, the 'key moment of self-contradiction' at the close of the book spreads an unheroic aura of defeat over the whole story – despite the final moment when it 'buries its head like an ostrich in the sands of chivalresque romance' with the time-honoured promise of a sequel ('Their eldest son, named Hipòlit after his father, lived all his life like a magnificent lord and did many singular deeds of chivalry, which the present book does not recount but leaves to the histories which were written about him', chapter 487). In this perspective, death in bed rather than in battle or in the lists can be seen as an apt and worthy end, encapsulating in its ironic matter-of-factness all the preceding elements of anti-heroic realism in the book, including Tirant's series of equally absurd premonitory mishaps.

One of these mishaps provides such a striking counterpart to his eventual death that it is worth examining further.[17] On the first night he spends naked in Carmesina's bed, Tirant is surprised and breaks his leg in a fall from her chamber window (chapter 233). While a farcical chase ensues in Carmesina's room, with the Empress, her ladies and the Emperor all hunting for the 'rat' in their nightgowns, Tirant lies moaning 'like a damsel in distress' in the flower-bed below and delivers himself of the following lover's parody of the traditional deathbed *Commendatio animae* (chapter 234):

> With desire of a kindred companion to requite my pain – all finished with this world and on the way down to the sad and tenebrous palaces, since multiplying my groans cannot restore my miserable life – I am content to die; life without you, lady princess, seems utterly odious to me. So the cause of my death may be manifest for ever, I pray to God, since all my delight in this life is at an end and it is time for my soul to leave its body – Oh Lord God eternal, who art full of all mercies, grant me your grace that I may die in the arms of that most virtuous princess, that my soul may repose in peace in the world hereafter.

In the dark, his men cannot recognize their captain from this girlish whining ('In God's name tell us, are you a dead soul in torment or some mortal in distress?'). Afraid that it may be the Emperor's guards, Tirant then shams the death he implored a moment before:

> I was a baptized Christian in life, but now I am being punished for my sins

---

[17] The parallel is drawn by Alemany (1995:23), who cites chapter 163 (falling from a horse), chapter 202 (being dropped into the sea), chapter 233 (catching a cold from standing in his underwear while waiting to enter Carmesina's bed), chapter 301 (falling flat on his back facing the moon) and chapter 399 (fainting from love) as further examples of the 'caustic and festive' vein which makes the book a bourgeois *contrafactum* of aristocratic romance.

by being made a ghost. I am invisible unless I choose to take shape. The devils down here hack my flesh and bones into pieces which they throw in the air, and if you remain you will share the cruel torments I suffer.

This puts the men into a comic agony of indecisive terror. Crossing themselves and babbling prayers, the Viscount of Branches suggests retreating for a crucifix and holy water, but Hipòlit plucks up courage to creep forward, his sword held out like a cross and a pious commination on his lips. At last they recognize Tirant and carry him away, leaving the ladies upstairs 'still marvelling that a rat could cause such turmoil'.

The merry humour of this ludicrous *simulacrum* of death, which surely belongs more to the *fabliaux* of cuckoldry exemplified by Chaucer's Miller's Tale than to a fiction of chivalry, appears to foreshadow many of the ironic implications of the ending. At all events, Tirant's bogus death as Don Juan caught with his trousers down makes mockery of the Prologue's proud assertion that honour, glory and eternal fame are due to 'men . . . who risk death for the commonwealth, for we read that . . . brave knights have always preferred death in battle to shameful flight'; or, indeed, of Tirant's own claim to the Viuda Reposada a few chapters later: 'Alas, how dark the blindness of those who love inordinately, . . . and how brave the despair of those who, shunning the dangers of living and dying in sin, prefer to abandon this life for the kingdom of heaven!' (chapter 269). For all his play-acting, Love really has unmanned Tirant and turned him into a living ghost; and the *flatus vocis* of his blasphemous prayer, emasculated voice, and trembling evocation of the demons and torments of Hell bear more than a hint of the lachrymose rhetoric of his actual dying.

An even more striking foreshadowing of Tirant's and Carmesina's deaths occurs on the announcement of a disastrous defeat of the Greek armies by the Turks in chapters 288–92. The Emperor greets the news with a grief exactly modelled on that of a medieval funeral ('oh grieving widows, make new lamentations, tear your hair, scratch your faces with your nails, and dress in mourning, for the flower of chivalry is lost!', chapter 288). Weeping and wailing sweep through the palace, and Tirant is summoned to find Carmesina in a swoon, the Empress with clothes torn and breasts exposed for frantic clawing, and the Emperor sitting dumbstruck on the floor. The despairing doctors declare the princess dead, upon which Tirant falls and again breaks his leg 'worse than the first time', with blood pouring from his nose and ears in a coma which lasts thirty-six hours (chapter 290). At last he calls for a crucifix and once more pronounces the *Confiteor* and *Commendatio animae*, receives the last rites from the cardinal, announces that his hour has come, and with comforting words to all and sundry drops back on his pillow and closes his eyes. But the frantic lamentations of his friends rouse him once again, and the whole performance is repeated a second time (chapter 291). Carmesina has already betaken herself to her chamber with a kitchen knife ready to commit suicide, but in the end a sagacious Jewess finds a simple remedy: the alarm of a Turkish raid is raised, and Tirant instantly gets out of bed ready for battle (chapter 292). And there is further irony to this comic charade, for while the palace is under the erroneous impression that Tirant's fatal grief is provoked by the military disaster, it is in fact the result of the Viuda Reposada's *trompe l'œil* trick to reveal Carmesina in carnal relations with her black gardener (chapters 282–6). The whole scene is illuminated with the superb humour of this *double entendre*, which reaches the summit of comedy in Tirant's hilarious dying wish that his sepulchre be adorned with 'black Moorish heads with these words inscribed around them: *The hateful cause of Tirant lo Blanc's demise*', and in the ludicrous blasphemy of his commendation of his soul to Christ:

> Almighty Jesus, I die for love as You died to save mankind! For love you endured beatings, wounds and torture, just as I endured the sorrow of beholding a black Moor. Only You have suffered like me, and as Your holy mother endured infinite grief at the foot of the cross, so I endured mine with two mirrors and a cord.

Delightfully enough, the bemused spectators 'marvelled at these pious words, holding him in their opinion a good Christian' (chapter 291).[18]

The narrator twice makes fun, therefore, of his hero's sham death; and he seems thereby to alert us – seems on purpose to alert us, given the clear cross-references to the *ars bene moriendi* in all three scenes – to the possibility that the actual death, when it comes, need not necessarily be taken seriously. Furthermore, he shows himself ready to laugh at the innumerable guises of real dying elsewhere in the book, many of which are exploited as opportunities for humour or spleen. The absurd strangulation from a burst gall-bladder of the head-banging, man-eating giant Kirieleison of Montalbà (chapter 80) and the mock death by disgrace of his fat and wheezing brother Tomàs appear to be Martorell's thinly-disguised revenge on his rival Gonzalo de Híjar, *comendador mayor* of Montalbán de Aragón.[19] Similar spite is present in the unseemly glee that greets the hanging, drawing and quartering of some jurists responsible for a dispute between the guilds of blacksmiths and weavers at the King of England's wedding ('as quickly as he could the duke had two gallows raised high, and hoist three lawyers on each, hanging them by their feet to show them the utmost honour, nor did he leave before they had sent their wretched souls to Hell', which the King receives with

---

[18] This recalls the bystanders' view of Tirant on his deathbed as 'not a knight but a saintly monk' (chapter 468). Hauf acutely calls the tragicomic precedent in chapter 291 a 'first lesson in the good death' (1995:143).

[19] Riquer 1990a:120–2; for Gonzalo de Híjar see ibid. 89–93. Death from ruptured bile, followed by eating by hyenas, is also the fate of the treacherous Duke of Andria (chapter 146).

'pleasure' and the commons praise as a 'virtuous act', chapter 41), which recalls Martorell's bombastic railing against the same profession in the cartels of challenge of his own litigation against Joan de Montpalau.[20] Racial, religious and social prejudice is given free rein in the matter-of-fact disposal of characters who might be considered surplus to requirements in the aristocratic world of late-medieval Christendom: the Calabrian philosopher kills a pimp by skewering him through the forehead with a roasting-spit in an alehouse quarrel over whether rabbit takes preference over mutton (chapter 110), fourteen hundred villainous Genoese traitors are tricked into walking into 'a dungeon full of snakes, vipers and other loathsome animals' (chapter 99), the Sultan of Cairo is thrown to his own lions after the failure of his siege of Rhodes (chapter 106), and the innocent and unsuspecting black slave Lauseta is seized by the hair and butchered at the door of his hut while 'donning some red breeches' (chapter 286), all without a trace of compunction or gravity. Equally short shrift is given to the Viuda Reposada's suicide (chapter 416). Her soul goes to Hell – 'Pluto's tenebrous kingdom' – unshriven and unhouselled, but the narrative is remarkable for its absence of recrimination (Carmesina has her honourably buried in Hagia Sophia) and for the levity with which the widow is portrayed even in death as a silly old woman made ridiculous by climacteric lust:

> It is the old tale: when their need is greatest, the harder women think the more useless is the course they choose, being by nature frivolous and fickle. Finally, unable to find another remedy and panicked by her lack of courage, she decided to poison herself so subtly that no one would detect it, lest they burn her body or feed it to the dogs. She poured some orpiment used to make depilatories into a cup of water and drank it. Then, leaving her door open, she undressed and got into bed. When she was lying down she started screaming loudly that she was dying. Her maids . . . rushed to her aid, but they found the widow in her death throes, though still shouting.

After which the narrator remarks unconcernedly; 'Here the book leaves the Viuda Reposada', and goes rejoicing on his way.[21] A little more respect is

---

[20] For Vargas Llosa the episode betrays the 'alarmed fury of a feudal lord at the rising bourgeoisie' (1991:17). On Martorell's correspondence with Joan de Monpalau see Riquer's introduction to Martorell and Galba 1982:33–4, and the appendix of the same edition (Letter IV, 30 May 1437: 'to trade letters and insults is not the act of knights and gentlemen, but of women and jurists who defend themselves only with pen and tongue' (1203); Monpalau's reply, 4 June 1437: 'it is clear which of us has decided to employ doctors in law and the craft of notaries and use the foxy tricks of women' (1205)). When the dastardly Duke of Macedonia attempts to submit Tirant's challenge to law, the hero replies: 'my hands are busy with more urgent matters than scribbling and litigation' (chapter 154); the Duke gets his deserts by being run through with a lance in the ensuing battle (chapter 157).

[21] For the malicious intent of undressing 'with the door open' cf. the widow's

accorded to deaths in battle or tourney, as in the miracle by which the bodies of Christian martyrs of a battle are made to lie 'gazing heavenwards, their hands clasped, smelling sweet' and ready to go 'straight to Heaven' whereas the Saracens lie 'face down and stinking like dogs' (chapter 340), but the book hides nothing of the brutal senselessness of 'the abject art of war'.[22]

All this would seem to provide support for an ironic reading of *Tirant lo Blanc*'s ending, and hence for Beltrán's view of the anti-heroic implications of Tirant's and Carmesina's deaths. Drawing on contemporary texts by Joan Roís de Corella and others, Hauf has sought to go further, recontextualizing the book's fatal connection between lust and death in the mentalities of the time. His conclusions suggest not the elegiac tone of disabused *fin-de-siècle* weariness detected by Beltrán, but an altogether tougher satiric note of ideological disapproval. Tirant is indeed one of those 'vain and pompous' men who waste their lives in the pursuit of glory and pleasure, for these are vanities inherent in the chivalric codes of honour and courtly love; yet by these very codes he stands condemned, for his seduction of his lord's daughter is a grave and dishonourable disloyalty. So tellingly does the disguised Plaerdemavida put this case for the prosecution against Tirant when she pleads on behalf of her Saracen mistress's city, accusing him of having 'tempted Carmesina with supplications and sought to affront her parents by stealing into her chamber, crowning himself emperor', that he once again falls into a death-like swoon from which it seems he can only be roused by having his head cradled between her naked breasts (chapters 351–7).[23] From this perspective, the deaths at the end of *Tirant lo Blanc* could be seen as offering a Christian lesson on mortality, sin and the vanity of earthly life. As such, the book forms part of that abundant fifteenth-century sententious and exemplary literature, written chiefly in the vernacular and addressed for the most part to noble and knightly readers, which concerned itself with the falls of princes, with the ever-turning wheel of mutability, and with the remedies of both

---

desperate striptease in chapters 284–6. Compare the tender suicide of her counterpart in *Curial e Güelfa*, the Moorish princess Camar, who also falls hopelessly in love with the hero but dies a Christian with a speech full of reminiscences of Virgil and Ovid (Waley 1982:238–45). She too appears naked, tied to a stake to be eaten by lions at the order of her jealous Moorish suitor, but only to give Curial the chance to save her from disgrace by killing the lions (and not by biting them to death, ibid. 246–7).

[22] The last phrase is quoted from Vargas Llosa's pages on the book's violence (1991:13–16).

[23] Hauf 1995. Plaerdemavida's accusation recalls another incidence of truth in jest, the Turkish galley-slave Galançó's unwitting description of Tirant to his face as a 'French devil . . . whose base and ugly name means usurper', who will 'get the emperor's daughter pregnant and the mother too, after which he will slay the father . . . and lo and behold the next thing you know he will be emperor of Constantinople'. Tirant roars with laughter, but the charge is uncomfortable (chapter 163).

prosperous and adverse Fortune, 'that perpetual enemy of virtue' (chapter 281).

To conclude, there is much to persuade us in the various bathetic, ironic, anti-heroic (elegiac-moral) and anti-chivalric (satiric-moral) readings of the end of *Tirant lo Blanc* expounded above. And yet it seems to me they do not entirely convince, either singly or together. All flounder sooner or later on the rock of the narrative's seemingly inexhaustible range of conflicting tones and attitudes. Few readers have dared confess, as Llorenç Riber did, to uncontrollable tears of sorrow at the deaths of the protagonists, yet a candid critic must surely admit that the Mallorcan canon's emotion was neither unreasonable nor unworthy of a Christian.[24] Coromines, while applauding Riquer's attribution of the 'tasteless, fatuous, pallid appendage' of the ending to the rascally Galba, saves from anathema two chapters of the narrative of Carmesina's death and seems thereby to put his finger on an important point. The heroine's decision not to wail and beat her breast at Tirant's death, but instead to dress solemnly in her bridal clothes and bear her grief with dignity 'until the moment comes to reveal her sorrow' (chapter 472), is a striking and moving portrayal of her ardent but self-controlled character ('a polar volcano capped with ice'); and when she embraces and kisses her lover's body, 'mingling her warm tears with Tirant's cold ones', and with trembling hands prizes open his dead eyes and presses tears into them 'so that he might seem to mourn her bereavement' (chapter 473), Coromines finds it 'a dazzling triumph of style and an ending of genius'.[25] Surely no one would disagree – except that a few pages later, after three days of doleful exequies 'which would have moved the cruellest heart to tears', commons and clergy 'lose all desire to lament for a whole year' (chapter 481) and are 'much solaced' at the announcement of Hipòlit's and the Empress's marriage, 'since they were weary of mourning and had feared it might last for many months or years' (chapter 483). This, as Espadaler remarks, is 'an unmistakable leg-pull', a touch of burlesque whose only conceivable purpose is to mock the reader whose heart has, indeed, been incautiously moved to tears by the preceding narrative.[26]

---

[24] Espadaler 1993:261–2.
[25] Coromines 1971:373 (in the course of a tirade against Galba as a 'jumped-up copy editor with pretensions to co-authorship' who puffed out the narrative with 'horrible paragraphs' of 'redundant, emphatic, jumbled and fattily bombastic' rhetoric and a 'deformed vegetation' of 'undigested pedantry' – not to mention writing shorter chapters than Martorell becuse he was on piece-work). The pathos seems to evade Riquer, who, in an argument about priority in the scene's numerous borrowings of Roís de Corella's *History of Hero and Leander* (cf. note 8 above), evinces sarcasm at the absurdity of hot tears mixing with cold – in the original, Leander's body was wet because he had just drowned in the Hellespont, but 'is it logical that Tirant's corpse should have tears in its eyes, even cold ones, when it was long dead, and pickled to boot?' (Riquer 1990a:300).
[26] Espadaler 1993:263.

The tonal complexity of such a story, which combines bathos, pathos, realism, fantasy and irony in endless kaleidoscopic variations, seems too extraordinary to bear any single moral. We are drawn to consider a final explanation for the emotional roller-coaster of the ending, which is that the narrator intended the protagonists' death to mix tragic and comic effects, not for any didactic purpose, but for reasons of art. The aesthetic principle involved may bewilder an incautious modern reader. In a subtle and suggestive article, Espadaler identifies in the narrative of the protagonists' deaths two separate strains: one ideal, ironic and dispassionately masculine, and the other, seen particularly in the extravagant faintings, gestures and lamentations, corresponding to a more emotive, earthy and passionate rhetoric which the author explicitly designates as feminine. Such, for example, are the 'female words' of the Countess of Warwick's intemperate lamentation, which mimic a kind of death, at her saintly husband William's decision to leave her for a pilgrimage to the Holy Land.[27]

For Espadaler, the explanation for *Tirant lo Blanc*'s ability to meld this variety of styles must be sought in the alien conditions of medieval orality. It may be so, but the suggestive parallel of a contemporary work, Fernando de Rojas's *Tragicomedia de Calisto y Melibea*, offers the no less interesting possibility that the complex tonality of Tirant's and Carmesina's deaths belong to a more specific late-fifteenth-century aesthetic of the tragicomic. Rojas's work also ends with the death of its hero from a silly fall, the laments and self-immolation of his lover, and the plaints and death from grief of her all-unsuspecting father; it, too, simultaneously juggles the ambiguous voices of sentimental tragedy, ironic burlesque and moral satire.[28] Both books share also, despite their distinct social contexts, a similar tendency to 'cover almost every theme' through the formalized persuasive techniques of an encyclopedic rhetoric which transcends both characterization and didactic consistency, and which, as Terry points out in relation to *Tirant lo Blanc*, discloses the density of the book's world through a 'comprehensiveness of perspectives' and a kind of narrative 'excess'.[29] In a pair of lucid articles Badia has

---

[27] Espadaler 1993. As so often, the extremes of feminine rhetoric in the countess's lament are based on a work by Joan Roís de Corella, this time *The Dolorous Plaint of Queen Hecuba*. The expression 'female words' (*paraules femelles*) occurs not only in *Tirant lo Blanc*, but also in Joan de Monpalau's reply to Martorell's sixth cartel of challenge, where it involves a conceit based on the grammatical genders of feminine *paraula* 'word' and masculine *fet* 'deed' (Martorell and Galba 1982:1213): 'words, which are female, come out of the mouth with little trouble, but to execute deeds, which are male, costs much more effort; so you may be said to have proved the old proverb, "Fine words butter no parsnips" [*del dir al far ha cent per centenar*]'. Compare also the quotes in note 20 above.

[28] For further discussion of this aspect of the *Tragicomedia de Calisto y Melibea* see Lawrance 1993. Another work that might be mentioned in connection with this aesthetic is Roís de Corella's *Tragedy of Caldesa*.

[29] Terry 1982, which corrects Alonso's simplistic division of the narrative into 'two

enlarged this notion of excess to include the extraordinary variety of sources and narrative forms which are assimilated in the book. The thick black-letter columns and massy folio format of the book would have encouraged an educated fifteenth-century reader to seek within, not only the entertaining 'history' of an exemplary but verisimilar story and the 'poetic fiction' of a fable with the 'hidden fruit . . . of moral knighthood and a theatre of good behaviour to abolish the tangles of vice and the ferocity of unnatural acts' (Dedication to Don Fernando of Portugal), but also a 'compendium of all the sciences, sacred and worldly', and a book of manners.[30] Small wonder that the narrative of the deaths becomes the platform for such an immense digest of speculative and curious discourse in speeches, prayers, laments, dialogues, didactic parentheses, letters and testaments, all elaborated with a mosaic of literary and erudite borrowings and authorities. It may be true that the manifold excess and perspectivism of the book's ambiguous and ironic presentation of the protagonists' deaths somewhat reduce their ideal stature, but it hugely increases the empathetic human drama of their destiny, retaining to the last that detached but lively pleasure in the infinite varieties of experienced life which is the book's greatest achievement.[31]

---

styles' (1961) and refines Vargas Llosa's notion of the 'total novel' and the author's creative 'ventriloquism' (1991:33–58;87–106). For a different but relevant approach see Vinaver's characterization of the contemporary narrative art of Sir Thomas Malory as 'an elaborate fabric woven of a number of themes which alternate with one another like the threads of a tapestry' (Malory 1971:vii).

[30] Badia 1993a and 1993b, which together constitute a crushing demolition of modern attempts to classify the book as anything so limited as a novel.

[31] It is a pleasure to record my gratitude to Lluís Cabré, who in conversation many years ago pointed out with customary *seny* that my temptation to laugh outright at the ending of *Tirant lo Blanc* was an anachronistic over-simplification – though he might not approve of any of the opinions I have advanced in this attempt to set the record straight.

Nine Problem Areas Concerning *Tirant lo Blanc*

JOSEP GUIA AND CURT WITTLIN

A book's quality and importance cannot be judged by the quantity of research published about it. Still, we can assume that, had *Tirant lo Blanc* been written in Castilian, ten times more studies would have been dedicated to it. Declared a classic, the novel would have become part of the curriculum in schools and universities in all Spanish-speaking countries. Year after year, large numbers of professors would have had to study and explain it. Many would have made publishable discoveries. But, written in Catalan, *Tirant* remained forgotten or inaccessible, in spite of Cervantes's praise that it is the 'world's best book'.

During the dark years of Franco's fascism, a *Tirant* in Castilian would not have had to share the fate of the vanquished Catalans. Publications about the novel during those years were few, almost limited to the admirable work of Martí de Riquer. In 1947 he edited the original *Tirant*, in regularized spelling. That same year Riquer began editing the early Castilian translation. In 1964 he adapted his introduction to that edition in his *Història de la literatura catalana*, and then reprinted it at the beginning of the reimpression of his Catalan *Tirant* in 1969. Those ninety pages became for just about everyone the basic introduction – all too often the only one – to the novel. What Menéndez Pidal had done for the *Poema de mio Cid*, Riquer has done for the *Tirant lo Blanc*.

And just as Pidal reversed, late in his life, his opinion concerning the single or dual authorship of the *Cid*, Riquer, in 1990, changed his views on the authorship of the *Tirant*. It is symptomatic that on the title page of his 1979 reimpression of the novel we read JOANOT MARTORELL in large letters, followed on the line below by MARTÍ JOAN DE GALBA in smaller size. But in his book *Aproximació al Tirant lo Blanc*, published in 1990, Riquer declares: 'There is not a single positive and solid argument which prevents us from assuming that Joanot Martorell was the only and exclusive author of the whole *Tirant lo Blanc*' (Riquer 1990:293, our translation).

Riquer is undoubtedly the greatest living specialist in *Tirant* studies. To voice doubts about his new hypothesis could be considered foolhardy, if not bad mannered. But since problems in literary history cannot be solved by simply counting the number of scholars who are for or against a given theory, progress will only be achieved if discussion is allowed to continue.

In 1490, in Valencia, 715 in-folio copies were printed of the voluminous *Tirant lo Blanc*. In 1497 a second printing was produced in Barcelona, with 300 copies. It is surprising that no early reference to the novel mentions its author(s). Only beginning with Nicolás Antonio's *Bibliotheca Hispanica Vetus* (Rome 1690) is it attributed to Joanot Martorell and Martí Joan de Galba, names found in the dedication and the colophon of the incunabula. The dedication contains this statement: 'I alone, Martorell, am responsible for this book. Nobody else should be blamed for possible mistakes, since I alone worked on it.' The colophon declares: 'Martorell died before finishing this book. The fourth and final part was translated by Sir Martí Joan de Galba Esq., at the request of Lady Isabel de Lloris.' Followers of the hypothesis of Martorell as sole author put all their trust in the dedication. Those who see *two* hands in the novel invoke the colophon in support of their belief in a dual authorship.

A recent new way of looking at the problem considers both dedication and colophon as fictitious, written by Joan Roiç de Corella (1435-97). Not only the style of Corella, but also dozens of extracts from his writings – not all of which are known or survive – can be found throughout the *Tirant*. Did Martorell imitate and plagiarize the much younger writer to such a degree? Did Galba possess the amazing ability to blend into Martorell's text all those words and phrases taken from Corella? Or did Corella himself work on the manuscript Martorell had handed over to Galba in early 1464, as a pawn for a loan, a year before he died?

The question of the authorship of the *Tirant* has all the elements of a detective story. Nobody, we believe, can yet claim to be able to present a complete, coherent and fully convincing view of what Martorell had written, between 2 January 1460 and early 1464, in those twenty-seven gatherings of loose pages he gave to the money-lender Galba, and of what happened to them in all those years until *Tirant lo Blanc* was printed in 1490. The assumption that the book from 1490 is identical with the manuscript Martorell had given to Galba in early 1464 is doubtful for many reasons and leaves too many questions unanswered.

The following pages are not our attempt at solving these questions. We are limiting ourselves to just pointing them out. Our readers are invited to ponder for themselves the importance and ramifications of each one, and to reflect on the strength of the solutions proposed.

1. The Dedication

As early as 1949, Martí de Riquer pointed out that the dedication of the *Tirant* is nothing but a 'scandalous plagiarism' of the dedication Enric de Villena had written in 1417 for his *Dotze treballs d'Hèrcules*. Villena himself was inspired by Jaume Conesa's prologue to his Catalan translation of the *Historia destructionis Troiae* by Guido delle Colonne (Guia 1996b). Once Pedro Cátedra had published Villena's dedication in 1988, as a foretaste of his still-awaited edition of the complete Catalan original, Riquer could present both pages, *Tirant* and Villena, in parallel columns (Riquer 1990a:275–78). The main changes we can observe result from three differences of circumstance: the persons addressed, the textual genre of the two books, and the fiction of the double translation.

a. The 'rei spectant'

Villena has addressed his *Hèrcules* from 1417 to a 'Molt noble i virtuós cavaller'. The *Tirant*, begun in 1460 but published only in 1490, is offered to the 'Molt excel.lent, virtuós e gloriós Príncep, rei spectant ... Don Ferrando de Portugal'. This 'King in waiting' keeps causing scholars considerable difficulties. Riquer (1990a:279–84) summarizes previous research and points out that only between 1438 and 1451 was Ferrando in line to inherit the crown of Portugal. But between August 1464 and March 1465 he was living at the court of his cousin, Peter the Constable, heir to the Catalan crown. Since Peter had no descendants, Ferrando could have been considered 'expecting' to inherit the Catalan crown. This is what Riquer now assumes. However, the question why Martorell, in 1460, should have wanted to offer his novel to Ferrando is not asked, nor why that allusion – incomprehensible or offensive to many readers already in Martorell's time – was not eliminated in the 1490 printing, just as it was in the Castilian translation of 1511.

A new approach to the problem asks if *rei spectant* does indeed mean 'king in waiting'. 'Spectant' could be a variant form of 'spectable'. which is used in Old Catalan in synonymic combinations with 'magnífic'. In his *Història de Josef* Corella calls Joseph in Egypt 'Visrey spectable', referring also to his 'espectabilitat'. Riquer is right in calling the expression *rei spectant* 'unusual' and 'surprising in courtly style' (1990a:178, 284). But it fits quite well Corella's creative use of language. If it was Corella who introduced the 'magnificent' King Ferdinand from Portugal into the dedication of the *Tirant*, he did it to refer the reader back to the times of Martorell, while also reinforcing his invention that there was once a Portuguese version of the novel.

The last words of the *Tirant*'s dedication are: 'This work was begun on the second day of January 1460.' Pointing out that novelists usually write and date dedications only after having completed their books, Riquer concludes that Martorell adapted Villena's page shortly after Ferrando had moved to Peter's court, and for whatever reason considered it important to recall the date when he had begun his novel. Nicolau d'Olwer (1961:133) has observed that so much of the *Tirant* is a compilation of materials previously assembled that Martorell might have wanted his statement to mean: 'Today I decided to combine into a book all those pages I have collected over the years.'

However, one of the few points Martorell changed in Villena's prologue is precisely that *Hèrcules* is a compilation.

Villena's *Hèrcules* is a compilation of several sources; the page which precedes the 1490 edition of the *Tirant* looks very much like it once was the introduction to a translation of a single text. Villena says that he 'puts together, collects . . . , searches for, collects, translates and puts in order' the deeds of Hercules he found described by 'historians and poets'. Martorell copied this allusion to 'historians and poets', but then states that the 'story and the deeds of Tirant are in the English language' and that he 'translated them from English into Portuguese and then from Portuguese into Valencian'. It is difficult to see why Martorell should have kept, from among all the verbs used by Villena, translated above, only 'espondre', which can mean 'to explain'; or 'to translate'. Martorell could honestly have thought that in his compilation of materials for the *Tirant* he did exactly what Villena had done preparing for his *Hèrcules*. He could have left Villena's dedication unchanged in this respect. Why did he not?

The answer, Wittlin believes (1993:207), is that the dedication we read at the beginning of the 1490 edition of the *Tirant* is *not* originally the dedication of the *Tirant*. It shows all the signs of having been composed for another book: a translation. There are strong indications that Martorell, having to while away many months of waiting in London in 1438 and 1439, when Ferrando became first in line to the throne of Portugal, had decided to translate the story of *Guy de Warwick*. The dedication we now read at the beginning of the *Tirant* makes much more sense as an introduction to that translation. While Villena excuses himself that his *Hèrcules* might have been presented in 'a better form', Martorell changed this to say that 'if I have made mistakes, they are due to difficulties with the language of the original'. Such disclaimers are commonplace in introductions to medieval translations. We can find one, for example, in Jaume Conesa's prologue to the *Històries troianes*, a prologue familiar to Villena *and* to the author of the dedication of the *Tirant* (Guia:1996a). It is quite usual for translators to indicate the date they begin a translation, and for chroniclers the date when they begin compiling documents. Martorell might have simply changed the date from that planned translation to the date when he started elaborating his novel using the materials concerning chivalry he had been assembling for years.

The dedication at the beginning of the *Tirant* printed in 1490 offers yet another statement that has no equivalent in Villena's prologue: 'And so that, should mistakes be found in this book, nobody else may be blamed for them, I, Joanot Martorell Esq., want to accept that blame myself, and nobody else with me.' Such insistence on 'mistakes' is rather strange in an introduction to a work of fiction, but was a standard topic in prologues to translations.

b. The fiction of the double translation

Assuming, with Guia (1996b), that the dedication of the *Tirant* is a page of fiction added by Roíç de Corella, it will be easier to find reasons for the fantasy of the obviously nonsensical statement – repeated in the colophon – that the *Tirant* was originally composed in English and thence translated into Portuguese and into Valencian. Let us observe first that any Bible in a modern language can be said to have been translated twice: first from Greek into Latin, and then from Latin into the vernacular. In 1993, Jordi Ventura published extracts from the proceedings of the Spanish Inquisition in Valencia against persons which had been involved in translating and publishing, in 1478, the so-called *Valencian Bible*. On 12 April 1483, Daniel Vives told the inquisitors how two translators 'undertook to emend a copy of a Bible written *en vulgar limosí* (that is, 'Old Catalan') . . . but had a difficult time changing those Limousin words into Valencian'. Vives also stated that he had been asked by the printers of the Bible to 'finish translating the third book of Esdras, which Doctor Pineda had begun translating', a statement that reminds us of the phrase in the colophon of the *Tirant* that Galba did 'finish and translate the fourth part of the book'.

Corella, professor of biblical studies, translator of the Psalms, possibly under inquisitorial orders to refrain from publishing, was certainly most interested in the proceedings against the persons involved with the 1478 edition of the Bible. We can only guess how he reacted to the burning of most of the six hundred vernacular Bibles printed. It is not too far-fetched to assume that, surreptitiously getting involved in the *Tirant lo Blanc*, he should have felt tempted to take some revenge. If we are not allowed – he might have thought – to use that marvellous new invention of printing to publish the Bible, which had gone through the hands of so many earnest translators, how about a 'translation' of a racy English novel?

2. The Colophon

The last page of the *Tirant* published in 1490 states that the book was

> translated from English into Portuguese and from thence into Valencian by the magnificent Sir Joanot Martorell Esq., who due to his death was only able to translate three parts. The fourth part, the end of the book, was translated by the magnificent Sir Martí Joan de Galba Esq., upon request by the noble Lady Isabel de Lloris.

When this colophon was printed, Galba had already been dead for half a year. It might have been the printer who added it, combining information he found in the dedication of the book with ideas he had learned haphazardly from Galba; it is strange, however, that he should call him 'mossèn' and 'cavaller', equivalent to our 'Sir' and 'Esquire', epithets Galba was not entitled to. On the other hand, if it was Corella who invented the colophon, just as he had rewritten the dedication, he may have done so to throw the Inquisition off track, calling Galba 'mossèn' and 'cavaller' on purpose, as a hint to insiders. Also, the expression 'lo fi del llibre' could be a play with words. 'Fi' not only means 'end', but also 'purpose' and 'perfection', just as 'lo més fi' means 'the finest, the best'. The colophon, whoever wrote it, is most certainly correct in pointing out that 'Martorell, because of his death, was not able to finish this novel.' If Martorell considered that what he had written between 1460 and 1464 was indeed 'finished', he was no longer alive to defend his 'copyright' should someone, between 1465 and 1490, have felt like changing things in those twenty-seven gatherings of unbound pages Martorell had given to Galba – in whose library was found a copy of them, described, to distinguish it from the other text, as 'tot acabat', 'all finished'.

As for Lady Isabel, she has recently been identified by Jaume Chiner (1993), but her contacts with Galba or Corella, and her role in publishing the *Tirant*, remain unknown. It should be mentioned that it could not have been a minor matter to involve a lady in the printing of a book considered by many rather 'risqué'.

Chiner has also made two more discoveries. Among the papers of the Lloris family, he found a single page of a *Tirant* manuscript. The text it presents is close to the 1490 edition – with space for rubrics left blank – but it does not permit any conclusions about the textual transmission, except that most important one, that Martorell's manuscript was not locked up at Galba's place between 1465 and 1490.

Secondly, Chiner came across proceedings of a court case from April 1465 launched by Martorell's heir against Galba. As the parties declared before the judge, Martorell, slightly over a year before his death, had given twenty-seven gatherings of pages containing *Lo Tiran* to Galba, as a pawn for a loan of 150 *sous* – the equivalent of about one hundred modern pounds – which he never repaid. The gatherings of unbound pages remained with Galba. What he did with them during the next twenty-five years, we do not know. However, when he died in 1490, the clerks who inventoried his possessions noted that, in addition to the 'book called Lo Tiran', there was also another, '*tot acabat* which is now at the printers'. This *tot acabat* is a clear echo of the statement in the colophon that Martorell 'had not been able to *acabar*, to finish', his project.

3. *Galba and the 'Fourth Part' of the Novel*

Until 1990 the standard theory was that Martorell had left his novel unfinished when he died and that it was left to Galba to complete it. But the answer to the question at which chapter the pawnbroker had to take over the composition remained constantly elusive. Riquer's hypothesis, which everyone considered convincing, was that Galba, after having started out making a literal copy of Martorell's manuscript, got more and more involved in the story, until 'he began adding details, especially speeches. His interventions became more and more extensive, but were always based on Martorell's shorter original' (Riquer 1949:83). 'After chapter 416 . . . it can be assumed that the overall responsibility is Galba's' (Riquer 1949:150 et seq.).

Space does not permit summarizing all the research done by scholars who tried to determine where that 'fourth part' begins, nor can we evaluate here the criteria applied by researchers in deciding which chapters are 'typical' of Martorell or of Galba. (Good references are found in Riquer 1990a:285–90 and in Chiner 1993:160–3.) It was unavoidable that many such judgements were based on intuitions and subjective assumptions. For instance: that Martorell was the imaginative, creative mind, Galba just a proof reader; that Martorell was totally realistic, while Galba would add supernatural elements (e.g. Espercius and the dragon, chapter 410 et seq., taken from Mandeville); that Martorell was interested in fights and battles, while Galba liked sermons and speeches; that Martorell quoted proverbs, Galba not; that Martorell used the traditional prose style, while Galba was infatuated with the new Valencian rhetoric, and so on. All these scholars felt that there were clear signs of a second hand in the novel, maybe not so much in content, but certainly in form and style.

Both A. Ferrando (1993:31) and C. Wittlin (1993:625), independently, hit upon the idea that 'quarta part' might not mean 'the fourth and last part' of the novel, but simply 'a fourth' of it; that is, that Galba (or 'whoever', as Ferrando has often been heard to say) revised Martorell's manuscript adding details, mostly of a stylistic nature, throughout the book, to an extent that then allowed him to tell the printers in 1490 that 'a fourth' of the *Tirant*, that is 25 per cent, came from him. Be that as it may, the colophon is probably quite right in stating that the printed version of the *Tirant* had become much longer than the old 'unfinished' manuscript, and that a large part of what was printed had not been written by Martorell.

Now that Martí de Riquer has declared that we should consider the 1490 edition of the *Tirant* a faithful transcription, without revisions or additions, of the manuscript Martorell had given to Galba in 1464, we can expect a series of studies that will attempt to show that passages heretofore judged superfluous interpolations are actually essential elements in the structural coherence of Martorell's master plan. (For a first example, see Perujo, 1995.) Undeniable – and undenied – *stylistic* incoherences will be said to be due to linguistic differences already present in Martorell's many sources, or to changes in Martorell's own style of writing.

4. Stylistic Incoherences in the 'Tirant'

In 1990 Martí de Riquer wrote:

> If it weren't for the colophon [of the 1490 edition], no one, absolutely no one, would ever have doubted that Martorell was the author of the entire *Tirant lo Blanc*, from the dedication to the concluding chapter 487.
>
> (1990a:291)

This proposition, impossible to put to the test, can be questioned. Riquer himself has written many a page where he contrasts the 'two styles intertwined in the prose of the *Tirant*' (e.g.1949:91). And just as some researchers showed much prejudice in ascribing admired chapters to Martorell, but uninspiring ones to Galba, others showed much inconsistency in judging the novel's form and style. An extreme example is Joan Coromines who, in a seminal article of 1956, calls two identical passages 'rhetorical and solemn' in chapter 3, which he considered written by Martorell, but 'horrible . . ., written by the sinful hand of Galba' when it reappears in chapter 474. Riquer, by assuming that those 'differences in language and style . . . show a logical stylistic evolution in an author who worked several years at writing such a long book' (1990a:291), replaced his earlier hypothesis of a second writer with one of a changing single writer. He does not explain why in the case of Martorell a stylistic evolution is 'logical', while other contemporary writers show no such change. There are also problems with the reference to 'several years', now reduced to just four years, and with the concept 'long book', since we do not know for sure how much original text there was in those twenty-seven gatherings of unbound pages Martorell gave to Galba in 1464.

But there are also other difficulties with the explanation that the style towards the end of the novel 'becomes more *baroque*, as if Martorell, while working on his long book, had become infected by the *Valencian prose style* of younger writers' (Riquer 1990a:293; 'younger writers' is a clear allusion to Corella). First, 'baroque' expressions appear throughout the *Tirant*. Riquer himself acknowledges in his introduction to Chiner 1993 that there is a sentence taken from Corella in chapter 20, as he has learned from Albert Hauf (1993a:78–9). Secondly, the comparison with an 'infection' suggests that Martorell himself began writing in that new style, that he imitated those 'younger writers'. However, we read in the *Tirant* not only *words* that echo that new style, but about one hundred and fifty *phrases* which have now been traced back to Joan Roíç de Corella. Obviously, if those 'quotations' were put there by Martorell, he did not so much imitate Corella's style, but rather plagiarize more and more frequently whole phrases of his, and this beginning in 1460. Even when it was assumed that Martorell had died in 1468, the common opinion was that he could not have finished his novel, and that, even more certainly, he did not have time to revise it. Riquer's new explanation, that Martorell completed his novel in early 1464, and even had time to go over it in order to interpolate phrases he copied from Corella, is difficult to believe.

Furthermore, 'style' means much more than just rhetorical artifices which could have been added mechanically during a revision. As Hauf shows in his masterful lecture (1993a), the feeling of 'déjà vu' one cannot avoid if one compares the *Tirant* with the surviving works of Corella, goes far beyond style. The phrases in the novel that are also found in Corella are so deftly woven into the new context that we would have to assume an amazing congruence in the thinking and feeling of the two writers. Hauf uses as an example the ideological underpinnings of all that talk in *Tirant* about fame and glory, and convincingly demonstrates the coherence of these ideas throughout the novel. That Galba could have achieved such a fusion of the words and thoughts of two other men while he was copying Martorell's manuscript, sprinkling dozens of quotations from Corella all over it, seems quite impossible. Hauf's many examples suggest a situation best described by the image that Martorell 'spoke through the mouth of Corella'. This impression, however, can also lead us to quite another view of what had really happened.

Paraphrasing Riquer's statement quoted above, we could say: 'If it weren't for the colophon and the dedication, people would have begun attributing *Tirant lo Blanc* to Joan Roíç de Corella many generations ago.'

5. *Lexical Incoherences*

Studies of disputed authorship had been made even before the arrival of the computer. The method used consists in comparing the lexicon of two texts, or of two parts of one long text, in order to quantify idiosyncrasies. It must first be ascertained that differences are not due to peculiarities in the topic or a change of source. Goertz (1967) was quite aware of this prerequisite when he compared the number of certain stylistic elements in descriptions of battles in different parts of the *Tirant*, or in speeches, or in prayers. He concluded that, with the possible exception of chapter 403, there seems to have been only one author at work.

Wittlin (1990) too had hoped that the starting point of that elusive 'fourth part' might be discovered by counting words, looking out for concentrations found only before or after a certain chapter. His research was much facilitated by the concordance of the 1490 edition of the *Tirant* prepared by Maria Brossa at the Centre de Tractament de Textos Catalans at the University of Barcelona. The premise of his study was that there are parts of the *Tirant* written by Martorell, and others revised or enlarged by Galba. But now that the more likely scenario is that a second author was at work throughout the book, the statistical method becomes unreliable. Still, it can direct us to passages that are worth a closer look.

A few examples: 'amistat' is used forty-one times, while there are only nine cases of 'amicícia', seven of which occur between chapters 368 and 378. 'Muntanya' is used ten times, but in chapters 343 and 344 we find four times 'mont'. 'Pusil.lànim' is used only three times, in chapters 374 and 379, where we find also other rare words and expressions, such as 'afalacs enganosos' and 'desenfrenades cogitacions'. 'Cogitacions' is used only three more times in the *Tirant*, all in chapter 376; the verb 'cogitar' is found in chapters 273 and 476, while the archaic 'cuidar' appears in chapters 132 and 153.

However one judges the usefulness of statistics in literary studies, it is obvious that a machine-readable text of the *Tirant* is a major desideratum. The electronic text should use regularized spelling to simplify searches. Even the transcription of numbers should be standardized, facilitating discoveries such as the following: there are dozens of examples in the *Tirant* where numbers of combatants, casualties or prisoners, are guessed at in round figures, such as 'ten thousand' or 'fifty thousand'. But in chapters 131, 159, 330 and 333 we find, for the same kind of items counted, the pseudo-precise numbers 1234, 11722, 35072, 44327 and 18237.

6. Passages Repeated in the 'Tirant'

The fact that certain passages can be found in two places in the *Tirant* was discovered by Nicolau d'Olwer in 1905, who pointed out that a paragraph from Pacs's *Doctrina moral* can be found in chapter 181 and chapter 328. The traditional assumption is that Martorell prepared himself for writing his novel by studying and copying medieval Catalan texts. The disorder in his collection of sources could have led to the reuse of certain extracts.

Other repetitions, however, are of a different kind. As already mentioned, there is a passage in chapter 3 of the *Tirant* that is repeated in chapter 474. The first describes the tearful separation of Guy of Warwick from his wife. Martorell, as we have speculated above, may have once translated a French life of that virtuous count; later he reworked those materials in his short *Guillem de Vàroic*. When starting out to compile the *Tirant*, he somewhat expanded the farewell scene. However, the speech of the countess contains a few lines that stand out for their elaborate vocabulary, syntax and content. The first sentence is grammatically incomplete. The lady speaking makes a convoluted allusion to her plan to commit suicide, an action totally unthinkable on the part of the countess. The speech, however, would make perfect sense in the mouth of Queen Dido, whose tragic story would fit very well among Corella's adaptations of classical tales. When the passage reappears a thousand pages later in the *Tirant*, it is in the Empress's lament about Carmesina's decision to let herself die of grief. The passage makes more sense here than in chapter 3, but we are left with a series of difficult questions. If the passage is by Martorell, writing in his second style, how can we explain the fact that he used it twice, and that it is the first use that seems out of context – in addition to the faulty syntax? Assuming that Galba had found this passage in another writer, or was capable of inventing it himself, would he have interpolated it in two places? If it was the author of the passage himself who interpolated it into the *Tirant*, why twice?

7. Corella Plagiarized in the 'Tirant'

a. Whole passages

We do not know if Corella had ever written an adaptation of the story of Dido. But there are several passages from surviving works of his that we find copied in the *Tirant*. The *Lletres* Corella attributed to Achilles and Polyxena are plagiarized by Diafebus, by the commander of Agramunt and Carmesina in their letters to Estefania, and by Plaerdemavida and Tirant, in chapters 188, 369 and 246 (Annicchiarico 1996). Lady Hope is using, in her speech in chapter 190, parts of Corella's *Lamentacions de Mirra* (Miralles 1977–78; Badia 1989). Carmesina too, in chapter 209, repeats exclamations made by the hapless Mirra (Miralles 1991). In chapter 323, Tirant speaks words to Queen Maragdina that Corella had used in a letter to Prince Charles of Viana (Moll 1934). In chapter 473 Carmesina repeats the complaint Corella had Hero say over Leander's dead body; Leander who, washed up on shore, had 'cold tears' on his face, while Tirant, embalmed, can be assumed to have been dry (Riquer 1949:18–20). The opening lines for Carmesina's lament are a quotation from Queen Hecuba's lamentation in Corella (Hauf 1993). The tombstone of Tirant and Carmesina in chapter 485 bears the same inscription Corella had put on Leander's grave (Riquer 1990a:298–301, with further examples). Corella's most famous literary invention, the *Tragèdia de Caldesa*, was well known to whoever wrote chapter 295 in the *Tirant*, using it also in other passages between chapters 268 and 305 (Garriga 1991).

About fifty such quotations from Corella had been detected by 1995, when Josep Guia announced that he had found about one hundred more.

b. Phrases and expressions

Discovering passages common to Corella's works and to the *Tirant* is a relatively straightforward matter. An old hypothesis (Coromines 1971:373, note 12) that, perhaps, it was Corella who plagiarized Martorell, has never been revived, and is, indeed, untenable. The question nowadays is: can we really assume, with a minimal degree of plausibility, that someone – Martorell, Galba, or whoever – had combed through all the works of Corella in order to extract dozens and dozens of words, expressions, phrases and passages, and then interpolated them most judiciously and – most of the time – flawlessly into draft versions of the *Tirant*? The chronology of Corella's writings has not yet been securely established. The texts most often plagiarized in the *Tirant*, adaptations of Ovidian and Trojan legends, are contemporary with the last years of Martorell's life. But there is growing evidence that even texts written by Corella *after* Martorell's death have been quoted in the *Tirant*.

What is even more interesting is that certain expressions that appear again and again in Corella's works, to the point of becoming shibboleths of his, can also be found in various parts of the *Tirant*. For example: at the beginning of the *Judgement of Paris* we learn that Corella was asked to add his prose allegorization of the classical tale to a poem sent to him by a friend with the words

> Per l'experiència manifesta que tinc de vostra verdadera amistat e condició afable, mossèn Joan Roís de Corella, he pres atreviment de demanar-vos, en singular gràcia, vullau acceptar la ploma, seguint l'estil de vostres elegants poesies, de la fingida *Visió de París* la verdadera al.legoria declarant escriure. E per abreujar part de vostre treball [I am sending you my verses].
> (Corella 1973:202)

This sentence is put into the mouth of Tirant's relatives in chapter 482, when they ask the Empress to marry Hipòlit: 'L'experiència manifesta que tenim de vostra amistat e condició afable, senyora excel.lentíssima, nos dóna atreviment de demanar-vos en singular gràcia vullau acceptar la nostra ambaixada'. It is echoed in chapter 445 of the *Tirant*, where the Emperor says: 'Per l'experiència manifesta que tinc de vostra molta virtut, Tirant, capità e fill meu, voldria e desige que per alleujar part de vostres treballs . . . me faríeu singular gràcia que . . .'. It is also used by the Count of Warwick telling his wife in chapter 3 of the *Tirant*: 'Experiència manifesta que tinc de vostra verdadera amor e condició afable, muller senyora, me fa sentir major dolor . . .'. If the following sentence were anonymous, would we not be inclined to believe it was written by the same hand that wrote the preceding examples? Lazarus's sisters tell Jesus: 'Per l'experiència que tenim de la tua profunda humilitat . . .'. The sentence is from the *Història de Santa Magdalena*, written by Corella after 1482.

It becomes obvious that we have to look out not only for repeated passages, but for reappearing expressions and analogous linguistic formulations. Some of these expressions might have been common stock in Valencia, and just a few examples in isolation would not permit any deductions. However, there is an abundance of such parallelisms between works of Corella and the *Tirant* (Guia 1996b). Concentrating now on examples from texts written *after* the death of Martorell, we find variations of the expression 'més angèlica que humana' (more angelical than human) in three works by Corella and in ten places in the *Tirant*. The alliteration 'verge ventre' (virgin womb) is used by Corella at least in four of his works, and can be found in three chapters in the *Tirant*. The expression 'ab un gran sospir que del retret del seu cor procehia' (with a great sigh which came from the depths of his/her heart) is used in

Josep, in *Magdalena* and in chapters 240, 375 and 474 of the *Tirant*. All four, Magdalene and Mary, Tirant and the King of Tunis, are praised as 'pilar on recolza' (pillars upon which rests . . .).

The search for parallelisms between the works of Corella and the *Tirant* should be carried one step further. Some researchers might try to explain away plagiarisms, quotations, allusions and echoes of Corella in the *Tirant* as having been made by Galba, or, given the chronology of the sources, by Martorell and Galba. But they will find it difficult to offer a believable description of how Martorell and/or Galba went about extracting from Corella's works all those phrases and passages, planning to interpolate them into the *Tirant*. We would have to assume that he/they were *students* of Corella, that he/they had become totally imbued with his linguistic, literary and even narrative style, to the point of giving up all their own creativity, limiting themselves to imitating the master. For example: Corella explains: 'The Lady Magdalena took . . . a castle called Magdaló, whence it could be named Magdalena, in accordance with her own name' (Corella 1913:309; text later than 1465); in chapter 222 of the *Tirant* we read: 'Thus they called themselves the men of Roca Salada [i.e. Salt Rock] since they . . . took a strong castle, which stood on a great rock which was all of good salt . . . And thus . . . they gave up their own names'. Similarly, just as the Pharaoh declares Joseph his viceroy 'ab pública crida' (in a public announcement), presenting him to the people 'en carro triunfal' (in a triumphal chariot) (Corella 1913:60; text later than 1465), the Emperor of Constantinople proclaims Tirant 'en pública crida', Caesar of the Empire, putting him 'en carro triunfal' (chapter 452). In that same amplification of the biblical story, Corella uses, when talking about Potiphar's wife, the words 'in accordance with the natural female condition . . . she was crying out in a loud voice' (1913:50), while in chapter 416 of the *Tirant* we read about the 'natura femenil' of the Viuda Reposada, who committed suicide 'continuament cridant' (continually crying out). That we should find similar words in similar contexts is of little consequence. It is more important to observe parallelisms in the treatment of the two female protagonists. It becomes obvious that only one mind was at work here. Creating the character of the Widow, or inventing non-biblical details about Potiphar's wife, the writer fell into a given frame of mind, remembering unconsciously terms used on the first occasion.

Who was that writer? If we believe the hypothesis that the *Tirant* from 1490 is a literal transcription of the manuscript Martorell had given to Galba in early 1464, we would have to assume that Martorell plagiarized Corella to an amazing degree, but that later Corella copied from the *Tirant* expressions that sound pretty much like Corella in the first place. Wittlin (1993:213 et seq.) observed that Martorell had made only few changes in the medieval texts he used as sources, and suggested that it might have been Galba who added rhetorical embellishments. For example: Ramon Llull begins his *Llibre de l'orde de cavalleria* with the words 'En una terra s'esdevenc que un savi cavaller . . .' (In a certain country it happened that a wise knight . . .). Martorell copies this sentence in his *Guillem de Vàroic*: 'En Anglaterra s'esdevenc que un savi cavaller . . .' (In England it happened that a wise knight . . .). But in chapter 2 of the *Tirant* we read: 'En la fèrtil, rica e delitosa illa d'Anglaterra habitava un cavaller . . .' (In the fertile, rich and delightful isle of England there dwelt a knight . . .). Corella, however, uses the lines 'A les fèrtils, daurades e pacífiques ribes de Colcos' (On the fertile, golden and peaceful shores of Colchos) in *Jason e Medea*, 'En la feroce bel.licosa província d'Espanya, en lo delitós ameníssim regne de València' (In the fierce, warlike province of Spain, in the delightful, most pleasant kingdom of Valencia) in his *Caldesa*, and 'en los florits e verts camps de la regió de Sichen' (in the flowering green fields of the region of Sichem) in the *Josep*. Instead of postulating a revision of Martorell's manuscript by Galba imitating the style of Corella, it seems simpler to assume that these Corellian phrases were put there by their author.

8. Division into Chapters

One aspect of the 1490 edition of the *Tirant* that even scholars who consider Martorell the only author are prepared to attribute to a second hand is the division into chapters and the addition of chapter headings. It is not uncommon that chapter divisions of medieval texts are due to copyists, revisors and publishers. For instance, according to a recent study by José M. Lucía, the *Libro del caballero Zifar* has thirteen chapters in the original, 34 in manuscript M, and 110 in the edition of 1512.

Two aspects of the way the *Tirant* is divided into 487 chapters attract attention. First, the very short chapters – two have just two lines – in the section transcribing the charter of the Order of the Garter (chapters 87–95). Secondly, how as the novel progresses more and more chapters become coextensive with a speech, a question, an answer, a letter and so on. The way such chapters are announced at the end of the previous chapter, how they begin and end, raises suspicions that they could have been interpolated. For instance, at the end of chapter 453 we learn that 'The Emperor announced throughout the city that Tirant should be considered his heir, Caesar of the Empire'. Chapter 454 transcribes that proclamation. In the following chapter, after the words 'Once Tirant had been declared the new Caesar of the Empire, the Emperor returned to his palace and . . .', the main plot continues. The ease with which such chapters are omitted in many a modern edition or translation of the *Tirant* should make us realize that it must have been just as easy for a writer versed in the rhetorical technique of the *amplificatio* to add them to the original, shorter, manuscript. Some scholars have wondered if those references to 'the book', as for example in expressions such as 'Here the book begins to talk about . . .' or 'Here the book stops talking about . . .', could be the sign of an interpolator.

In 1992 (186) Riquer went to some length in counting the formulae that announce or introduce speeches in the *Tirant*. He found the expression (or close variants thereof) 'féu principi a semblants paraules' (began the following words) ten times, 'no tardà de fer principi a tal resposta' (did not delay beginning such an answer) twenty-five times, 'li presentà paraules de semblant estil' (offered him/her words of the following style) eighteen times, 'féu principi a un tal parlar' (began such a speech) seventy-three times and so on. Quite correctly he considers them 'peculiar to and characteristic of' the *Tirant*, but his impression that 'they are somehow like Martorell's signature' should be formulated more carefully. Given the fact that these very same formulae are proportionally even more frequent in Corella, in all his surviving works, makes it just as likely that that author was Corella.

9. Manuscript 7811 of the Biblioteca Nacional of Madrid

No hypothetical account of the external history of the *Tirant* – any such hypothesis, basically, has to figure out what was in the manuscript Martorell gave to Galba in 1464 and what happened to it before *Tirant lo Blanc* was printed in 1490 – can be complete without a discussion of MS 7811 of the Biblioteca Nacional of Madrid. Martí de Riquer describes it in 1990a:255 et seq. This big but somewhat untidy codex of 537 folios offers transcriptions, made by various hands during the second half of the fifteenth century, of a variety of texts, all related to chivalry. The majority deal with imaginary or real duels among knights. Martorell's very own *Lletres de batalla* with his cousin Monpalau, with whom he wanted to fight a duel in London because Monpalau had seduced his sister, are transcribed in ff. 175–93. The text of Martorell's *Guillem de Vàroic* – written probably after he finished, or gave up, translating *Guy of Warwick* – can be found in ff. 164–71.

More surprisingly, the codex also contains texts used in the *Tirant*. There is the anonymous Catalan translation of Petrarch's *Letter to Niccolo Acciaiuoli*, presented – without hardly any changes, which needs explaining – in chapter 143 of the *Tirant* as a speech by Abdal.là Salomó. There is the fictitious letter of the Sultan of Babylon to the King of Cyprus, passages of which are copied in chapter 135 of the *Tirant*. There is the correspondence between Bernat de Vilarig and Joanot de la Serra, from 1452 and 1453, sentences of which can be found in chapters 146, 149 and 154 of the *Tirant*.

Finally we find in f. 532 – numbered also 132 – the beginning of a text with the title *Flor de cavalleria* (which can be translated as *Anthology of What is Best in Chivalry*), a book now lost but listed in the inventory of Galba's library. It begins with an explanation of the conditions that make warfare permissible, a topic also treated in chapter 9 of the *Tirant*. The single page does not offer much material for comparisons, but it is surprising to discover parallelisms between the beginning of the *Flor* and the Prologue of the *Tirant* in the expression 'viure perpetualment per glòria' and 'vida... perpetual per glòria' (to live perpetually through glory... perpetual life through glory). Another phrase seems to link three texts. The *Flor* refers to the 'time of Joshua and the Kings and the Maccabees, of the Greeks, Trojans and Romans and many others'. In the Prologue and in chapter 37 of the *Tirant* there is an allusion to 'Joshua..., Kings..., Judas Maccabeus..., Greeks, Trojans... Romans', and so on. In *Guillem de Vàroic* we just read 'Judas Maccabeus... and many others it would be tedious to relate'.

Who wrote the *Flor de cavalleria*? When? Where does all the material in MS 7811 come from? If it had been copied before Martorell claims to have begun compiling his *Tirant* – 2 January 1460 – we would be tempted to assume that it is his collection of materials he had assembled with a view to combining them, one day, into a book, perhaps a manual for knights. But many of the letters copied bear later dates.

Conclusion

In these pages we have limited ourselves to nine problem areas found in the *Tirant lo Blanc*, of which we only know the 1490 edition. There are many more, as we can see for instance in Perujo 1995 (222 et seq., with references to Riquer).

In chapter 1 we are told that the book will be divided into seven parts, but this scheme – which Martorell took over from his source for those chapters, Ramon Llull – is not maintained. While there are many descriptions of luxurious dresses for ladies, only after chapter 448 do we find mentions of 'cortapises' and 'mantilles'. Tirant's native language was Breton, but the author never explains how the hero communicated with people from England, Sicily, Greece and Africa; only the author of chapters 389 to 463 considers this kind of linguistic problem worthy of comment. The reader gets to know the character called Hipòlit as a loyal and grateful friend of Tirant, but when he reappears in chapter 479 'Galba presents him as a troublemaker ... who is pleased to learn that Tirant is dead' (Nicolau d'Olwer 1961:146; our translation). Plaerdemavida is one of the most endearing characters in the novel, but there are chapters where she is presented in a way that made Professor Coromines (1954:176 et seq.) wonder if they were written by a different hand. Coromines also found it hard to believe that one and the same author could in certain chapters introduce many precise place names, but mention only few in others, or else invent fantastic ones.

The internal incoherence observed in the *Tirant* that offers the most important new support for the hypothesis of two authors in the novel concerns the way Arab culture is presented. According to Maria Jesús Rubiera y

Mata (1993), Martorell was reasonably well informed about most aspects of Muslim life. But after chapter 300 we find statements which that first writer would not have made. There are drunken Muslims, a reference to a Muslim king of Christian Ethiopia, the suggestion that Mohammed was a divinity, misunderstandings concerning the Friday prayers, and so on.

It is quite possible that plausible reasons can be found to explain many of these internal inconsistencies without having to assume dual authorship of the novel. Many, but not all. The search for a complete and coherent explanation of all the stages in the long and murky history of everything which had happened between 2 January 1460, when Martorell began filling twenty-seven querns, and 20 November 1490, when the printers of *Tirant lo Blanc* added the second colophon to the one that mentions Galba and Lady Isabel, must continue.

Postscript

This paper was sent to the editor in September 1996. No changes were made to it at the proofreading stage. The two authors, however, would like to add the following notes:

Guia: After my book from 1996, I contrasted the *Tirant* and Corella – now especially his religious works – also in a chapter of my *Fraseologia i estil: Enigmes literaris a la Valencia del segle XV* (Valencia: Tres i Quatre) from 1998. I would also like to draw attention to a possible solution to the as yet unsolved problem of the ambigous statement made in *Don Quijote* about the *Tirant*, calling it 'el mejor libro del mundo', but adding 'merecía el que lo compuso . . . que le echaran a galeras'. Nicolas Fréret, in his 'Avertissement' to the French version of the *Tirant* from 1740 writes: 'J'ai idée d'avoir lu quelque part que l'auteur du roman de *Tirant le Blanc* était mort aux galères, mais je ne puis me rappeler dans quel livre'. Since, according to the DRAE, 'echar a galeras' often means just 'to condemn', one might wonder if Cervantes too had heard something about a 'condemnation' of the true author of the *Tirant*, Corella, condemned to silence by the Inquisition, according to an old document. Since Old-Spanish 'merecía' can mean 'do something deserving', and since any 'que' can stand for 'para que', the enigmatic sentence could be understood thus: 'He who composed the *Tirant* did a work of great merit; he did not deserve to be condemned for having written that amusing confabulation.'

Wittlin: The major new factor in Tirant-studies since 1996, from my point of view, are the discoveries that, just as Corella was used as a source of extracts for the *Tirant*, there are in this novel also very many fragments drawn from the Catalan translations of Colonne's *Històries troianes*, Ovid's *Heròides*, Seneca's plays, and of Boccaccio's *Fiammetta*. (See articles by Josep Pujol, Tomàs Martínez and Annamaria Annicchiarico.) While the argument, that the person who most easily could have put extracts from works of

Corella into the *Tirant* was Corella himself, seems self-evident, one finds it much more difficult to envisage Corella interpolating all those 'quotations' from Seneca, Boccaccio, etc. Colon has shown in 1999 that it is unlikely that Corella revised the *Tirant* since many of the words typical of his prose (*acerbíssim, bàlsem, deífic, durícia, especiós*, etc.) are not found in that novel. But if Martorell himself wrote the whole book, three-fourths of which are a quilt of plagiarized materials, then his mind must have worked along lines which should be investigated not by literary historians, but by psychologists.

BIBLIOGRAPHY

This bibliography only contains references that occur in the various articles. For a fuller bibliography, concentrating specifically on the *Tirant*, see Jean Marie Barberà, ed., *Actes del Col.loqui Internacional 'Tirant lo Blanc': Estudis crítics sobre 'Tirant lo Blanc' i el seu context* (Barcelona: Publicacions de l'Abadia de Montserrat, 1997), 477–84. See also the extensive bibliography, edited by Rafael Beltrán and Josep Izquierdo, in *Llengua i Literatura* 7 (1996), 345–405.

Alemany, Rafael, 1994. 'La mort de Tirant i el triomf d'Hipòlit o la crisi del món cavalleresc vista per un cavaller en crisi', in *La cultura catalana tra l'Umanesimo e il Barocco: Atti del V Convegno dell'Associazione Italiana di Studi Catalani* (Padua: Programma), 13–26.
Alemany, Rafael, 1995. 'En torno al desenlace del *Tirant lo Blanc*', in Juan Paredes, Enrique J. Nogueras Valdivieso and Lourdes Sánchez Rodrigo, ed., *Estudios sobre el 'Tirant lo Blanc'* (Granada: Universidad de Granada), 11–26.
Alonso, Dámaso, 1961. '*Tirant lo Blanc*, novela moderna', in his *Primavera temprana de la literatura europea* (Madrid: Ediciones Guadarrama), 201–53. Originally published in *Revista valenciana de filología* I (1951), 179–215.
Amador de los Ríos, José, 1969. *Historia crítica de la literatura española*, 7 vols [Madrid: José Rodríguez and Joaquín Muñoz, 1861–65] repr. Biblioteca Románica Hispánica, Facsímiles, 9 (Madrid: Gredos), VII, 385–9.
Annicchiarico, Annamaria, 1996. *Varianti corelliane e 'plagi' del Tirant: Achille e Polissena*, Biblioteca della ricerca: Cultura Straniera 72 (Fasano di Brindisi: Schena).
Annicchiarico, Annamaria, 1998. ' "Volgia de Pathos" e un'altra "connexió": Fiammetta e Corella nel Tirant lo Blanc', *Caplletra* 24, 25–44.
Anonymous (trans.), c.1489–91. *Arte de bien morir* (Saragossa: Hans Hurus).
Aramon i Serra, Ramon, ed., 1930–33. *Curial e Güelfa*, 3 vols (Barcelona: Barcino).
Ariès, Philippe, 1977. *L'homme devant la mort*, 2nd edn, 2 vols (Paris: Le Seuil).
Atiya, Aziz S., 1965. *The Crusade in the Later Middle Ages*, 2nd edn (New York: Kraus Reprints).
Auerbach, Erich, 1953. *Mimesis: the Representation of Reality in Western Literature* (Princeton: Princeton University Press).
Avalle-Arce, Juan Bautista, 1991. *Amadís de Gaula: el primitivo y el de Montalvo* (Mexico: FCE).
Aylward, Edward T., 1985. *Martorell's Tirant lo Blanch: a Program for Military*

and Social Reform in Fifteenth-Century Christendom, North Carolina Studies in the Romance Languages and Literatures 225 (Chapel Hill: University of North Carolina Press).
Aylward, Edward T., 1993. '*Tirant lo Blanc* comentado en los capítulos 6 y 21 del *Quijote* (1605): una relación invertida', in *Actes del Symposion 'Tirant lo Blanc'* (Barcelona: Quaderns Crema), 21–33.
Badel, Pierre-Yves, 1980. *Le Roman de la Rose au XIVe siècle: Étude de la réception de l'œuvre* (Geneva: Droz).
Badia, Lola, 1983–4. 'Frontí i Vegeci, mestres de cavalleria en català dels segles XIV i XV', *Boletín de la Real Academia de Buenas Letras de Barcelona* XXXIX, 191–215.
Badia, Lola, 1988. 'L'"humanisme català": formació i crisi d'un concepte historiogràfic', in her *De Bernat Metge a Joan Roís de Corella* (Barcelona: Quaderns Crema), 13–38.
Badia, Lola, 1989. 'De la *Faula* al *Tirant*, passant, sobretot, pel *Llibre de Fortuna e Prudència*', in *Quaderns Crema, deu anys* (Barcelona: Quaderns Crema), 17–57. Reprinted in Badia 1993b, 93–128.
Badia, Lola, 1991a. 'Traduccions al català dels segles XIV i XV i innovació cultural i literària', *Estudi General* 11, 31–50.
Badia, Lola, 1991b. 'El *Tirant*: la tradició i la moral', *Serra d'Or* 373, 56–9. Reprinted in Badia 1993b, 129–38.
Badia, Lola, 1993a. 'El *Tirant* en la tardor medieval catalana', in *Actes del Symposion Tirant lo Blanc* (Barcelona: Quaderns Crema), 35–99.
Badia, Lola, 1993b. *Tradició i modernitat als segles XIV i XV: Estudis de cultura literària i lectures d'Ausiàs March* (Valencia–Barcelona: Institut Universitari de Filologia Valenciana, Publicacions de l'Abadia de Montserrat).
Badia, Lola, 1994. 'La legitimació del discurs literari en vulgar segons Ferran Valentí', in Lola Badia and Albert Soler, ed., *Intel.lectuals i escriptors a la Baixa Edat Mitjana* (Barcelona: Curial, Publicacions de l'Abadia de Montserrat), 161–84.
Barberà, Jean Marie, 1997. 'L'anamorphose de la mort dans *Tirant lo* Blanc', in Barberà, ed., *Actes del Col.loqui Internacional Tirant lo Blanc, Aix-en-Provence, 21–22 October 1994* (Barcelona: Centre Aixois de Recherches Hispaniques, Institut Interuniversitari de Filologia Valenciana, Publicacions de l'Abadia de Montserrat), 261–84.
Beltrán, Rafael, 1983. *Tirant lo Blanc: evolució i revolta de la narració de cavalleries* (Valencia: Institut Alfons el Magnànim, Diputació de València).
Beltrán, Rafael, 1990. 'Las bodas sordas en *Tirant lo Blanc* y *La Celestina*', *Revista de Filología Española* LXX, 91–117.
Beltrán, Rafael, 1993. '*Tirant lo* Blanc i la biografia cavalleresca', in *Actes del Symposion Tirant lo Blanc* (Barcelona: Quaderns Crema), 101–32.
Beltrán, Rafael, 1997a. 'Urganda, Morgana y Sibila: el espectáculo de la nave profética en la literatura de caballerías', in Ian Macpherson and Ralph Penny, ed., *The Medieval Mind: Studies in Honour of Alan Deyermond* (London: Támesis), 21–47.
Beltrán, Rafael, 1997b. 'La muerte de Tirant: elementos para una autopsia', in *Actes del Col.loqui internacional Tirant lo Blanc, Aix-en-Provence, 21–22 October 1994* (Barcelona: Centre Aixois de Recherches Hispaniques, Institut

Interuniversitari de Filologia Valenciana, Publicacions de l'Abadia de Montserrat), 75–93.
Beltrán, Rafael, ed., 1997c. Gutierre Díez de Games, *El Victorial* (Salamanca: Universidad de Salamanca).
Beltrán, Rafael, in press. 'Conversaciones entre Plaerdemavida y Sharazade (más sobre *Orlando furioso*, V)', in *Actas del Coloquio 'Literatura caballeresca en Italia y España (1460–1550). Circulación y transformación de géneros, temas y argumentos desde el Medioevo'* (Cologne, 3–4 April, 1997).
Bensch, Stephen P., 1995. 'Early Catalan Contacts with Byzantium', in Larry J. Simon, ed., *Iberia and the Mediterranean World of the Middle Ages*, vol.1 (London: E.J. Brill), 131–60.
Bisson, T.N., 1986. *The Medieval Crown of Aragon: A Short History* (Oxford: Clarendon Press).
Bofarull, P. de, ed., 1857. Antoni Canals, *Carta de sant Bernat a sa germana*, in *Colección de documentos inéditos del Archivo de la Corona de Aragón* XIII, 415-652.
Bohigas, Pere, ed., 1947. *Tractats de cavalleria* (Barcelona: Barcino).
Booth, Wayne, 1983. *The Rhetoric of Fiction*, 2nd edn (Chicago: University of Chicago Press).
Boulton, D'Arcy J.D., 1987. *The Knights of the Crown: the Monarchical Orders of Knighthood in Later Medieval Europe, 1325–1520* (Woodbridge: The Boydell Press).
Boureau, Alain, 1988. *Le simple corps du roi: L'impossible sacralité des souverains français. XVe–XVIIIe siècle* (Paris: Les Éditions de Paris).
Bruni, Francesco, 1990. *Boccaccio: L'invenzione della letteratura mezzana* (Bologna: Il Mulino).
Bruni, Francesco, 1991. *Testi e chierici del medioevo* (Genoa: Marietti).
Carrillo de Huete, Pedro, 1946. *Crónica del Halconero de Juan II*, ed. Juan de Mata Carriazo, *Colección de Crónicas de España* 8 (Madrid: Espasa-Calpe).
Cátedra, Pedro M., 1988. 'Sobre la obra catalana de Enrique de Villena', in *Homenaje a Eugenio Asensio* (Madrid: Gredos), 127–40.
Cátedra, Pedro M., ed., 1989. Enrique de Villena, *Traducción y glosas de la 'Eneida'*, 2 vols (Salamanca: Diputación de Salamanca).
Cátedra, Pedro M., 1993. 'Los *Doze Trabajos de Hércules* en el *Tirant*: (Lecturas de la obra de Villena en Castilla y Aragón)', in *Actes del Symposion Tirant lo Blanc* (Barcelona: Quaderns Crema), 171–206.
Cervantes Saavedra, Miguel de, 1950. *Don Quixote*, tr. J.M. Cohen (Harmondsworth: Penguin Books).
Cervantes Saavedra, Miguel de, 1978. *El ingenioso hidalgo Don Quijote de la Mancha*, ed. Luis Andrés Murillo, 2 vols (Madrid: Castalia).
Cervantes Saavedra, Miguel de, 1992. *Don Quixote*, tr. Charles Jarvis [1742]. The World's Classics (Oxford: Oxford University Press).
Chiner, Jaume, 1991. 'Batalla a ultrança per Joanot Martorell', *A sol post* 2, 83–127.
Chiner, Jaume and Jesús Villalmanzo, 1992. *La pluma y la espada: Estudio documental sobre Joanot Martorell y su familia (1373–1483)* (Valencia: Ajuntament de Valencia).

Chiner, Jaume, 1993. *El viure novel.lesc: Biografia de Joanot Martorell* (Alcoy: Marfil).
Cingolani, Stefano M., 1994. 'Finzione della realtà e realtà della finzione: Considerazioni sui modelli culturali del *Curial e Güelfa*, in *Intel.lectuals i escriptors a la Baixa Edat Mitjana*, ed. Lola Badia and Albert Soler (Barcelona: Curial, Publicacions de l'Abadia de Montserrat 1994), 129–59.
Cingolani, Stefano M., 1995–96. 'Clàssics i pseudoclàssics al *Tirant lo Blanc*', *Boletín de la Real Academia de Buenas Letras de Barcelona* XLV, 361–88.
Cocozzella, Peter, 1993. '*Roques* and Pageantry: *Artifici* as a Function of Joanot Martorell's Dramatic Text', in '*Tirant lo Blanc': Text and Context (Proceedings of the Second Catalan Symposium)* (New York: Peter Lang), 19–37.
Codex Justinianus, 1541. *Codicis de Iustiniani sacratiss. Principis ex repetita praelectione libri XII* (Basle: apud Johannes Hervagio, 1541).
Cohn, Dorrit, 1978. *Transparent Minds: Narrative Modes for Presenting Consciousness in Fiction* (Princeton: Princeton University Press).
Colon, Germà, 1999. 'Entre el *Cartoixà* de Corella i el *Tirant*', in Vincent Martines, ed., *Estudis sobre Joan Roís de Corella*, Alcoi: Marfil, 125–32).
Conlon, D.J., ed., 1969. *Le romant de Guy de Warwick et de Herolt d'Ardenne* (Chapel Hill: University of North Carolina Press).
Contamine, Philippe, 1992. *La guerre au Moyen Âge* (Paris: Presses Universitaires de France).
Copeland, Rita, 1991. *Rhetoric, Hermeneutics and Translation in the Middle Ages: Academic Traditions and Vernacular Texts* (Cambridge: Cambridge University Press).
Corella, Joan Roís de, 1913. *Obres*, ed. Ramon Miquel i Planas (Barcelona: Biblioteca Catalana).
Corella, Joan Roís de, 1983. *Obra profana*, ed. Jordi Carbonell (Valencia: Albatros, 1973. Reprinted Valencia: Tres i Quatre).
Coromines, Joan, 1971. 'Sobre l'estil i manera de Martí Joan de Galba i els de Joanot Martorell', originally published in *Homenatge a Carles Riba* (Barcelona: Janés, 1954), 168–84. Reprinted in his *Lleures i converses d'un filòleg* (Barcelona: Club Editor), 363–78.
Cortijo Ocaña, Antonio, 1995. 'La traducción portuguesa de la *Confessio Amantis* de John Gower', *Euphrosyne: Revista de Filología Clásica* XXIII, 457–66.
De Courcelles, Dominique, 1996. 'Vœu chevalresque et vœu de croisade dans le roman de *Tirant lo Blanc* (1460–1490): La fin de l'empire chrétien d'Orient', *Cahiers du Centre de Recherches Historiques* XVI, 75–90.
Delumeau, Jean, 1989. *El miedo en Occidente (s. XV–XVIII): La ciudad sitiada* (Madrid: Taurus).
Dionisotti, Carlo, 1965. 'Proposta per Guido Giudice', *Rivista di cultura classica e medievale* VII, 453–66.
Dressendörfer, Peter, 1989. 'Los "Moros" y la "Reconquista": la dimensión histórica de un malentendido fundamental', in C. Strosetski and M. Tietz, ed., *Akten des Deutschen Hispanistentages Passau 26.2–1.3 1987. Einheit und Vielfalt in der Iberoromania: Geschichte und Gegenwart* (Hamburg: Buske), 25–34.

Duran, Eulàlia and Joan Requesens, 1997. *Profecia i poder al Renaixement* (Valencia: Tres i Quatre, 1997).
Dutton, Brian and Joaquín González Cuenca, ed., 1993. *Cancionero de Juan Alfonso de Baena* (Madrid: Visor).
Eberenz, Rolf,1982. 'Diàleg i llenguatge col.loquial al *Tirant lo Blanc*', in Luis López Molina, ed., *Miscelánea de estudios hispánicos: homenaje de los hispanistas de Suiza a Ramon Sugranyes de Franch* (Barcelona: Publicacions de l'Abadia de Montserrat), 55–67.
Eco, Umberto, 1994. *Six Walks in the Fictional Woods* (Cambridge MA: Harvard University Press).
Egidio Romano, 1607. *De regimine principum libri III* (Rome: Bartolomeo Zanetto).
Eisenberg, Daniel, 1982. *Romances of Chivalry in the Spanish Golden Age*, Juan de la Cuesta Monographs (Newark, Delaware).
Eiximenis, Francesc, 1483–84. *Primer libre del volum appellat Crestià* and *Dotzèn libre appellat Crestià* (Valencia: Lambert Palmart).
Elliott, J.H., 1986. *The Count-Duke of Olivares: The Statesman in an Age of Decline* (New Haven and London: Yale University Press).
Epalza, Mikel de, 1987. *Jésus otage. Juifs, chrétiens et musulmans en Espagne (VI–XVII s.)* (Paris, 1987).
Espadaler, Anton M., 1984. *Una reina per a Curial* (Barcelona: Quaderns Crema).
Espadaler, Anton M., 1993. 'Paraula de Joanot Martorell: sobre els principis estètics del *Tirant lo Blanc*', in *Actes del Symposion Tirant lo Blanc* (Barcelona: Quaderns Crema), 261–71.
Ferrando, Antoni, 1995. 'Del *Tiran* de 1460–4 al *Tirant* de 1490', in *Actes del Novè Col.loqui de l'AILLC* (Alacant-Elx, 1991), vol. 2 (Barcelona: Publicacions de l'Abadia de Montserrat, 1993), 25–68. Reprinted in Juan Paredes, Enrique J. Nogueras Valdivieso and Lourdes Sánchez Rodrigo, ed., *Estudios sobre el 'Tirant lo Blanc'* (Granada: Universidad de Granada), 75–109.
Flavio Vegecio, 1982. *Epitoma rei militaris*, in María Teresa Calleja Berdones, ed., 'El "Epitoma rei militaris" de Vegecio: Edición y estudio de los libros I y II' (Madrid: Universidad Complutense, unpublished doctoral thesis, 1982), and Felisa del Barrio, ed., 'El "Epitoma rei militaris" de Vegecio: Edición y estudio de los libros III y IV' (Madrid: Universidad Complutense, unpublished doctoral thesis, 1982).
Frye, Northrop, 1957. *Anatomy of Criticism: Four Essays* (Princeton NJ: Princeton University Press).
Fuster, Joan, 1993. 'Consideracions sobre el *Tirant*', in *Actes del Novè Col.loqui de l'AILLC* (Alacant-Elx, 1991), vol. 2 (Barcelona: Publicacions de l'Abadia de Montserrat), 5–23. Reprinted in Fuster, *Obres completes, VII: Llengua, literatura, història* (Barcelona: Edicions 62, 1994), 256–77.
Gallina, Annamaria, ed., 1967. Domenico Cavalca, *Mirall de la Creu: Versió catalana del segle XV, per Pere Busquets*, 2 vols (Barcelona: Barcino).
García, Santiago, 1976. 'Un manuscrito inédito valenciano del siglo XV, titulado *Art de ben morir*', *Anales valentinos* IV, 371–414.
Garriga, Carles, 1991. 'Caldesa i Carmesina: Roís de Corella plagiat en el *Tirant*

lo Blanc', in *ELLC* 23 = *Miscel.lània Jordi Carbonell*, II (Barcelona: Publicacions de l'Abadia de Montserrat), 17–27.
Gaucher, Elisabeth, 1994. *La biographie chevalresque: Typologie d'un genre (XIIIe–XVe siècle)* (Paris: Champion).
Gili i Gaya, S., 1947–48. 'Noves recerques sobre *Tirant lo Blanch*', *Estudis Romànics* I, 138–9.
Goertz, Wolf, 1967. 'Zur Frage der Einheit des *Tirant lo Blanc*', *Romanisches Jahrbuch* XVIII, 249–67.
Gómez Moreno, Ángel, 1985. 'La *militia* clásica y la caballería medieval; las lecturas *de re militari* entre Medioevo y Renacimiento', *Euphrosyne: Revista de Filología Clásica* XXIII, 83–97.
González-Casanova, Roberto, 1994. 'Western Narratives of Eastern Adventurers: the Cultural Poetics and Politics of Catalan Expansion, 1300–1500', *Catalan Review* 8, 1–2, 211–27.
Griffin, Nathaniel Edward, ed., 1936. Guido de Columnis, *Historia Destructionis Troiae* (Cambridge MA: The Medieval Academy of America. Reprinted New York: Kraus, 1970).
Grilli, Giuseppe, 1994. *Dal 'Tirant' al 'Quijote'*, Biblioteca de Filologia Romanza 36 (Bari: Adriatica).
Guadalajara Medina, José, 1996. *Las profecías del Anticristo en la Edad Media* (Madrid: Gredos).
Guenée, Bernard, 1980. *Histoire et culture historique dans l'Occident médiéval* (Paris: Aubier).
Guenée, Bernard, 1991. *L'Occident aux XIVe et XVe siècles: Les états* (Paris: Presses Universitaires de France).
Guia, Josep, 1995. 'Introducció a la fraseologia del *Tirant*', *Afers* 20, 129–42.
Guia, Josep, 1996a. 'Corella també en menjava, d'olives', *Revista de Catalunya* CV, 83–114.
Guia, Josep, 1996b. *Descobrint l'autor de 'Tirant lo Blanc'. De Martorell a Corella* (Catarroja: Afers).
Guia, Josep and Maria Conca, in press. 'Manlleus fraseològics i altres intertextualitzacions de la traducció catalana de la *Historia destructionis Troiae* al *Tirant lo Blanc*', *VI Convegno dell'Associazione Italiana di Studi Catalani* (Cagliari, 1995).
Guiu de Columpnes, 1916. *Les Històries troianes (traduïdes al català en el XIVèn segle per Jaume Conesa)*, ed. Ramon Miquel i Planas (Barcelona: Biblioteca Catalana).
Haebler, Conrado, 1903–17. *Bibliografía ibérica del siglo XV: enumeración de todos los libros impresos en España y Portugal hasta el año de 1500 con notas críticas*, 2 vols (The Hague: Martinus Nijhoff and Leipzig: Karl W. Hiersemann).
Haro, Marta, 1995. *Los compendios de castigos del siglo XIII: técnicas narrativas y contenido ético*, Anejos de *Cuadernos de Filología* 14 (Valencia: Departamento de Filología Española, Universidad de Valencia).
Haro, Marta, 1996. *La imagen del poder real a través de los compendios de castigos del siglo XIII*, Papers of the Medieval Hispanic Research Seminar (London: Dept. of Hispanic Studies, Queen Mary and Westfield College).
Hart, Thomas R., 1993. '*Tirant lo Blanc*: Between Romance and Epic', in *Letters*

and Society in Fifteenth-Century Spain: Studies Presented to P.E. Russell on his Eightieth Birthday, ed. Alan Deyermond and Jeremy Lawrance (Llangranog: Dolphin Books), 59–68.
Hauf, Albert G., 1989. 'El parany historiogràfic. Nota al pròleg del *Tirant*', *Saó* 1, 19–23.
Hauf, Albert G., 1990. 'Artur a Constantinoble: Entorn a un curiós episodi del *Tirant lo Blanc*', *L'Aiguadolç (Homenatge al 'Tirant lo Blanc')*, 12–13, 13–31.
Hauf, Albert G., 1993a. '*Tirant lo Blanc*: algunes qüestions que planteja la connexió corelliana', in *Actes del Novè Col.loqui de l'AILLC* (Alacant-Elx, 1991), vol. 2 (Barcelona: Publicacions de l'Abadia de Montserrat), 69–116.
Hauf, Albert G., 1993b. 'Tres cartes d'amor: contribució a l'estudi del gènere epistolar en el *Tirant lo Blanc*', in *Actes del Symposion Tirant lo Blanc* (Barcelona: Quaderns Crema), 379–409.
Hauf, Albert G., 1994. ' "La dama de Rodes": Tècnica i "energia boccacciana" en un novellino del *Tirant lo Blanc*', in *Miscel.lània Joan Fuster. Estudis de Llengua i Literatura* VIII, ed. Antoni Ferrando and Albert Hauf (Barcelona: Publicacions de l'Abadia de Montserrat), 79–118.
Hauf, Albert G., 1995. '*Tirant lo Blanc* : ¿novela anticaballeresca? Algunas cuestiones que plantea la conexión corelliana', in Juan Paredes, Enrique J. Nogueras and Lourdes Sánchez Rodrigo, ed., *Estudios sobre el 'Tirant lo Blanc*' (Granada: Universidad de Granada), 111–51.
Hauf, Albert G., 1996. 'Texto y contexto de "La flor de las Historias de Oriente": un programa de colaboración cristiano-mongólica', in *Juan Fernández de Heredia y su época*, ed. A. Egido and J.M. Enguita (Saragossa: Institución 'Fernando el Católico'), 111–54.
Hauf, Albert G. and Josep Escartí, ed., 1990. *Tirant lo Blanc*. See under Martorell and Galba, 1990.
Hillgarth, J.N., 1975. 'The problem of a Catalan Mediterranean Empire: 1229–1327', *The English Historical Review*, Supplement 8, 1–54.
Hillgarth, J.N., 1976. *The Spanish Kingdoms: 1250–1516*, vol.1 (Oxford: Clarendon Press).
Hocks, Else, 1942. *Pius II und der Halbmond* (Freiburg: Herder).
Housely, Norman, 1992. *The Later Crusades: from Lyons to Alcazar: 1274–1580* (Oxford: Oxford University Press).
Huizinga, Johan, 1985. *El otoño de la Edad Media*, tr. José Gaos (Madrid: Alianza Universidad). (English translation, *The Waning of the Middle Ages*, London: E. Arnold, 1923).
Hutcheon, Linda, 1988. *A Poetics of Postmodernism: History, Theory, Fiction* (New York and London: Routledge).
Jaffe, Samuel, 1978. 'Gottfried von Strassburg and the Rhetoric of History', in James J. Murphy, ed., *Medieval Eloquence: Studies in the Theory and Practice of Medieval Rhetoric* (Berkeley: University of California Press), 288–318.
Jaume I, 1991. *Llibre dels fets*, ed. Josep M. Pujol. Tria de clàssics 3 (Barcelona: Teide).
Jónsson, Einar Már, 1995. *Le miroir: Naissance d'un genre littéraire* (Paris: Les Belles Lettres).

Kamen, Henry, 1986. *La sociedad europea 1500–1700* (Madrid: Alianza Universidad).
Kamen, Henry, 1993. *The Phoenix and the Flame: Catalonia and the Counter Reformation* (New Haven: Yale University Press 1993).
Kantorowicz, Ernst H., 1957. *The King's Two Bodies: A Study in Medieval Political Theology* (Princeton: Princeton University Press).
Kedar, Benjamin Z., 1984. *Crusade and Mission: European Approaches toward the Muslims* (Princeton: Princeton University Press).
Keen, Maurice, 1986. *La caballería* (Barcelona: Ariel).
Köhler, Erich, 1991. *La aventura caballeresca: Ideal y realidad en la narrativa cortés* (Barcelona: Sirmio). Original edn, 1957.
Krynen, Jacques, 1993. *L'Empire du roi: Idées et croyances politiques en France, XIIIe–XVe siècle* (Paris: Gallimard).
Kundera, Milan, 1988. *The Art of the Novel*, tr. Linda Asher (New York: Harper and Row).
Laiou, Angelici E., 1972. *Constantinople and the Latins: the Foreign Policy of Ambrosius II, 1282–1328* (Cambridge MA: Harvard University Press).
La Sale, Antoine de, 1931. *Little John of Saintré*, tr. Irvine Gray, Broadway Medieval Library (London: Routledge).
Lawrance, Jeremy, 1979. *Un tratado de Alonso de Cartagena sobre la educación y los estudios literarios* (Bellaterra: Universitat Autònoma de Barcelona).
Lawrance, Jeremy, 1986. 'On Fifteenth-Century Spanish Vernacular Humanism', in *Medieval and Renaissance Studies in Honour of Robert Brian Tate* (Oxford: Dolphin).
Lawrance, Jeremy, 1993. 'On the title *Tragicomedia de Calisto y Melibea*', in Alan Deyermond and Jeremy Lawrance, eds, *Letters and Society in Fifteenth-Century Spain: Studies Presented to P.E. Russell on his Eightieth Birthday* (Llangranog: Dolphin Books), 79–92.
Lawrance, Jeremy, 1998. 'La muerte y el morir en las letras ibéricas al fin de la Edad Media', in Aengus M. Ward et al., ed., *Actas del XII Congreso de la Asociación Internacional de Hispanistas, 21–26 de agosto de 1995, Birmingham*, 7 vols (Birmingham: Dept of Hispanic Studies, University of Birmingham), I: *Medieval y lingüística*, 1–26.
Lee, Harold, Marjorie Reeves and Giulio Silano, 1989. *Western Mediterranean Prophecy: The School of Joachim of Fiore and the Fourteenth-Century 'Breviloquium'* (Toronto: Pontifical Institute of Medieval Studies).
Lida de Malkiel, María Rosa, 1962. *La originalidad artística de 'La Celestina'* (Buenos Aires: Eudeba).
Lida de Malkiel, María Rosa, 1966. 'Para la génesis del *Auto de la Sibila Casandra*', in her *Estudios de literatura española y comparada* (Buenos Aires: Eudeba), 157–72.
Limorti i Payà, Paül, 1993. 'Notes al pròleg i a la dedicatòria del *Tirant*', in *Actes del Novè Col.loqui de l'AILLC* (Alacant-Elx, 1991), vol. 2 (Barcelona: Publicacions de l'Abadia de Montserrat), 147–58.
Llull, Ramon, 1972. *Doctrina pueril*, ed. by Gret Schib (Barcelona: Barcino).
Llull, Ramon, 1988. *Llibre de l'orde de cavalleria*, ed. Albert Soler i Llopart (Barcelona: Barcino).
Lowe, Alfonso, 1972. *The Catalan Vengeance* (London: Routledge).

Lucía, José M., 1993. 'Hacia la partición original del *Libro del cavallero Zifar*', in *Actas del V Congreso de la AHLM* (Granada: Universidad de Granada), 4 vols, III, 111–30.
Malory, Sir Thomas, 1971. *Works*, ed. Eugène Vinaver, 2nd edn, Oxford Standard Authors (Oxford: Oxford University Press).
Marcos Casquero, Manuel A., ed., 1996. Guido delle Colonne, *Historia de la destrucción de Troya* (Madrid: Akal).
Marinescu, Constantin, 1953–54. 'Du nouveau sur *Tirant lo Blanc*', *Estudis Romànics* IV, 137–203.
Marinescu, Constantin, 1994. *La politique orientale d'Alfonse V, Roi d'Aragon, Roi de Naples (1416–68)*, revised by M.J. Ferrer i Mallol (Barcelona: Institut d'Estudis Catalans).
Martín, José Luis, ed., 1991. Pero López de Ayala, *Crónicas* (Barcelona: Planeta).
Martínez Romero, Tomàs, ed., 1995. Seneca, *Tragèdies: Traducció medieval catalana amb comentaris del segle XIV de Nicolau Trevet*, 2 vols (Barcelona: Barcino).
Martínez Romero, Tomàs, 1998. *Un clàssic entre clàssics: Sobre traduccions i recepcions de Sèneca a l'època medieval* (Valencia–Barcelona: Institut Interuniversitari de Filologia Valenciana, Publicacions de l'Abadia de Montserrat).
Martínez, Tomàs, 1998. 'De la comtessa de Varoic a la princess Carmensina: per la presència de Sèneca al Tirant lo Blanc', in *Actes . . . Aix*, listed under Barberà, 285–305.
Martorell, Joanot and Martí Joan de Galba, 1947. *Tirant lo Blanc*, ed. Martí de Riquer (Barcelona: Selecta).
Martorell, Joanot and Martí Joan de Galba, 1974. *Tirante el blanco*, ed. Martí de Riquer, 5 vols, Clásicos Castellanos 188–92 (Madrid: Espasa-Calpe).
Martorell, Joanot and Martí Joan de Galba, 1979. *Tirant lo Blanc*, ed. Martí de Riquer (Barcelona: Ariel)
Martorell, Joanot, and Martí Joan de Galba, 1982. *Tirant lo Blanc i altres escrits*, ed. by Martí de Riquer (Barcelona: Ariel).
Martorell, Joanot and Martí Joan de Galba, 1984. *Tirant lo Blanc*, tr. David H. Rosenthal (London and New York: Macmillan and Schocken Books. Reprinted Baltimore and London: The Johns Hopkins University Press, 1996).
Martorell, Joanot and Martí Joan de Galba, 1990a. *Tirant lo Blanc*, . ed. by Albert G. Hauf, 2 vols. Clàssics valencians 7–8 (Valencia: Conselleria de Cultura, Educació i Ciència de la Generalitat Valenciana).
Martorell, Joanot and Martí Joan de Galba, 1990b. *Tirante el Blanco: Traducción castellana del siglo XVI* (Barcelona: Planeta).
Massip, Francesc, 1996. 'El món de l'espectacle en *Tirant lo Blanc* (primera aproximació)', in *Formes teatrals de la tradició medieval*, ed. Francesc Massip (Barcelona: Institut del Teatre de la Diputació de Barcelona), 151–62.
Menéndez Pelayo, Marcelino, 1943. *Orígenes de la novela*, 4 vols [Nueva Biblioteca de Autores Españoles, I,VII,XIV,XXI. Madrid: Bailly-Baillière, 1905–15], 2nd edn, Edición Nacional de las Obras Completas de Menéndez Pelayo, 13–16 (Santander: Consejo Superior de Investigaciones Científicas).
Mensa i Valls, Jaume, 1998. *Les raons d'un anunci apocalíptic: La polèmica*

escatològica entre Arnau de Vilanova i els filòsofs i teòlogs professionals (1297–1305): anàlisi dels arguments i de les argumentacions (Barcelona: Facultat de Teologia).

Minnis, A.J., 1988. *Medieval Theory of Authorship: Scholastic Literary Attitudes in the Later Middle Ages*, 2nd edn (Aldershot: Wildwood House).

Miquel i Planas, Ramon, ed., 1914. *Llibre anomenat Valerio Màximo dels dits y fets memorables: Traducció catalana del XIVèn segle per frare Antoni Canals* (Barcelona: Biblioteca Catalana).

Miquel i Planas, Ramon, ed., 1916. *Les Històries Troyanes de Guiu de Columpnes, traduïdes al català en el XIVèn segle per En Jaume Conesa* (Barcelona: Biblioteca Catalana).

Miralles, Carles, 1977–78. 'Raons de Mirra en boca d'Esperança: Sobre un plagi de Roís de Corella en el *Tirant lo Blanc*', *Boletín de la Real Academia de Buenas Letras de Barcelona* XXXVII, 141–7.

Miralles, Carles, 1991. 'Raons de Mirra en boca de Carmesina: Encara un altre plagi de Roís de Corella en el *Tirant lo Blanc*', in *ELLC* 23 = *Miscel.lània Jordi Carbonell* II (Barcelona: Publicacions de l'Abadia de Montserrat).

Moll, Francesc de Borja, 1934. 'Rudiments de versificació en el *Tirant lo Blanc*', *Bolletí del Diccionari de la llengua catalana* 15, 169–72.

Nicolau d'Olwer, Lluís, 1905. 'Sobre les fonts catalanes del *Tirant lo Blanch*', *Revista de Bibliografia Catalana* 5, 5–37.

Nicolau d'Olwer, Lluís, 1961. '*Tirant lo Blanch*: examen de algunas cuestiones', *Nueva Revista de Filología Hispánica* 15, 131–54.

Nieto Soria, José Manuel, 1993. *Ceremonias de la realeza: Propaganda y legitimación en la Castilla Trastámara* (Madrid: Nerea).

Oleza Simó, Joan, 1992. '*Tirant lo Blanch* y la ansiedad de ficción del caballero Martorell', in *Historias y ficciones: coloquio sobre la literatura del siglo XV*, ed. R. Beltrán, J.L. Canet and J. Ll. Sirera (Valencia: Universitat de València), 323–35.

Olson, Glending, 1982. *Literature as Recreation in the Later Middle Ages* (Ithaca: Cornell University Press).

Padoan, Giorgio, ed., 1994. Giovanni Boccaccio, *Esposizioni sopra la Commedia di Dante*, 2 vols (Milan: Mondadori).

Panormita, Antonio Becadelli el, 1990. *Dels feyts e dits del gran rey Alfonso. Versió catalana del segle XV de Jordi de Centelles*, ed. E. Duran (Barcelona: Barcino), 73–4.

Parkes, Malcolm B., 1991. 'The Influence of the Concepts of *Ordinatio* and *Compilatio* on the Development of the Book', in his *Scribes, Scripts and Readers: Studies in the Communication, Presentation and Dissemination of Medieval Texts* (London: The Hambledon Press).

Patterson, Lee, 1987. *Negotiating the Past: the Historical Understanding of Medieval Literature* (Madison: University of Wisconsin Press).

Perujo, Joan, 1995. *La coherència estructural del 'Tirant lo Blanc'* (Alicante: Instituto de Cultura Juan Gil-Albert).

Pou y Martí, José, 1996. *Visionarios, beguinos y fraticelos catalanes (siglos XIII–XV)* (Alicante: Instituto de Cultura Juan Gil-Albert).

Pujol, Josep, 1994. '*Gaya vel gaudiosa, et alio nomine inveniendi scientia*: Les idees sobre la poesia en llengua vulgar als segles XIV i XV', in Lola Badia and Albert Soler, ed., *Intel.lectuals i escriptors a la Baixa Edat Mitjana* (Barcelona: Curial–Publicacions de l'Abadia de Montserrat), 69–94.

Pujol, Josep, 1995–96. 'El desenllaç tràgic del *Tirant lo Blanc*, les *Troianes* de Sèneca i les idees de tragèdia al segle XV', *Boletín de la Real Academia de Buenas Letras de Barcelona* XLV, 29–66.

Pujol, Josep, 1996. '*Psallite sapientier*: la gaia ciència en els sermons de Felip de Malla de 1413 (Estudi i edició)', *Cultura Neolatina* LVI, 177–250.

Pujol, Josep, 1997. 'De Guido delle Colonne a l'Ovidi epistolar: Sobre el rendiment narratiu i retòric d'unes fonts del *Tirant lo Blanc*', in Tomàs Martínez, ed., *De literatura i cultura a la València medieval*, *Anuari de l'Agrupació Borrianenca de Cultura* VIII, 133–74.

Pujol, Josep, 1998. ' "Micer Johan Bocaci" i mossèn Joanot Martorell: presències del *Decameron* i de la *Fiammetta* al *Tirant lo Blanc*', *Llengua & Literatura* 9, 49–100.

Pujol, Josep, 1999. 'Boccaccio al *Tirant lo Blanc*: les "questioni d'amore" del *Filocolo*', in *Actes del VIIè Congrés de l'Associació Hispànica de Literatura Medieval* (Castelló de la Plana, 22–26 de Setembre de 1997) (Castelló: Universitat Jaume I), III, 181–97.

Ramos, Rafael, 1995. '*Tirant lo Blanc*, *Lancelot du Lac* y el *Llibre de l'orde de cavalleria*', *La Corónica* XXIII, 2, 74–87.

Reeves, Marjorie, 1992–93. *The Influence of Prophecy in the Later Middle Ages*, 2nd edn (Notre Dame: University of Notre Dame Press).

Renau, Xavier, 1991. 'Martí Joan de Galba: Vida i llinatge', *Serra d'Or* 375, 46–8.

Renedo, Xavier, 1995–96. 'Raó i intuició en Plaerdemavida', *Boletín de la Real Academia de Buenas Letras de Barcelona* XLV, 317–60.

Renedo, Xavier, 1996. 'Turpia feminarum incessa lascivarum (El joc teatral en el capítol 283 del *Tirant lo Blanc*)', in *Formes teatrals de la tradició medieval*, ed. Francesc Massip (Barcelona: Institut del Teatre de la Diputació de Barcelona), 209–16.

Reynaud, Georges, 1988. 'La fin de la croisade du pape Calixte III: l'assassinat du Comte Ulrich de Gili', *Sharq al-Andalus* (Alicante) V, 187–92.

Riquer, Martí de, 1949. *Nuevas contribuciones a las fuentes del 'Tirant lo Blanc'* (Barcelona: Biblioteca Central de la Diputación de Barcelona).

Riquer, Martí de, 1964. *Història de la literatura catalana*, vol. III (Barcelona: Ariel. Reprinted 1983).

Riquer, Martí de, 1973. 'L'art militar al *Tirant lo Blanc*', in *In Memoriam Carles Riba (1959–69)* (Barcelona: Ariel), 325–38.

Riquer, Martí de, 1990a. *Aproximació al 'Tirant lo Blanc'* (Barcelona: Quaderns Crema).

Riquer, Martí de, 1990b: see Martorell and Galba, 1990b.

Riquer, Martí de, 1992. *'Tirant lo Blanc': novela de historia y de ficción* (Barcelona: Sirmio).

Riquer, Martí and Mario Vargas Llosa, 1972. *El combate imaginario: Las cartas de batalla de Joanot Martorell* (Barcelona: Seix Barral).

Riu Riu, Manuel, 1989. *Manual de Historia de España: Edad Media (711–1500)* (Madrid: Espasa-Calpe).

Rodríguez Velasco, Jesús D., 1996a. *El debate sobre la caballería en el siglo XV* (Valladolid: Junta de Castilla y León).
Rodríguez Velasco, Jesús D., 1996b. 'La historiografía como base argumentativa de la literatura ético-política en Europa, *ca.* 1100–1350', *Epos* 12, 177–205.
Rojas, Fernando de, 1991. *Comedia o Tragicomedia de Calisto y Melibea (La Celestina)*, ed. Peter E. Russell (Madrid: Castalia).
Romeu i Figueras, J., 1994. '*Ficció que féu la Reprovada Viuda a Tirant*: Comentaris al capítol 283 de *Tirant lo Blanc*', in his *Lectura de textos medievals i renaixentistes* (Valencia–Barcelona: Institut Universitari de Filologia Valenciana, Publicacions de l'Abadia de Montserrat), 163–75.
Rubiera y Mata, María Jesús, 1990. 'El món cavalleresc àrab i el món cavalleresc del *Tirant*', *Afers* 10, 267–74.
Rubiera y Mata, María Jesús, 1993. *Tirant contra el Islam* (Altea: Aitana).
Rubió i Balaguer, Jordi, 1987. *Història i historiografia (Obres de Jordi Rubió i Balaguer VI)* (Barcelona: Publicacions de l'Abadia de Montserrat).
Russell, P.E., 1969. '*Don Quixote* as a Funny Book', *Modern Language Review* LXIV, 312–26.
Russell, P.E., 1985. *Traducciones y traductores en la península ibérica (1400–1550)* (Bellaterra: Universitat Autònoma de Barcelona).
Sales Dasí, Emilio, 1991. '*Tirant lo Blanc* i la mítica cavalleria medieval', in Antoni Ferrando and Albert Hauf, ed., *Miscel.lània Joan Fuster: Estudis de Llengua i Literatura*, IV (Barcelona: Publicacions de l'Abadia de Montserrat), 97–117.
Sanchis Sivera, Josep, ed., 1932. *Dietari del Capellà d'Anfós el Magnànim* (Valencia: Acción Bibliográfica Valenciana).
Scaglione, Aldo, 1991. *Knights at Court: Courtliness, Chivalry and Courtesy from Ottonian Germany to the Italian Renaissance* (Berkeley: University of California Press).
Segre, Cesare, 1993. 'La comunicación indirecta en *Tirant lo Blanc*', in *Actes del Symposion Tirant lo Blanc* (Barcelona: Quaderns Crema), 573–86.
Sobrequés Vidal, Santiago, 1952. 'Sobre el ideal de la cruzada en Alfonso V', *Historia* XIX, 232–52.
Sutherland, D.R., 1961. 'The Love Meditation in Courtly Literature', in *Studies in Medieval French Presented to Alfred Ewert* (Oxford: Blackwell), 165–93.
Terry, Arthur, 1982. 'Character and Role in *Tirant lo Blanc*', in R.B. Tate, ed., *Essays in Narrative Fiction in the Iberian Peninsula in Honour of Frank Pierce* (Oxford: Dolphin), 177–95.
Thomas Aquinas, St, 1978. *Summa Theologiae*, ed. Fratres Ordinis Praedicatorum, 5 vols (Madrid: Biblioteca de Autores Cristianos).
Turró i Torrent, Jaume, 1991. 'Sobre el *Curial*, Virgili i Petrarca', in Antoni Ferrando and Albert Hauf, ed., *Miscel.lània Joan Fuster*, III. *Estudis de Llengua i Literatura* (Barcelona: Publicacions de l'Abadia de Montserrat), 149–68.
Vargas Llosa, Mario, 1991. 'Carta de batalla por *Tirant lo Blanc*', in his *Carta de batalla por 'Tirant lo Blanc'* (Barcelona: Seix Barral), 9–58. Repr. from *Revista de Occidente* LXX (1969), 1–21.
Vargas Llosa, Mario, 1993. '*Tirant lo Blanc*: las palabras como hechos', in *Actes del Symposion Tirant lo Blanc* (Barcelona: Quaderns Crema), 587–603.

Ventura, Jordi, 1978. *Inquisició espanyola i cultura renaixentista del País Valencià* (Valencia: Tres i Quatre)
Ventura, Jordi, 1993. *La Biblia valenciana* (Barcelona: Curial).
Vincentius Bellovacensis (Vincent of Beauvais), 1624. *Speculum Historiale* (Douai: B. Belleri. Reprinted Graz: Akademische Druck- u. Verlagsanstalt, 1965).
Waley, Pamela, tr., 1982. *Curial and Guelfa* (London: Allen and Unwin).
Weiss, Julian, 1990. *The Poet's Art: Literary Theory in Castile c. 1400–60* (Oxford: The Society for the Study of Medieval Languages and Literature).
Weiss, Julian, 1992. 'La *Quistión entre dos cavalleros*: Un nuevo tratado político del siglo XV', *Revista de Literatura Medieval* IV, 9–46.
Wittlin, Curt, 1990. 'Pistes per a descobrir canvis introduïts per Martí Joan de Galba en el *Tirant lo Blanc* de Joanot Martorell', *Afers* 10, 313–27.
Wittlin, Curt, 1993. 'Dels manuscrits a l'edició: el *Tirant*, elaborat per Martorell el 1460 usant materials preexistents, revisat després en valenciana prosa per Galba', in *Actes del Symposion Tirant lo Blanc* (Barcelona: Quaderns Crema), 605–33. Reprinted in his *De la traducció*, 203–24.
Wittlin, Curt, 1995. 'La influència lingüística de la traducció catalana de les *Històries troianes* sobre el *Tirant lo Blanc*', in *Segon Congrés Internacional de la Llengua Catalana*, VIII (Valencia: Institut de Filologia Valenciana, 1989), 751–7. Reprinted in his *De la traducció literal a la creació literària* (Valencia–Barcelona: Institut de Filologia Valenciana, Publicacions de l'Abadia de Montserrat), 193–202.
Yates, Alan, 1980. 'Tirant lo Blanc: the Ambiguous Hero', in John England, ed., *Hispanic Studies in Honour of Frank Pierce* (Sheffield: Dept of Hispanic Studies, University of Sheffield), 181–98.
Zumthor, Paul, 1989. *La letra y la voz: de la 'literatura' medieval*, tr. J. Presa (Madrid: Cátedra).

INDEX

Alemany, Rafael, 100n7
Al-Farari, 12
Alfons IV (the Magnanimous), 77–80
Alfonso X of Castile, 13, 36
Alonso, Dámaso, 84
Amadís de Gaula, 3, 48
Aquinas, St Thomas, 8–9
Ariosto, Ludovico, 26
Auerbach, Erich, 19
Avicenna, 12
Aylward, E.J., 47
Badia, Lola, 10, 29n2, 97n12, 106–07
Baena, Juan Alfonso de, 31, 36
Beltrán, Rafael, 92n2, 97n12, 100, 104
Bisson, T.N., 51
Boccaccio, Giovanni, 36n15, 41, 42, 70
Borgia, Alfonso (Pope Calixtus III), 81, 82
Bouvet, Honoré, 2, 4
Busquets, Fra Pere, 34n10
Cabré, Lluís, 107n31
Canals, Antoni, 29n2, 31, 35, 38n17, 43
Cartagena, Alonso de, 43
Cato, 10
Celestina, La, 18, 26n13, 85, 106
Cervantes Saavedra, Miguel de, 45–46, 58, 84, 88, 97
Cerverí de Girona, 55
Chiner, Jaume, 114
Cicero, 1, 11, 31, 36
Cohn, Dorrit, 90
Conesa, Jaume, 41, 111, 112
Copeland, Rita, 34n12
Corella, Joan Roiç de, 2, 29n2, 39, 40, 41, 92, 104, 106n27, 110, 111, 113, 116, 117,119–22, 123
Coromines, Joan, 105, 124
Curial e Güelfa, 38, 41, 42, 48, 66, 93, 104n21
Dante, 36
De la Marche, Olivier, 2
De la Sale, Antoine, 94

Delle Colonne, Guido, 29n2, 35, 36, 39, 40, 42
Desclot, Bernat, 51, 55
Díez de Games, Gutierre, 31, 94
Dressendörfer, Peter, 50
Eberenz, Rolf, 84
Eco, Umberto, 88
Egidius Romanus, 8, 9, 12, 13
Eisenberg, Daniel, 46
Eiximenis, Francesc, 37, 71, 72, 75, 76, 77
Elliott, John H., 85
Espadaler, Anton M., 105, 106
Fernando of Portugal, Prince, 55, 111–12
Ferrando, Antoni, 115
Ferrer, Fra Joan, 74
Ferrer, St Vicent, 75
Flor de cavalleria, 123–24
Frontinus, 1, 3n2, 37, 71n1
Frye, Northrop, 97–98
Fuster, Joan, 46n2
Galba, Martí Joan de, viii, 2, 62–63, 64, 65, 67, 88, 98, 110, 113–15, 116, 117, 121, 125
Garter, Order of the, 6, 122
Gassull, Jaume, 46n2
Gerson, Jean, 43
Goertz, Wolf, 117
González-Casanova, Roberto, 51, 52, 56
Gower, John, 34n11
Grilli, Giuseppe, 20
Guia, Josep, 120
Guillem de Vàroic, 3, 4, 39, 96n9, 122, 123
Gumiel, Diego de, 48
Hauf, Albert, vii, 2, 3n2, 26n12, 32, 83, 96, 104, 116, 117
Híjar, Gonzalo de, 102
Hillgarth, J.N., 50n6, 56n11
Housely, Norman, 49, 50
Hunyadi, John, 64, 67, 82
Hutcheon, Linda, 45n1

Iser, Wolfgang, 58n12
Jaume I, 51, 52, 94–95
Justinian, 1
Keen, Maurice, 22
Koran, 72n2
Kundera, Milan, 90
Le Chastelain, Georges, 2
Legnano, Giovanni, 4
Libro del caballero Zifar, 122
Libro intitulado de bien morir, 96, 99
Lida de Malkiel, María Rosa, 88
Livy, 37
Llull, Ramon, 3, 5, 32, 52, 54, 55, 64, 121, 122
López de Ayala, Pero, 32n10, 35
Luke, St, 31
Malla, Felip de, 36
Malory, Sir Thomas, 93, 95, 107n29
March, Ausiàs, 42
Martorell, Joanot, passim
Massip, Francesc, 21, 22, 25
Menéndez Pelayo, Marcelino, 98
Monpalau, Joan de, 29n3, 103n20, 106n27, 123
Mort Artu, 57
Muntaner, Ramon, 37, 38, 39, 40, 51, 52, 58
Nicolau d'Olwer, Lluís, 111–12, 118, 124
Oleza Simó, Joan, 23, 49
Olivares, Gaspar de Guzmán, Conde Duque de, 85–86
Ovid, 18, 27, 29n2, 39, 40, 41, 42
Pamphilus, 18, 20n3
Patterson, Lee, 58
Pere III, 51
Perujo, Joan, 16n1, 115, 124
Petrarca, Francesco, 123
Petronius, 19
Renedo, Xavier, 26n11
Riber, Llorenç, 105

Richard of Bury, 36
Riquer, Martí de, vii, 3n2, 6, 14, 23n7, 24–25, 31n5, 36, 48n4, 51n10, 56, 59, 71n1, 83, 92, 98n15, 102n19, 103n20, 105n25, 109, 110–11, 115, 116, 123
Rodríguez de Padrón, Juan, 40
Roger de Flor, 52
Rojas, Fernando de, 18, 26n13, 85, 86, 106
Romant de Guy de Warwick, 3, 94
Rosenthal, David, 84
Rubiera y Mata, María Jesús, 125
Ruiz, Juan, Arcipreste de Hita. 18, 31
Russell, Peter, 87, 88
Sallust, 32, 37, 38
Sánchez de Badajoz, Diego, 24
Santillana, Marqués de, 31
Sassoferrato, Bartolo de, 2, 4
Segre, Cesare, 16, 89
Seneca, 29n2, 39, 41, 42
Sutherland, D.R., 86
Terry, Arthur, 87, 89, 106n29
Toroella, Guillem de, 24n10, 57
Troyes, Chrétien de, 4, 48
Valentí, Ferran, 31, 33, 42
Valera, Diego de, 2, 4
Valerius Maximus, 37, 38n17
Vargas Llosa, Mario, 46, 86, 90, 103n20, 104, 106n29
Vegetius, Flavius, 1, 3n2, 13, 32, 37
Ventura, Jordi, 113
Vicente, Gil, 24
Vilanova, Arnau de, 75
Vilaragut, Jaume de, 60
Villena, Enric de, 31, 33, 34n13, 36, 111, 112
Vincent of Beauvais, 37
Voeux du Faisan, 4, 49
Wittlin, Curt, 115, 117, 121
Yates, Alan, 87